Bloom's Literary Themes

∾⤫⤬

Alienation
The American Dream
Civil Disobedience
Dark Humor
Death and Dying
Enslavement and Emancipation
Exploration and Colonization
The Grotesque
The Hero's Journey
Human Sexuality
The Labyrinth
Rebirth and Renewal
Sin and Redemption
The Sublime
The Taboo
The Trickster

Bloom's Literary Themes

EXPLORATION AND COLONIZATION

Bloom's Literary Themes

EXPLORATION AND COLONIZATION

Edited and with an introduction by
Harold Bloom
Sterling Professor of the Humanities
Yale University

Volume Editor
Blake Hobby

 BLOOM'S
LITERARY CRITICISM
An imprint of Infobase Publishing

Bloom's Literary Themes: Exploration and Colonization

Bloom's Literary Criticism
An imprint of Infobase Publishing
132 West 31st Street
New York NY 10001

Library of Congress Cataloging-in-Publication Data
Exploration and colonization / edited and with an introduction by Harold Bloom ; volume editor, Blake Hobby.
    p. cm. —(Bloom's literary themes)
  Includes bibliographical references and index.
  ISBN 978-1-60413-442-1 (hc : alk. paper)
  1. Colonies in literature. 2. Geography in literature. I. Bloom, Harold. II. Hobby, Blake. III. Title. IV. Series.
  PN56.C63E97 2010
  809'.93358—dc22
                    2009053495

Bloom's Literary Criticism books are available at special discounts when purchased in bulk quantities for businesses, associations, institutions, or sales promotions. Please call our Special Sales Department in New York at (212) 967-8800 or (800) 322-8755.

You can find Bloom's Literary Criticism on the World Wide Web at
http://www.chelseahouse.com

Text design by Kerry Casey
Cover design by Takeshi Takahashi
Composition by IBT Global, Inc.
Cover printed by IBT Global, Inc., Troy, NY
Book printed and bound by IBT Global, Inc., Troy, NY
Date printed: March 2010
Printed in the United States of America

10 9 8 7 6 5 4 3 2 1

This book is printed on acid-free paper.

Contents

Series Introduction by Harold Bloom:
Themes and Metaphors   xi

Volume Introduction by Harold Bloom   xv

The Works of Bartolomé de Las Casas   1
    "Preface" by Sir Arthur Helps, in
      The Life of Las Casas: The Apostle of the Indies (1868)

Ceremony (Leslie Marmon Silko)   7
    "Towards a National Indian Literature: Cultural
      Authenticity in Nationalism" by Simon J. Ortiz, in
      MELUS (1981)

The Writings of Christopher Columbus   15
    "Reading Columbus" by Margarita Zamora,
      in *Reading Columbus* (1993)

The Cure at Troy (Seamus Heaney) and *Philoctetes* (Sophocles)   31
    "Seamus Heaney, Colonialism, and the Cure:
      Sophoclean Re-Visions" by Hugh Denard, in
      PAJ: A Journal of Performance and Art (2000)

"The Guest" (Albert Camus)   57
    "Ambiguity and Colonialism in Albert Camus's
      'The Guest'" by Michael D. Sollars

Heart of Darkness (Joseph Conrad)   67
   "Close Encounters of the Absurd Kind in Joseph
   Conrad's *Heart of Darkness*" by Jonathan Wright

The Iliad (Homer)   83
   "*The Iliad*" by Charles Moorman, in *Kings and
   Captains: Variations on a Heroic Theme* (1971)

The Novels of Toni Morrison   99
   "Periodizing Toni Morrison's work from *The Bluest
   Eye* to *Jazz*: the importance of *Tar Baby*" by Malin
   Walther Pereira, in *MELUS* (1997)

"My Kinsman, Major Molineux" (Nathaniel Hawthorne)   115
   "'That Evening of Ambiguity and Weariness': Readerly
   Exploration in Hawthorne's 'My Kinsman, Major
   Molineux'" by Robert C. Evans

One Hundred Years of Solitude (Gabriel García Márquez)   123
   "History, Erasure, and Magic Realism: Exploration,
   Colonization, and *One Hundred Years of Solitude*" by
   Jeffrey Gray

A Passage to India (E.M. Forster)   133
   "Forster's Critique of Imperialism in *A Passage to India*"
   by Hunt Hawkins, in *South Atlantic Review* (1983)

Robinson Crusoe (Daniel Defoe)   147
   "The Fetishism of Commodities and the Secret
   Thereof" by Karl Marx, in *Capital: A Critique of
   Political Economy* (1867)

The Plays of Wole Soyinka   151
   "Wole Soyinka and the Nobel Prize for Literature" by
   Bruce King, in *Sewanee Review* (1988)

The Works of Jonathan Swift   159
   "The Irish Tracts" by David Ward, in *Jonathan Swift:
   An Introductory Essay* (1973)

Contents

The Tempest (William Shakespeare)   179
"'Had I Plantation of this Isle, My Lord—':
Exploration and Colonization in Shakespeare's *The
Tempest*" by Robert C. Evans

Things Fall Apart (Chinua Achebe)   191
"Exploration and Colonization in Chinua Achebe's
Things Fall Apart" by Eric Sterling

"United Fruit Co." (Pablo Neruda)   201
"'United Fruit Co.,' *Canto General*, and Neruda's
Critique of Capitalism" by Jeffrey Gray

Waiting for the Barbarians (J.M. Coetzee)   213
"*Waiting For the Barbarians:* Narrative, History,
and the Other" by Lorena Russell

Wide Sargasso Sea (Jean Rhys)   225
"Exploration and Colonization in *Wide Sargasso Sea*"
by Merritt Moseley

*The Woman Warrior: Memoirs of a Girlhood
Among Ghosts* (Maxine Hong Kingston)   235
"Maxine Hong Kingston's *Woman Warrior*: Filiality
and Woman's Autobiographical Storytelling" by
Sidonie Smith, in *A Poetics of Women's Autobiography*
(1987)

Acknowledgments   253

Index   255

Series Introduction by Harold Bloom:
Themes and Metaphors

1. Topos and Trope

What we now call a theme or topic or subject initially was named a *topos*, ancient Greek for "place." Literary *topoi* are commonplaces, but also arguments or assertions. A topos can be regarded as literal when opposed to a trope or turning which is figurative and which can be a metaphor or some related departure from the literal: ironies, synecdoches (part for whole), metonymies (representations by contiguity) or hyperboles (overstatements). Themes and metaphors engender one another in all significant literary compositions.

As a theoretician of the relation between the matter and the rhetoric of high literature, I tend to define metaphor as a figure of desire rather than a figure of knowledge. We welcome literary metaphor because it enables fictions to persuade us of beautiful untrue things, as Oscar Wilde phrased it. Literary *topoi* can be regarded as places where we store information, in order to amplify the themes that interest us.

This series of volumes, *Bloom's Literary Themes*, offers students and general readers helpful essays on such perpetually crucial topics as the Hero's Journey, the Labyrinth, the Sublime, Death and Dying, the Taboo, the Trickster and many more. These subjects are chosen for their prevalence yet also for their centrality. They express the whole concern of human existence now in the twenty-first century of the Common Era. Some of the topics would have seemed odd at another time, another land: the American Dream, Enslavement and Emancipation, Civil Disobedience.

I suspect though that our current preoccupations would have existed always and everywhere, under other names. Tropes change across the centuries: The irony of one age is rarely the irony of another. But the themes of great literature, though immensely varied, undergo transmemberment and show up barely disguised in different contexts. The power of imaginative literature relies upon three constants: aesthetic splendor, cognitive power, wisdom. These are not bound by societal constraints or resentments, and ultimately are universals, and so not culture-bound. Shakespeare, except for the world's scriptures, is the one universal author, whether he is read and played in Bulgaria or Indonesia or wherever. His supremacy at creating human beings breaks through even the barrier of language and puts everyone on his stage. This means that the matter of his work has migrated everywhere, reinforcing the common places we all inhabit in his themes.

2. CONTEST AS BOTH THEME AND TROPE

Great writing or the Sublime rarely emanates directly from themes since all authors are mediated by forerunners and by contemporary rivals. Nietzsche enhanced our awareness of the agonistic foundations of ancient Greek literature and culture, from Hesiod's contest with Homer on to the Hellenistic critic Longinus in his treatise *On the Sublime*. Even Shakespeare had to begin by overcoming Christopher Marlowe, only a few months his senior. William Faulkner stemmed from the Polish-English novelist Joseph Conrad, and our best living author of prose fiction, Philip Roth, is inconceivable without his descent from the major Jewish literary phenomenon of the twentieth century, Franz Kafka of Prague, who wrote the most lucid German since Goethe.

The contest with past achievement is the hidden theme of all major canonical literature in Western tradition. Literary influence is both an overwhelming metaphor for literature itself, and a common topic for all criticism, whether or not the critic knows her immersion in the incessant flood.

Every theme in this series touches upon a contest with anteriority, whether with the presence of death, the hero's quest, the overcoming of taboos, or all of the other concerns, volume by volume. From Monteverdi through Bach to Stravinsky, or from the Italian Renaissance through the agon of Matisse and Picasso, the history of all the arts demonstrates the same patterns as literature's thematic struggle with itself. Our country's great original art, jazz, is illuminated by what the great creators called "cutting contests," from Louis Armstrong and Duke Ellington on to the emergence of Charlie Parker's Bop or revisionist jazz.

A literary theme, however authentic, would come to nothing without rhetorical eloquence or mastery of metaphor. But to experience the study of the common places of invention is an apt training in the apprehension of aesthetic value in poetry and in prose.

Volume Introduction by Harold Bloom

In my eightieth year I am still not virtuous enough to embrace "post-colonialism", so this brief introduction will confine itself to the *literary* theme of exploration. Homer's Odysseus (Ulysses in Latin) is the founder of imaginative exploration, and is prominent not only in *The Odyssey* but in many subsequent masterpieces, sometimes under his own name – as in Tennyson's dramatic monologue – but also in other beings, including Satan in John Milton's *Paradise Lost*, and the genial Leopold Bloom in James Joyce's *Ulysses*.

Homer's Odysseus is admirable but dangerous, a great survivor. You would not want to be in the same boat as Odysseus; he would survive, and you, like all his mariners, would drown. Endlessly resourceful, the cunning Odysseus explores from island to island, in his drive to return home to his own island kingdom of Ithaca, and to his wife Penelope and son Telemachus. Since the sea-god Poseidon is determined to destroy him, the exploratory drive of Odysseus becomes a model for survival in a very difficult cosmos.

In the *Inferno*, Dante revises Ulysses into an explorer of unknown realms, too restless in his settled existence to enjoy what he had struggled to reattain. Placed down in Hell as an evil counselor of his final shipmates, he is punished eternally for his last voyage into a forbidden knowledge. And yet his journey of exploration has a clear analogue in Dante's own voyage, in the *Commedia*, through Hell, Purgatory, and Paradise.

This ambiguity is explored superbly by Alfred Lord Tennyson in his *Ulysses*, where the Greek hero recounts his own final voyage. Satan, in *Paradise Lost*, heroically had explored chaos on his way to view Eden, there to revenge himself upon God by bringing about the Fall of Adam and Eve. Tennyson's Ulysses echoes Satan's: "And courage never to submit or yield/ And what is else not to be overcome?" This transmutes to Tennyson's hero ending by crying out: "To strive, to seek, to find, and not to yield."

The grand culmination of the Ulysses Theme of Exploration, Endurance, and Survival comes on Bloomsday in Joyce's *Ulysses* when the ordinary yet quietly heroic Poldy gloriously sustains the hazards of city life in Dublin. Curious, kind, gentle, infinitely humane Poldy finds his spiritual son in Joyce's surrogate, Stephen Dedalus, the artist as a young man. What Poldy triumphantly explores is still our daily round of urban life, a century later.

THE WORKS OF BARTOLOMÉ DE LAS CASAS

"Preface"
by Sir Arthur Helps, in *The Life of Las Casas:*
The Apostle of the Indies (1868)

INTRODUCTION

Bartolomé de Las Casas, first Bishop of Chiapas, bore witness to the first of many European efforts to colonize, exploit, and subjugate other cultures. In the excerpt below, Sir Arthur Helps praises Las Casas's humanitarian sympathies and his intellect, both of which helped change the colonizing practices of Spain. As Helps reports, Las Casas was praised even by his enemies, one of who describes him as "most subtle, most vigilant, and most fluent, compared with whom the Ulysses of Homer was inert and stuttering." Such qualities made Las Casas an ideal recorder of Spain's efforts to explore and colonize the New World.

The life of Las Casas appears to me one of the most interesting, indeed I may say the most interesting, of all those that I have ever studied; and I think it is more than the natural prejudice of a writer for his hero, that inclines me to look upon him as one of the most remarkable

Helps, Sir Arthur. "Preface." *The Life of Las Casas: The Apostle of the Indies.* London: Bell and Daldy, 1868. v-xv.

personages that has ever appeared in history. It is well known that he has ever been put in the foremost rank of philanthropists; but he had other qualifications which were also extraordinary. He was not a mere philanthropist, possessed only with one idea. He had one of those large minds which take an interest in everything. As an historian, a man of letters, a colonist, a missionary, a theologian, an active ruler in the Church, a man of business, and an observer of natural history and science, he holds a very high position amongst the notable men of his own age. The ways, the customs, the religion, the policy, the laws, of the new people whom he saw, the new animals, the new trees, the new herbs, were all observed and chronicled by him.

In an age eminently superstitious, he was entirely devoid of superstition. At a period when the most extravagant ideas as to the divine rights of kings prevailed, he took occasion to remind kings themselves to their faces, that they are only permitted to govern for the good of the people; and dared to upbraid Philip the Second for his neglect of Spanish and Indian affairs, through busying himself with Flemish, English, and French policy.

At a period when brute force was universally appealed to in all matters, but more especially in those that pertained to religion, he contended before Juntas and Royal Councils that missionary enterprise is a thing that should stand independent of all military support; that a missionary should go forth with his life in his hand, relying only on the protection that God will vouchsafe him, and depending neither upon civil nor military assistance. In fact his works would, even in the present day, form the best manual extant for missionaries.

He had certainly great advantages: he lived in most stirring times; he was associated with the greatest personages of his day; and he had the privilege of taking part in the discovery and colonization of a new world.

Eloquent, devoted, charitable, fervent, sometimes too fervent, yet very skilful in managing men, he will doubtless remind the reader of his prototype, Saint Paul; and it was very fitting that he should have been called, as he was, the "Apostle of the Indies."

Notwithstanding our experience, largely confirmed by history, of the ingenuity often manifested in neglecting to confer honour upon those who most deserve it, one cannot help wondering that the Romish Church never thought of enrolling Las Casas as a saint, amongst such fellow-labourers as Saint Charles of Borromeo, or Saint Francis of Assisi.

His life is very interesting, if only from this circumstance, that, perhaps more than any man of his time, he rose to great heights of power and influence, and then, to use a phrase of his own, fell sheer down "into terrible abysses." His spirit, however, almost always rose indomitable: and the "abysses" did not long retain him as their captive.

Among his singular advantages must be mentioned his great physical powers, and tenacity of life. I do not remember that he ever mentions being ill. He exceeded in his journeyings his renowned master and friend, Charles the Fifth, and he lived fully as laborious a life as did that monarch.

When Charles, a youth of sixteen, came to the throne. Las Casas was a man of about forty, of great power and Influence, He soon won the young king's attachment; during the whole of whose active life he worked vigorously with him at Indian affairs; and when, broken in health and in spirit, Charles retired to San Yuste, Las Casas was in full vigour, and had his way with Philip the Second, not, however, without the aid of the Imperial recluse. For almost the last business which Charles attended to was one in which the dying monarch gave his warm support to his friend Las Casas.

With Charles's grandfather, Ferdinand the Catholic, Las Casas had also worked at Indian affairs; and, with his usual sincerity, had not failed to inform that king of many truths which concerned his soul and the welfare of his kingdom.

Columbus, Cardinal Ximenes, Cortes, Pizarro, Vasco Nuñez, Gattinara the great Flemish statesman, were all known to Las Casas: in fact, he saw generations of notable men—statesmen, monarchs, inventors, discoverers, and conquerors—rise, flourish, and die; and he had continually to recommence his arduous conflict with new statesmen, new conquerors, and new kings. He survived Ferdinand fifty years, Charles the Fifth eight years, Columbus sixty years, Cortes nineteen years, Ximenes forty-nine years, Pizarro twenty-five years, and Gattinara thirty-seven years.

He was twenty-eight years old when he commenced his first voyage to the Indies; and he was still in full vigour, not failing in sight, hearing, or intellect, when, at ninety-two years of age, he contended before Philip the Second's ministers in favour of the Guatemalans having Courts of Justice of their own. Having left the pleasant climate of Valladolid, doubtless excited by the cause he was urging, and denying himself the rest he required, he was unable to bear up against that treacherous air of Madrid, of which the proverb justly says, "though it will not blow out a candle, it will yet kill a man," and so, was cut off, prematurely, as I always feel, in the ninety-second year of his age.

His powers, like those of a great statesman of our own time, decidedly improved as he grew older. He became, I believe, a better writer, a more eloquent speaker, and a much wider and more tolerant thinker towards the end of his life. His best treatise[1] (in my judgment) was written when he was ninety years of age, and is even now, when its topics have been worn somewhat threadbare, a most interesting work.

To show that I have not exaggerated his great natural powers as well as his learning, I need only refer to his celebrated controversy with Sepulveda. This Sepulveda was then the greatest scholar in Spain, and was backed, moreover, by other learned men; but Las Casas was quite a match for them all. In argument he was decidedly superior. Texts, quotations, conclusions of Councils, opinions of fathers and school-men were showered down upon him. He met them all with weapons readily produced from the same armouries, and showed that he too had not in vain studied his Saint Thomas Aquinas and his Aristotle. His great opponent, Sepulveda, in a private letter describing the controversy, speaks of Las Casas as "most subtle, most vigilant, and most fluent, compared with whom the Ulysses of Homer was inert and stuttering." Las Casas, at the time of the controversy, was seventy-six years of age.

The reader of this introduction will perhaps think that if Las Casas is such a man as I have described, and his life is of such exceeding interest, it is strange that, comparatively speaking, so little has been heard about him. This, however, can be easily explained. His life can only be fully pourtrayed after reference to books, manuscripts, and official documents of the greatest rarity, not within the reach even of scholars, until recent years. The government of Spain has of late years thrown open to all students, in the most unreserved manner, its literary treasures, and afforded every facility for their study. In modern times, too, the Americans have taken great pains to investigate the early records of America, and have always been remarkably generous, in the use they have allowed to be made of the documents which they have rescued and brought together.[2]

There are few men to whom, up to the present time, the words which Shakespeare makes Mark Antony say of Caesar, would more apply than to Las Casas:—

"The evil that men do lives after them,
The good is oft interred with their bones."

At one inauspicious moment of his life he advised a course which has ever since been the one blot upon his well-earned fame, and too often has this advice been the only thing which, when the name of Las Casas has been mentioned, has occurred to men's minds respecting him. He certainly did advise that negroes should be brought to the New World. I think, however, I have amply shown in the "Spanish Conquest" that he was not the first to give this advice, and that it had long before been largely acted upon. It is also to be remembered, that this advice, to introduce negroes, was but a very small part of his general scheme. Had that been carried into effect as a whole, it would have afforded the most efficient protection for negroes, Indians, and for all those who were to be subject to the Spanish Colonial Empire.

However, Las Casas makes no such defence for himself, but thus frankly owns his great error, saying, in his history, "This advice, that licence should be given to bring negro slaves to these lands, the Clerigo Casas first gave, not considering the injustice with which the Portuguese take them and make them slaves; which advice, after he had apprehended the nature of the thing, he would not have given for all he had in the world. For he always held that they had been made slaves unjustly, and tyrannically; for the same reason holds good of them as of the Indians."[3]

This one error must not be allowed to overshadow the long and noble career of one, who never, as far as I am aware, on any other occasion, yielded to worldly policy; who, for nearly sixty years, held fast to a grand cause, never growing weary of it; and who confronted great statesmen, potent churchmen, and mighty kings, with perfect fearlessness, in defence of an injured, a calumniated, and down-trodden race,—a race totally unable to protect themselves from the advance of a pseudo-civilization which destroyed as much as it civilized.

Notes

1. On Peru.
2. A short letter of Las Casas—not a marave pocket— an enterprising American at a sum amounting to more than ten

thousand maravedis, and the purchaser was but too glad if his purchase could be of any use to an historian.

3. It is a curious fact in history, that this suggestion of Las Casas tended, as far as it was adopted, to check the importation of negroes into the New World. The licence to import was restricted, for a term of eight years, to the number of 4000, whereas the emperor had been requested to allow the importation of negroes without any restriction whatever.

CEREMONY
(LESLIE MARMON SILKO)

"Towards a National Indian Literature: Cultural Authenticity in Nationalism" by Simon J. Ortiz, in *MELUS* (1981)

INTRODUCTION

Simon J. Ortiz explores the way Leslie Marmon Silko's *Ceremony* relies upon the oral tradition as a subject. To Ortiz, the oral tradition has been for the Native peoples a means of resistance against colonial forces, a way of maintaining the "Native American voice," which shows "the creative ability of Indian people to gather in many forms of the sociopolitical colonizing force which beset them and to make these forms meaningful in their own terms. In fact, it is a celebration of the human spirit and the Indian struggle for liberation."

Uncle Steve—Dzeerlai, which was his Acqumeh name—was not a literate man and he certainly was not literary. He is gone now, into the earth and back north as the Acqumeh people say, but I remember him clearly. He was a subsistence farmer, and he labored for the railroad during his working years; I remember him in his grimy working clothes. But I remember him most vividly as he sang and danced and

---

Ortiz, Simon J. "Towards a National Indian Literature: Cultural Authenticity in Nationalism." *MELUS* 8.2 (Summer 1981) 7–12.

told stories—not literary stories, mind you, but it was all literature nevertheless.

On fiesta days, Steve wore a clean, good shirt and a bright purple or blue or red neckerchief knotted at his tightly buttoned shirt collar. Prancing and dipping, he would wave his beat-up hat, and he would holler, Juana, Juana! Or Pedro, Pedro! It would depend on which fiesta day it was, and other men and younger ones would follow his lead. Juana! Pedro! It was a joyous and vigorous sight to behold, Uncle Dzeerlai expressing his vitality from within the hold of our Acqumeh Indian world.

There may be some question about why Uncle Steve was shouting Juana and Pedro, obviously Spanish names, non-Indian names. I will explain. In the summer months of June, July, and August, there are in the Pueblo Indian communities of New Mexico celebrations on Catholic saints' days. Persons whose names are particular saints' names honor those names by giving to the community and its people. In turn, the people honor those names by receiving. The persons named after the saints such as John or Peter—Juan, Pedro—throw from housetops gifts like bread, cookies, crackerjacks, washcloths, other things, and the people catching and receiving dance and holler the names. It will rain then and the earth will be sustained; it will be a community fulfilled in its most complete sense of giving and receiving, in one word: sharing. And in sharing, there is strength and continuance.

But there is more than that here. Obviously, there is an overtone that this is a Catholic Christian ritual celebration because of the significance of the saints' names and days on the Catholic calendar. But just as obviously, when the celebration is held within the Acqumeh community, it is an Acqumeh ceremony. It is Acqumeh and Indian (or Native American or American Indian if one prefers those terms) in the truest and most authentic sense. This is so because this celebration speaks of the creative ability of Indian people to gather in many forms of the sociopolitical colonizing force which beset them and to make these forms meaningful in their own terms. In fact, it is a celebration of the human spirit and the Indian struggle for liberation.

Many Christian religious rituals brought to the Southwest (which in the 16th century was the northern frontier of the Spanish New World) are no longer Spanish. They are now Indian because of the creative development that the native people applied to them. Present-day Native American or Indian literature is evidence of this in the very same way. And because in every case where European culture was cast upon Indian people of this nation there was similar creative response and development, it can be observed that this was the primary element of a nationalistic impulse to make use of foreign ritual, ideas, and material in their own—Indian—terms. Today's writing by Indian authors is a continuation of that elemental impulse.

Let me tell you more about Dzeerlai. I have a memory of him as he and other men sang at one Acqumeh event. He is serious and his face is concentrated upon the song, meaning, and the event that is taking place during this particular afternoon in early September. Santiago and Chapiyuh have come to Acqu. They enter from the south, coming exactly upon the route that Juan de Onate's soldiers took when they razed Acqu in the winter of 1598.

Santiago was the patron saint of the Spanish soldiers, and the name seemed to have been their war cry as well. On this afternoon, as he steps upon the solid stone of Acqu, Santiago is dressed in ostentatious finery. His clothes have a sheen and glitter that anyone can marvel at and envy. He wears a cowboy ten-gallon hat and there are heavy revolvers strapped to his hips. The spurs on his fancy boots jingle and spin as he and his horse prance about. As Santiago waves a white-gloved hand at the crowds of Acqumeh people lining his route and grins ludicrously with a smile painted rigidly on a pink face, the people still marvel but they check their envy. They laugh at Santiago and the hobby horse steed stuck between his legs.

Alongside, and slightly behind to his right, is another figure, Chapiyuh. His name is abrupt in the mouth. He doesn't walk; he stomps as he wears heavy leather thick-soled boots like a storm-trooper. Chapiyuh has a hood over his face with slits cut in it for eyes. He wears the dark flowing robes of a Franciscan priest secured with a rough rope at his waist. In one hand Chapiyuh carries a bullwhip which he cracks or a length of chain, and in the other hand he carried the book, the Bible. As he stomps along heavily, he makes threatening gestures to the people and they shrink away. Children whimper and cling desperately to their mothers' dresses.

There are prayer narratives for what is happening, and there are songs. Uncle Steven and his partners sang for what was happening all along the route that Santiago and Chapiyuh took into Acqu. It is necessary that there be prayer and song because it is important, and no one will forget then; no one will regard it as less than momentous.

It is the only way in which event and experience, such as the entry of the Spaniard to the Western Hemisphere, can become significant and realized in the people's own terms. And this, of course, is what happens in literature, to bring about meaning and meaningfulness. This perception and meaningfulness has to happen; otherwise, the hard experience of the Euroamerican colonization of the lands and people of the Western Hemisphere would be driven into the dark recesses of the indigenous mind and psyche. And this kind of repression is always a poison and detriment to creative growth and expression.

As one can see, most of this perception and expression has been possible through the oral tradition which includes prayer, song, drama-ritual, narrative or storytelling, much of it within ceremony—some of it outside of ceremony—which is religious and social. Indeed, through the past five centuries the oral tradition has been the most reliable method by which Indian culture and community integrity have been maintained. And, certainly, it is within this tradition that authenticity is most apparent and evident.

Uncle Steve and his singer-partners were naturally authentic as they sought to make a lesson of history significant, and they did so within the context of the Acqumeh community. There is no question of the authenticity of the ritual drama in that case. But there is more than the context that makes the drama—and any subsequent literary expression of it—authentic. Steve was only one in a long line of storytellers and singers who have given expression to the experience of Indian people in the Americas. Throughout the difficult experience of colonization to the present, Indian women and men have struggled to create meaning of their lives in very definite and systematic ways. The ways or methods have been important, but they are important only because of the reason for the struggle. And it is that reason—the struggle against colonialism—which has given substance to what is authentic.

Since colonization began in the 15th century with the arrival of the Spaniard priest, militarist, and fortune and slave seeker upon the shores of this hemisphere, Indian songmakers and storytellers have created a body of oral literature which speaks crucially about the experience of colonization. Like the drama and the characters described above, the indigenous peoples of the Americas have taken the languages of the colonialists and used them for their own purposes. Some would argue that this means that Indian people have succumbed or become educated into a different linguistic system and have forgotten or have been forced to forsake their native selves. This is simply not true. Along with their native languages, Indian women and men have carried on their lives and their expression through the use of the newer languages, particularly Spanish, French, and English, and they have used these languages on their own terms. This is the crucial item that has to be understood, that it is entirely possible for a people to retain and maintain their lives through the use of any language. There is not a question of authenticity here; rather it is the way that Indian people have creatively responded to forced colonization. And this response has been one of resistance; there is no clearer word for it than resistance.

It has been this resistance—political, armed, spiritual—which has been carried out by the oral tradition. The continued use of the oral tradition today is evidence that the resistance is on-going. Its use, in fact, is what has given rise to the surge of literature created by contemporary Indian authors. And it is this literature, based upon continuing resistance, which has given a particularly nationalistic character to the Native American voice.

Consider Antoine, the boy-character through whose eyes the idea of the novel, *Wind from an Enemy Sky*, by D'Arcy McNickle is realized. Antoine is witness to the tumultuous and terrible events that face and cause change among his Little Elk people. McNickle not only has us see through Antoine's immediate youthful eyes but also through the knowledge related by Bull, his grandfather, and other kinfolk. We come to see not only a panorama of the early 20th century as experienced by the Little Elk people but also of the national Indian experience. Antoine, through his actions, thought, and understanding shows what kind of decisions become necessary, and even though the novel ends with no victory for the Little Elk people, we realize that the boy and his people have fought as valorously and courageously as they have been able, and that McNickle, as an Indian writer, has provided us a literary experience of it.

Abel in N. Scott Momaday's novel, *House Made of Dawn*, is unlike Antoine, but he carries on a similar struggle not only for identity and survival but, more, to keep integral what is most precious to him: the spiritual knowledge which will guide him throughout his life as it has guided those before him. It is knowledge of this life source that Momaday denotes as the strength which inspires the resistance of the people from whom Abel comes, and it will be what will help them to overcome. Surely, it is what proves to be the element which enables Abel to endure prison, city life, indignities cast upon him, and finally it is what helps him to return to himself and run in the dawn so that life will go on. Momaday concludes his novel by the affirmation that dawn will always come and renewal of life will be possible through resistance against forces which would destroy life. It is by the affirmation of knowledge of source and place and spiritual return that resistance is realized.

Ceremony, the novel by Leslie M. Silko, is a special and most complete example of this affirmation and what it means in terms of Indian resistance, its use as literary theme, and its significance in the development of a national Indian literature. Tayo, the protagonist in the usual sense, in the novel is not "pure blood" Indian; rather he is of mixed blood, a mestizo. He, like many Indian people of whom he is a reflection, is faced with circumstances which seemingly are beyond his ability to control. After a return home to his Indian community from military service in World War II, Tayo is still not home. He, like others, is far away from himself, and it is only through a tracking of the pathways of life, or rebuilding through ceremony of life, that he is able at last to return to himself and to ongoing life. Along the way, Silko, the novelist, has Tayo and other characters experience and describe the forces of colonialism as "witchery" which has waylaid Indian people and their values and prevents return to their sources. But Tayo does return, not by magic or mysticism or some abstract revelation; instead the return is achieved through a ceremony of story, the tracing of story, rebuilding of story, and the creation of story.

It is in this ritual that return and reaffirmation is most realized, for how else can it be. Story is to engender life, and *Ceremony* speaks upon the very process by which story, whether in oral or written form, substantiates life, continues it, and creates it. It is this very process that Indian people have depended upon in their most critical times. Indeed, without it, the oral tradition would not exist as significantly as it does today, and there would likely be no basis for present-day Indian writing, much less Indian people. But because of the insistence to keep telling and creating stories, Indian life continues, and it is this resistance against loss that has made that life possible. Tayo in *Ceremony* will live on, wealthy with story and tradition, because he realizes the use and value of the ritual of storymaking which is his own and his people's lives in the making. "It is never easy," Silko writes; it is always a struggle and because it is a struggle for life it is salvation and affirmation.

The struggle to maintain life and the resistance against loss put up by Antoine, Abel, and Tayo, in their separate entities, illustrate a theme, national in character and scope, common to all American native people and to all people indigenous to lands which have suffered imperialism and colonialism. In the decade of the 70s, it has been the predominant subject and theme that has concerned Indian writers. And it has been the oral tradition which has carried this concern in the hearts of Indian people until today it is being expressed not only in the novel but in poetry and drama as well.

Nevertheless, it is not the oral tradition as transmitted from ages past alone which is the inspiration and source for contemporary Indian literature. It is also because of the acknowledgement by Indian writers of a responsibility to advocate for their people's self-government, sovereignty, and control of land and natural resources; and to look also at racism, political and economic oppression, sexism, supremacism, and the needless and wasteful exploitation of land and people, especially in the U.S., that Indian literature is developing a character of nationalism which indeed it should have. It is this character which will prove to be the heart and fibre and story of an America which has heretofore too often feared its deepest and most honest emotions of love and compassion. It is this story, wealthy in being without an illusion of dominant power and capitalistic abundance, that is the most authentic.

Bob Hall in *Southern Exposure* wrote, describing the textile workers' struggle in the South, that the themes of family, community, religion, humor, and rage are the most common among the workers in their stories and music. He could have added "most authentic" to common, and he could have been commenting upon Indian people for it is those very themes that Indian literature of today considers. The voice given these themes is the most culturally authentic as these are fundamental to human dignity, creativity, and integrity. This voice is that authentic one that my nonliterary Uncle Steve, wearing a beat-up cowboy hat and bright blue neckerchief, expressed at Acqu as he struggled to teach history, knowledge of our community, and understanding of how life continues. Indeed, like that ceremony at Acqu, depicting Santiago, the conquistador-saint, and Chapiyuh, the inquisitor-missionary, the voice is not a mere dramatic expression of a sociohistorical experience, but it is a persistent call by a people determined to be free; it is an authentic voice for liberation. And finally, it is the voice of countless other non-literary Indian women and men of this nation who live a daily life of struggle to achieve and maintain meaning which gives the most authentic character to a national Indian literature.

THE WRITINGS OF
CHRISTOPHER COLUMBUS

"Reading Columbus"
by Margarita Zamora,
in *Reading Columbus* (1993)

INTRODUCTION

In the this chapter from her study *Reading Columbus*,
Margarita Zamora compares alternate versions of explorer
Christopher Columbus's announcement of his landfall on a
new continent. Noting the "creative tension" attendant upon
interpreting an author's intended meanings, Zamora explores
"the role reading has played in the writing of the history of
the Discovery." Columbus's letter, which was widely circulated across Europe, determined how people viewed his
voyage and whether further efforts at colonization deserved
to be funded. Thus, Zamora's study of the letter illuminates
the motivations and historical circumstances surrounding
Europe's fledgling efforts at exploration and colonization.

Christopher Columbus's act of writing to the Crown to announce the
Discovery was an event almost as momentous as the act of discovering
itself. Not only did his letter make the fact of the historical event

---

Zamora, Margarita. "Reading Columbus." *Reading Columbus.* Berkeley, CA:
University of California Press, 1993. 9–20.

known to others, but the very future of the enterprise depended on how it was represented to those who were in the position to decide its fate.

Like writing, reading has consequences, and our thoughts today about Columbus's first voyage are at least as much the result of how the Columbian texts were read as of the manner in which they were written. This essay considers the earliest readings of Columbian writing through a comparative lens, focusing on two versions of the announcement of the Discovery. Both were presumably written by Columbus, although, as I note below, that is a matter of some debate. The dispute over the actual authorship of these versions aside, however, the significant variations between the two texts suggest that one constitutes a reading of the other, an emendation of the original scriptural act that created a new and different image of the Discovery.

Of course, not every act of reading literally constitutes a new text. But reading is always, if only in a metaphorical sense, a rewriting. As readers, we privilege certain aspects of the text, repress others, misunderstand some, and perhaps on occasion even understand only too well the story before us. Readings are, in any case, always in creative tension with the text. In underscoring the generative quality of the act of reading, my purpose is to explore the role reading has played in the writing of the history of the Discovery.

As the *Diario* of the first navigation tells it, on 14 February 1493, in the midst of a life-threatening storm, Columbus wrote to Ferdinand and Isabella, announcing the Discovery. He sealed the letter inside a barrel, along with a note asking whoever found it to deliver it to the sovereigns unopened, with the promise of a substantial reward if the instructions were followed; he then tossed the barrel overboard to the fate of the wind and the waves.[1] Given the raging storm and the fact that Columbus had not yet sighted any land, although he calculated that he was sailing in the vicinity of the Azores, the composition of this letter seems more an act of desperation than of premature optimism. On 4 March he wrote to the king of Portugal and to the Spanish sovereigns again. According to the *Diario*, Columbus had managed to find his way to tranquil waters in the mouth of the Tagus River on that day, and both letters were apparently posted overland.

Two other letters, both dated 15 February 1493, also announcing the Discovery, have been ascribed to Columbus. One was addressed to Luis de Santángel, the other to Rafaél (Gabriel) Sánchez. Both these men were officials of the Crown of Aragon who had been instrumental in facilitating the Columbian enterprise. Neither of these letters, however, are mentioned in the *Diario*, and the place of composition stated in the letters contradicts Columbus's itinerary.[2]

Until quite recently the only versions of the announcement known to have survived were the almost identical texts of the letters addressed to Santángel and Sánchez. Within a few months of Columbus's return, these had been published in various editions and in three different languages throughout Europe. The letter of 14 February apparently was lost at sea. The only remaining traces of it are the references in the *Diario* and in subsequent histories derived from that account of the first navigation.[3] The letters of 4 March, to João II of Portugal and to Isabella and Ferdinand, also disappeared without a trace, but probably for the opposite reason—not because they were lost en route to the addressees, but because they indeed were received and read. As official documents of considerable import, they undoubtedly would have been copied and the originals handled with utmost care. Nonetheless, until 1989 we had only references to their existence: the *Diario* mentions the letter to the Portuguese king; the postscript of the published letters to Santángel and Sánchez mentions the letter to the Spanish sovereigns; and correspondence from the Crown to Columbus acknowledges receipt of a letter that most scholars believe was probably the text of 4 March. But the letters themselves fell victim to accident or, more likely, to deliberate suppression by officials treating them as state secrets at the Portuguese and Castilian courts. They were wholly lost to us until 1989, when Antonio Rumeu de Armas published an undated and unsigned copy of the 4 March letter, based on a manuscript of uncertain origin, probably from the mid-sixteenth century.[4]

The letters dated 15 February to Santángel and Sánchez, on the contrary, were so vigorously and widely circulated that they appear to have been part of a concerted propaganda campaign. After thorough study of the enigmas surrounding the composition and publication of the letters to Santángel and Sánchez, Demetrio Ramos Pérez concluded that the evidence overwhelmingly suggests they are a sanitized version of another text (probably the letter of 4 March to Ferdinand and Isabella), composed by officials at court (perhaps by Santángel himself) to broadcast the official version of the Discovery.[5] Moving beyond the letters' inconsistencies concerning dates and place of composition, Ramos shows how the letters of 15 February responded to the political climate in Europe during the months immediately following the conclusion of the first voyage.

Some of Ramos's assumptions about the lost letter to Ferdinand and Isabella of 4 March have proved inaccurate in light of Rumeu's edition. Yet the thrust of Ramos's argument that the version of 15 February was composed as propaganda, appears to be strengthened by the 4 March text. Though similar, the February and March versions offer fundamentally distinct representations of the Discovery.

If one accepts the hypothesis that Columbus himself authored the originals of each of these announcements of the Discovery, then all three letters can be considered distillations of the *diario* of the first voyage; that is, products of Columbus reading himself. Both Ramos and Rumeu have tested a similar hypothesis and found that the correlation of specific passages is often very close, although the letters also present significant divergences from the *Diario*. The fundamental problem with this approach, however, is that all of the surviving versions of the itinerary of the first voyage are secondhand. Ferdinand Columbus and Las Casas both quoted or paraphrased extensively from the *diario* of the navigation in their accounts of that voyage, but their texts can only be considered reconstitutions of whatever Columbus may have written. Even Las Casas's edition of the *Diario*, the closest version we have to Columbus's own account, is a highly edited summary of a copy of the text, composed by Las Casas in the sixteenth century.[6] Two other factors also tend to undermine any conclusions drawn from such a comparative analysis. First, no holographs of these texts are available. The closest extant versions of the original letter of 15 February are an archival copy of the text addressed to Santángel and the surviving first editions of the published texts. The copy of the letter of 4 March to Ferdinand and Isabella published by Rumeu is some 150 years removed from the original. Such lacunae make it essentially impossible to draw any solid conclusions about the sources of the variations or even the significance of the similarities.

With Rumeu's publication of the 4 March letter, however, two different versions of the announcement of the Discovery are now available. Indisputably, one of them is a reading of the other. And while it may be impossible to verify with absolute certainty which of these texts was the original and which the revision, or to determine who did the rewriting, a comparison of the two versions provides an opportunity to consider the consequences that the earliest readings of Columbian writing have had on our understanding of the Discovery.

Rumeu (1:27–41) contends that Columbus must have penned two different versions of the announcement, one addressed to the Crown and the other to Santángel and to Sánchez, all of which he then sent to court together on 4 March 1493. Ramos, on the other hand, proposes that someone, probably Santángel himself, composed the version of 15 February specifically for publication, working from either a letter Columbus sent him or, more likely, the letter of 4 March to the sovereigns.[7] In any case, it is difficult to dispute that a pen other than Columbus's intervened in the 15 February version, especially if one is persuaded by Ramos and Rumeu that its publication must have been carried out with the Crown's blessing and under official supervision.

A comparison of the letter to Santángel with the letter of 4 March strongly suggests that the former underwent stylistic revision on its way to publication. Generally more concise and better organized than the royal version, the Santángel text systematically summarizes various passages that are more elaborate in the letter to Isabella and Ferdinand. Many of these concern the technical aspects of the exploration, such as the recording of distances, directions, geographical information received from the Indians, and so on. The descriptions of people and landscape in the letter to Santángel tend to be of a more general character, often collapsing details given in the 4 March letter about particular islands into sweeping characterizations of all the islands as a group. Some revisions seem to have been undertaken for the purpose of resolving ambiguities or contradictions in the 4 March text. In the letter to Santángel, for example, a passage describing Columbus's predicament and actions on the north coast of Cuba and explaining his critical decision to cut short the exploration of what he thought was the mainland differs from its 4 March counterpart not only in its specific wording but also in the greater degree of detail it provides with respect to Columbus's thoughts and actions (see Appendix, note 4).

Other changes, however, cannot be attributed to the reviser's desire for economy or clarity, simply to facilitate reading. By far the more interesting differences are those which suggest that the royal text was systematically censored on its way to becoming the public version of the announcement. It is in this redactive process, whose traces emerge between the lines of text when the two versions are compared, that a particular way of reading the Discovery unfolds.

The *Santa María* disaster is a case in point. The letter to the sovereigns tells of leaving behind the flagship to serve in building a fortification for the Spaniards who were to remain at La Navidad. It does not mention, however, what the *Diario* entry for 25 December amply explains: that it became necessary to abandon the vessel and leave the men on the island after the *Santa María* had run aground on a reef, due to the negligence and cowardice of some of the crew, and was unfit for the return trip. Despite Columbus's reticence, the implications of Spanish misconduct must have been clear. Deliberately, it would seem, no reference whatsoever to the fate of the *Santa María* appears in the Santángel version.

Ships are in fact a prominent topic in the letter of 4 March. Columbus proffers elaborate observations on the advantages of using smaller vessels for exploration and apologetically explains that he had taken larger ones against his better judgment, bowing to pressure from a fearful crew that was reluctant to trust the smaller ships in oceanic navigation. None of these comments appear in the 15 February version, perhaps because they were considered potentially useful to rival expeditions, or perhaps to delete the implication of cowardice among the crew. Whatever the reason, these passages were purged from the public announcement.

Also absent from the 15 February version is any mention of the treachery of Martín Alonso Pinzón, captain of the *Pinta*, who vexed Columbus throughout the voyage, according to the *Diario* and an allusion to "one from Palos" in the letter of 4 March. The full extent of Columbus's complaint about Pinzón is difficult to ascertain because the manuscript of the 4 March copy is severely damaged in this section, but it is evident that Columbus wanted to alert the Crown to Pinzón's insubordination and self-interest in straying from the rest of the fleet to explore on his own. The Santángel letter, however, is completely silent on this issue. Nor does it mention another source of friction—the generalized resistance to the project Columbus encountered at court prior to his departure. The 4 March letter, on the other hand, lingers on the ridicule and ill treatment Columbus had to endure from his detractors, seeming to relish the implicit "I told you so."

Other differences between the royal and public versions of the announcement may seem insignificant at first but, on closer examination, reveal important semantic alterations. Consider, for example, the following almost identical passages:

Quanto tienen y tenían davan por qualquiera cosa que por
ella se le diese, hasta tomar un pedazo de vidrio o de escudilla
rrota o cosa semejante, quiera fuese oro quier fuese otra cosa
de qualquier valor; los cavos de las agujetas de cuero ovo un
marinero más de dos castellanos y medio; y destas cosas ay diez
mill de contar. ("Carta a los Reyes"; Rumeu, 2:437)

Everything they have or had they gave for whatever one gave
them in exchange, even taking a piece of glass or broken
crockery or some such thing, for gold or some other thing
of whatever value. One sailor got more than two and a half
castellanos [in gold] for the ends of leather latchets. There are
ten thousand like occurrences to tell. (Morison, 183)

Yo defendí que no se les diesen cosas tan siviles como pedazos
de escudillas rotas y pedazos de vidrio roto y cabos de agugetas;
haunque cuando ellos esto podían llegar, les parescía haver la
mejor ioya del mundo; qúe se acertó haver un marinero por una
agugeta, de oro de peso de dos castellanos y medio, y otros de
otras cosas que muy menos valían, mucho más. ("Carta a Luis
de Santángel"; Varela, 142; emphasis added)

I forbade that they should be given things so worthless as
pieces of broken crockery and broken glass, and lace points,
although when they were able to get them, they thought they
had the best jewel in the world; thus it was learned that a sailor
for a lace point received gold to the weight of two and a half
castellanos, and others much more for other things which were
worth much less. (Morison, 183)

Both passages deal with the highly favorable rate of exchange the
Europeans obtained from the Taínos owing to their portrayed generosity or naiveté (or, more likely, to their different value system). In
each text the same anecdote of the sailor who managed to negotiate a
nice chunk of gold for a leather latchet is presented as a sort of paradigm of present and future transactions. But in the Santángel version
the added words "Yo defendí" and "haunque cuando" affect not just
the tone, but the entire import of the passage. For what in the letter

to Isabella and Ferdinand was simply an example of the potential for exploiting future trading partners is transformed in the letter to Santángel into a situation created and welcomed by the Indians themselves, despite Columbus's explicit sanctions against such crass abuse. The two short phrases added to the Santángel text turn the Indians into the instigators who invite and perpetuate the uneven negotiations Columbus gallantly tried to prevent—a consummate example of blaming the victim.

Simple differences in the organization of the two texts also produce important semantic variations. For example, consider the passages that describe the Indians' reception of the Spaniards:

> generalmente en quantas tierras yo aya andado, creieron y creen que yo, con estos navíos y gente, venía del çielo, y con este acatamiento me rreçibían, y oy, en el día, están en el mesmo propósito ni se an quitado dello, por mucha conversaçión que ayan tenido con ellos; y luego en llegando a qualquiera poblazón, los hombres y mugeres y niños acidan dando bozes por las casas: "Benid, benid a ver la gente del çielo." ("Carta a los Reyes"; Rumeu, 2:437)

> generally, in whatever lands I traveled, they believed and believe that I, together with these ships and people, came from heaven, and they greeted me with such veneration. And today, this very day, they are of the same mind, nor have they strayed from it, despite all the contact they [the Spaniards at La Navidad] may have had with them. And then upon arriving at whatever settlement, the men, women, and children go from house to house calling out, "Come, come and see the people from heaven!" (Morison, 184)

> y creían muy firme que yo con estos navíos y gente venía del cielo ... Oy en día los traigo que siempre están de propósito que vengo del cielo, por mucha conversación que ayan havido conmigo. Y estos eran los primeros a pronunciarlo adonde yo llegava, y los otros andavan corriendo de casa en casa y a las villas cercanas con bozes altas "Venit, venit a ver la gente del cielo." Así todos, hombres como mugeres, después de haver el corazón seguro de nos, venían que non quedavan grande ni pequeño, y todos traían

algo de comer y de bever, que davan con un amor maravilloso. ("Carta a Luis de Santángel"; Varela, 142–43)

and they are still of the opinion that I come from the sky[8] in spite of all the intercourse which they have had with me, and they were the first to announce this wherever I went, and the others went running from house to house and to the neighboring towns with loud cries of, "Come! Come! See the people from the sky!" They all came, men and women alike, as soon as they had confidence in us, so that not one, big or little, remained behind, and all brought something to eat and drink which they gave us with marvelous love. (Morison, 184)

In isolation, the passage in the letter to Santángel appears to be primarily an expansive paraphrase, a rhetorical intensification that employs repetition, additional modifiers, and detail to recreate more vibrantly the scene of arrival. But, more importantly, the passage has also been relocated and recontextualized. In the letter of 4 March these observations appeared immediately preceding the passage describing the opportunities for exploitative barter, a juxtaposition that highlighted the patently unheavenly conduct of the Christians in response to their hosts' generous and reverent reception. In the letter to Santángel, the welcoming of the Europeans as divine beings follows the mention of the sanctions Columbus placed on unfair trading. Thus the scene of arrival now effectively confirms and even underscores the Admiral's laudable ethical comportment, and the reverential reception given to the Europeans by the Indians appears well-deserved.

Moreover, in the letter to Santángel, the passage immediately preceding that of the arrival describes the evangelical dimension of the expedition and Columbus's generosity toward the Indians. In repositioning and recontextualizing the scene of arrival, the letter in effect redefines the terms of exchange: The crass exploitation of the natives related in the royal missive is refashioned into a reciprocal interaction that bespeaks the noble Christian character of the Spaniards. The letter that announces the Discovery to Christian European readers presents the image of a paternal Columbus who brings the word of God to the heathens and seeks to protect them not so much from Spanish greed as from their own naiveté, a man worthy of the Indians' adoration and the Crown's favor.

Perhaps the most striking difference between the letter to the sovereigns and the published letter to Santángel is the deletion of several concluding paragraphs in the latter. Three of these paragraphs contain direct petitions to the Crown for favors and the fulfillment of the honors and rewards promised Columbus in the "Capitulaciones de Santa Fe" (17 April 1492). Specifically, these include a request for the concession of favors for services rendered, together with a letter of petition to the Pope asking for a cardinalate for Columbus's legitimate son Diego, and a request for the appointment of Pedro de Villacorta, a Columbus favorite, to the post of paymaster of the Indies. The nature of the petitions themselves is probably not as significant as is the fact that the royal letter contains them while the Santángel version does not. Such petitions, of course, would have been inappropriate, indeed irrelevant, in a letter addressed to anyone but the Crown, and they may have been omitted by Columbus himself if he in fact wrote the original version of the letter to Santángel (even before the idea of publication came into play).

Nonetheless, the petitions in the royal letter significantly color the reader's conceptualization of the Discovery in underscoring the contractual character of the enterprise. As the petitions remind us, Columbus's fate rested in the Crown's perception of the success or failure of his endeavor. The purpose of the letter announcing the Discovery to the royal sponsors of the expedition was not simply to transmit an objective account of what Columbus witnessed and experienced. Rather, it was a fairly transparent attempt to advocate for the protagonist's interests before Isabella and Ferdinand. From this perspective, every observation on the lands and peoples is marked by the contractual pragmatics that determine and define the acts of writing and of reading. Nowhere is this more evident than in Columbus's supplication that "la honrra me sea dada según el serviçio" (441; honor be bestowed upon me according to [the quality of] my service). In the final analysis, the announcement of the Discovery in the letter of 4 March is the account of the quality of the service rendered by the protagonist and a petition for commensurate compensation.

Ferdinand and Isabella seemed to have recognized Columbus's announcement as such a request, as their response of 30 March indicates:

Don Cristóbal Colón, nuestro almirante del Mar Océano e visorrey y gobernador de las islas que se han descubierto en las Indias: vimos vuestras letras, y hobimos mucho placer en saber lo que por ellas nos escribistes, y de haberos dado Dios tan buen fin en vuestro trabajo, y encaminado bien en lo que comenzaste, en que él será mucho servido, y nosotros asimismo y nuestros reinos recibir tanto provecho.... Placerá a Dios que demás de lo que en esto le servides, por ello recibiréis de Nos muchas mercedes, *las cuales creed que se vos harán con* (sic) *vuestros servicios e trabajos lo merescen.* (Rumeu, 1:35; emphasis added)

Don Cristóbal Colón, our admiral of the Ocean Sea and viceroy and governor of the islands that have been discovered in the Indies: we read your letters, and derived great pleasure from learning what you wrote to us in them, and that God has given such success to your labor, and set what you began on such a good path, in which He, and we also, will be well served, and our kingdoms will receive so much profit.... It will please God that besides the service you have rendered to Him, you will receive from Us many favors for it, *which favors you can trust will be granted unto you according to the merit of your services and labors.* (emphasis added)

In the salutation the Crown explicitly acknowledges and confirms the titles of admiral, viceroy, and governor promised to Columbus in the "Capitulaciones." Moreover, echoing his letter of 4 March, this letter directly links the bestowal of royal favors to his labors and the quality of his service. In deleting the contractual pragmatics of Columbus's announcement, the Santángel version redefined the Discovery—from an enterprise marked by significant national and private interests to a heroic, selfless mission on behalf of Christendom.

Yet another paragraph from the letter to the sovereigns, but absent from the Santángel version, contains arguably the most important contribution the recent publication of the 4 March letter has made to our understanding of the Columbian enterprise. Columbus asserts that the project was undertaken for the expressed purpose of helping to finance a Spanish military campaign to reconquer the Holy Land:

Concluio aquí: que mediante la graçia divinal, de aquél ques comienço de todas cosas virtuosas y buenas y que da favor y victoria a todos aquéllos que van en su camino, que de oy en siete años yo podré pagar a Vuestras Altezas çinco mill de cavallo y çinquenta mill de pie en la guerra e conquista de Iherusalem, *sobre el qual propósito se tomó esta empresa.* (Rumeu, 2:440; emphasis added)

I conclude here: that through the divine grace of He who is the origin of all good and virtuous things, who favors and gives victory to all those who walk in His path, that in seven years from today I will be able to pay Your Highnesses for five thousand cavalry and fifty thousand foot soldiers for the war and conquest of Jerusalem, *for which purpose this enterprise was undertaken.* (emphasis added)

The topic of the reconquest of Jerusalem becomes very prominent in Columbian discourse from the third voyage on. The passage cited above is repeated almost verbatim in a letter Columbus addressed to Pope Alexander VI in 1502 (Varela, 312). The recovery of Jerusalem is also a principal theme of the *Libro de las profecías* and of two letters, one addressed to Queen Isabella; the other to the sovereigns together, both written in 1501. The royal missive of 4 March strongly suggests that the project had already been discussed with the Crown prior to the inception of the first voyage. And yet such a remarkable statement of purpose, which would undoubtedly have impressed any Christian reader, does not appear in the version of the letter published precisely to broadcast the news of the voyage's success throughout Christendom.[9] This deletion is even more perplexing if one is persuaded by Ramos's contention that the letter's publication was intended not only for general propaganda but specifically to thwart Portuguese pretensions at the Vatican and to pave the way for Castilian negotiations for a bull of concession of the newly found lands from the Pope.[10] In any case, the Crown may have felt the commitment to evangelization proclaimed in the letter was sufficient to ensure that the Church would be well-disposed toward the enterprise without the additional, and much more costly, commitment to a campaign for the Holy Land. Whatever the reasons, the link between the Discovery and the reconquest of Jerusalem was dropped from the published version, rendering the enterprise of Discovery less religiously committed and certainly less messianic than Columbus seems to have intended.[11]

Thus the active promotion of the Santángel version of Columbus's announcement of the Discovery, together with the suppression of the royal version, created a revised image of the event that was the product of reading at least as much as of the original scriptural act, whatever that may have been. For almost five hundred years our sense of the Discovery has been the product of a reading that appears to have been little concerned with the objective representation of the geographical and anthropological aspects of the lands in question, or with historical accuracy. The Santángel version was much more interested in its own reception; that is, it was fashioned for the readers it sought to engage and the reactions it hoped to elicit. So, undoubtedly, was the letter of 4 March to the sovereigns that the Santángel text supplanted in the public arena, although it did so in significantly different ways, as we have seen.

The first mediation in the transmission of Columbian writing to future readers was an erasure, as Rojas suggested in the prologue to *Celestina*, a reading that eradicated one text and created another. The 15 February Santángel/Sánchez texts replaced the royal missive as the "original" announcements of the Discovery, and the surrogate versions were invested with all the privilege and authority of primogeniture. The unprecedented blanketing of Europe with copies and translations of the 15 February version of the announcement all but ensured that it would be the one transmitted to posterity. A sobering reminder that acts of reading, like storms at sea and other acts of God or Fate, have the power to erase—and to rewrite—the text of history.

NOTES

1. He strapped another barrel with like contents to the ship's stern (Varela, 127). Ferdinand Columbus, in his account of the first voyage, quotes his father's words regarding this first letter announcing the Discovery:

    > escribí en un pergamino, con la brevedad que el tiempo exigía, cómo yo dejaba descubiertas aquellas tierras que les había prometido; en cuántos días y por qué camino lo había logrado; la bondad del país y la condición de sus habitantes, y cómo quedaban los vasallos de

Vuestras Altezas en posesión de todo lo que se había descubierto. Cuya escritura, cerrada y sellada, dirigí a Vuestras Altezas con el porte, es a saber, promesa de mil ducados a aquél que la presentara sin abrir. A fin de que si hombres extranjeros la encontrasen, no se valiesen del aviso que dentro había, con la avidez del porte. Muy luego hice que me llevaran un gran barril, y habiendo envuelto la escritura en una tela encerada, y metido ésta en torta u hogaza de cera, la puse en el barril. Y bien sujeto con sus aros, lo eché al mar, creyendo todos que sería alguna devoción. Y porque pensé que podría suceder que no llegase a salvamento, y los navíos aun caminaban para acercarse a Castilla, hice otro atado semejante al primero, y lo puse en lo alto de la popa para que, si se hundía el navío, quedase el barril sobre las olas a merced de la tormenta. (Fernando Colón, *Vida del Almirante Don Cristóbal Colón* [Mexico: Fondo de Cultura Económica, 1947], 123, chap. 37)

I wrote on a parchment, as briefly as the state of things required, how I had discovered those lands as I had promised to do; the length of the voyage and the route thither; the goodness of the country and the customs of its inhabitants; and how I had left Your Highnesses' vassals in possession of all I had discovered. This writing, folded and sealed, I addressed to Your Highnesses with a written promise of 1,000 ducats to whoever should deliver it sealed to you; this I did so that if it should fall into the hands of foreigners, they would be restrained by the reward from divulging the information it contained to others. I straightway [*sic*] had a great wooden barrel brought to me, and having wrapped the writing in a waxed cloth and put it in a cake or loaf of wax, I dropped it into the barrel, which I made secure with hoops and cast into the sea; and all thought this was an act of devotion. I still feared the barrel might not reach safety, but as the ships meanwhile were drawing closer to Castile I lashed a similar cask at the head of the stern, so that if the ship sank, it might float on the waves at the mercy of the storm. (Fernando

Colón, *The Life of the Admiral Christopher Columbus by His
Son Ferdinand*, ed. and trans. Benjamin Keen [Westport,
Conn.: Greenwood Press, 1978], 92)

2. According to the *Diario*, Columbus would have been off the
   coast of the Azores on 15 February 1493, not the Canaries, as the
   15 February letter claims. The patent discrepancy supports the
   argument that the text could not have been written by Columbus
   or, at least, must have been altered after leaving his hands.

3. Ferdinand Columbus's *Vida del Almirante* and Bartolomé de
   Las Casas's *Historia de las Indias*.

4. For the background on this copy, see Rumeu, 1:19–20. Rumeu
   considers the manuscript an authentic sixteenth-century
   transcription, perhaps two or three copies or more removed
   from the original and containing a few insignificant errors. For
   another evaluation of the authenticity of the *Libro Copiador*,
   see P. E. Taviani, C. Varela, J. Gil, and M. Conti, eds., *Relazione
   e lettere sul secundo, terzo, e quarto viaggio* (Nuova Raccolta
   Colombiana), 2 vols. (Rome, Istituto Poligrafico e Zecca dello
   Stato, 1992), 1:163–82. The authenticity of the manuscript is
   likely to be a topic of debate in years to come, however, as more
   specialists have the opportunity to evaluate it.

5. Demetrio Ramos Pérez, *La primera noticia de America*
   (Valladolid: Seminario Americanista de la Universidad de
   Valladolid, 1986). The value of this study, which has not yet
   received the attention it deserves, is enhanced by Ramos's
   inclusion of a transcription and facsimile of the archival copy of
   the letter of 15 February addressed to Santángel.

6. The extent and consequences of Las Casas's editing is the subject
   of "All these are the Admiral's exact words," later in this volume.

7. See Ramos, *La primera noticia de America*, 74–86. He further
   argues that there was no letter addressed to Sánchez, but rather
   that the translator, of the Latin version, the only one that names
   Sánchez as an addressee, confused him with Santángel.

8. I disagree with Morison's translation of *cielo* in this context as
   "sky," rather than "heaven"; both the 4 March and 15 February
   letters imply that the Indians took the Spaniards for divine
   beings, venerating them and making offerings to them as such.

9. The letter was published in Rome, Florence, Barcelona, Basel,
   Paris, and Amsterdam.

10. See Ramos, *La primera noticia de América*, 62–67.
11. On the evolving importance of Jerusalem within the Columbian articulation of Discovery, see "Voyage to Paradise," in [*Reading Columbus*].

THE CURE AT TROY
(SEAMUS HEANEY)

AND

PHILOCTETES
(SOPHOCLES)

"Seamus Heaney, Colonialism, and the Cure: Sophoclean Re-Visions"
by Hugh Denard, in *PAJ:*
A Journal of Performance and Art (2000)

INTRODUCTION

In this analysis of *The Cure at Troy*, Nobel Laureate Seamus Heaney's recasting of Sophocles' play *Philoctetes*, Hugh Denard explores how Heaney's version offers many allegorical possibilities for understanding Irish terrorism and British colonialism. For Denard, colonization presupposes the superiority of the colonizer to the colonized, constituting "a grievance-perpetuating myth" that promotes a "culture of victims and victors." Heaney's Irish reworking of Sophocles' play, as Denard notes, was invoked by many Irish seeking peace in the 1990s. Thus "*The Cure at Troy* both represents, and is *itself*, symbolically, a groundbreaking, postcolonial voice" within both an historical and literary context. Denard concludes that Heaney's work constitutes "a vision of a radical reconciliatory future for Northern Ireland" during a time when such optimistic dreams were had by few.

Denard, Hugh. "Seamus Heaney, Colonialism, and the Cure: Sophoclean Re-Visions." *PAJ: A Journal of Performance and Art* 22. 3 (September 2000): 1–18.

In November 1990, the election to the Irish presidency of Mary
Robinson heralded an overnight transformation of the iconography
of State in the Republic of Ireland. Robinson was a progressive young
constitutional lawyer and a brave champion of civil rights; her election to this largely symbolic role was seen by many to mark a national
"coming of age." It was certainly one of the most clearly defined and
defining moments in Irish history since partition. In her inauguration
speech she set the tone for her Presidency with the words:

> History says, *Don't hope*
> *On this side of the grave.*
> But then, once in a lifetime
> The longed-for tidal wave
> Of justice can rise up,
> And hope and history rhyme.
>
> So hope for a great sea-change
> On the far side of revenge.
> Believe that a further shore
> Is reachable from here.[1]

These words were drawn from Seamus Heaney's version of Sophocles'
Philoctetes, entitled *The Cure at Troy*.

Four years later, on August 31, 1994, the IRA announced its first
ceasefire in twenty-five years, this marking the opening of a new
chapter of different possibilities, and different fears, throughout the
island of Ireland. A striking symmetry revealed itself on December
1 of the following year when, mirroring Robinson's inaugural speech,
Bill Clinton recited the same words from *The Cure at Troy* as he stood
on the steps of the Bank of Ireland, bringing the weight of American
influence and dollars to bear on the Northern Irish peace process.
The Bank, still crowned by symbols of royal authority from its days
as the Irish Houses of Commons and Lords under British rule, faces
the front gates of Trinity College, which was established in 1592 by
Elizabeth I to be the educational foundation for the Anglicization of
Ireland. The symbolism of the occasion was unmistakable.

Also in 1995, Jacques Santer, President of the European Commission, addressed the Forum for Peace and Reconciliation in Dublin
Castle; he too looked to *The Cure at Troy* for a vocabulary through

which he could express his aspiration that "history and hope can be made to rhyme" in Ireland. Indeed, shortly after his visit, Judge Catherine McGuinness, the Chair of the Forum, wrote in the *Irish Times* that "these words could be a motto for the forum, set up as it was in the climate of hope and optimism induced by the paramilitary ceasefires." Heaney had not yet been awarded the Nobel Prize for Literature (1995) nor the Whitbread Prize for his translation of *Beowulf* (2000), but nonetheless, there are surely few dramatic texts which can claim to have acquired such prominence in the political affairs of modern times.

Among the various narratives of identity which have shaped political and social discourses in Northern Ireland, those which have themselves been structured by the discourse of colonialism have perhaps been the most decisive. Heaney's work boldly opened up a dialogue between its Sophoclean model and the culture and politics of Northern Ireland. To the Sophoclean representation of a wounded, embittered Philoctetes, Heaney brought the experience of suffering in Northern Ireland. To the Northern Irish crisis, the Sophoclean model brought a vision of miraculous redemption which, in Heaney's version, avoided merely aestheticizing "The Troubles" by the toughness and realism of its tenor, and the long shadows of irony with which it concludes. But in this article, I propose a reading of Seamus Heaney's *The Cure at Troy* which does not merely take place within colonial discourse, but rather which takes Heaney's version as a pretext for subjecting that discourse itself to interrogation. Challenging its value as a template for historical and political narratives in and of Northern Ireland, I arrive at the following conclusions:

Colonial discourse itself, as an interpretative paradigm or episteme, has served to lock Catholics and Protestants (and critics and analysts of the crisis) into accepting the seemingly inescapable, historically determined roles of colonized and colonist respectively. These roles, manifested in a culture of victims and victors, has exercised a malign influence upon all aspects of life in Northern Ireland against which the politics of reconciliation continually has had to pit itself. Notwithstanding the apparent exhaustion of colonial discourse as an adequate paradigm for making sense of relations between Catholics and Protestants in Northern Ireland in present times, colonial discourse *continues* to be preserved and exploited in various ways as a grievance-perpetuating myth. Challenging this arid legacy, however, it can be argued that, in fact, neither of the mythically "pure" identities of colonist and colonized remain intact indefinitely; the process of colonialism in fact produces a hybrid, "postcolonial" consciousness in both the historical colonist and colonized. *The Cure at Troy* allows us to observe what happens when this shared hybridity is recognized and is made the basis of new relationships based on respect for both the wounds and the worth of the historical "Other." *The Cure at Troy* therefore constitutes an important part of a new, postcolonial mythology in Northern Ireland. Conceived at a meeting of the Field Day Theatre Company directorate in December 1989, and premièred the following October, the version embodied these insights well in advance of their later incorporation in the institutions which were set up by the Good Friday Agreement and ratified by referenda north and south of the border. To that extent, *The Cure at Troy* both represents, and is *itself*, symbolically, a groundbreaking, postcolonial voice.

* * *

Heaney's version represented the latest contribution to a century-long tradition of such translations in Ireland, beginning with Yeats's versions of *Oedipus the King* and *Oedipus at Colonus* in 1926 and 1927 respectively. Like Yeats, Heaney worked from a selection of prior translations. Derek Walcott and others at Harvard advised on details of classical scholarship, resulting in a blank verse text, with a number of choruses which have no antecedent in the Greek play. On the whole, Heaney's version is characterized by a conservative attentiveness to the dignity of the Greek original, in contrast to more robustly independent versions of Greek tragedy by, for instance, Brecht, Fugard, Soyinka, or Anouilh. As with his illustrious predecessors in the project of reworking Greek tragedy, through creating allegorical apertures, the project enabled Heaney to explore and articulate the interface between history and myth (ancient and modern). Moreover, Greek tragedy could be represented as an "honest broker" between rival pieties in Northern Ireland; its supposedly eternal verities enshrined within the edifice of canonical authority—notions particularly attractive to a culture transfixed by atavistic conceptions of the past: Sophocles was ripe for revisionism.

The version employs a number of terms which draw attention to connections between the culture(s) of Northern Ireland and the characters in the play. Immediately prior to the arrival of the *deus ex machina*, Hercules, the Chorus speaks the words:

> The innocent in gaols
> Beat on their bars together.
> A hunger-striker's father
> Stands in the graveyard dumb.
> The police widow in veils
> Faints at the funeral home.[2]

These words and phrases are among the many which evoke the public rhetoric and attitudes that "the troubles" in Northern Ireland have produced: "traitor," "that alliance," "Never. No. No matter how I'm besieged," "What sort of surrender do you want?" "Where's the ambush?" "There's a courage / And dignity in ordinary people / That can be breathtaking," "tainted with their guilt / Just by association," "turncoat," to name but a few. Heaney recalls that his version was:

> ... full of echoes that worked within the first circle of vigilance
> and suspicion in the North. The word "traitor" for example is a
> faintly old-fashioned word within the larger acoustic of English,
> but within the British establishment and the Northern Orange
> idiom ..."Traitor" is a great Paisley word. It's loaded with a big
> common voltage, and that's what you want.[3]

On a more general level, the language also serves to locate the version in a recognizably Irish context, with terms such as "slabbering," "canny" and "canniness," "hagged" (for "hacked"), "clouts," "is his head away?" "shake-down," "wheesht!" "that put me wild," "I am astray," "blather?" "shilly-shallying." "This is it ..." becoming a statement of bewilderment, and the vernacular Heaney gives to the Sophoclean Merchant character, especially the use of the present simple in describing past events ("So Odysseus organises a night raid," etc.), is also recognizably Irish. In addition, there are a couple of well-known Heaneyisms woven into the version, which are associated with his attempts to address the question of what poets' responses to crisis in their polities should be: "You should govern your tongue and present a true case"—Heaney has a volume of essays called *The Government of the Tongue*.[4] As Neoptolemus prepares to rectify an injustice, he says:

"I'm going to redress the balance," which is reminiscent of its usage in Heaney's essay "The Redress of Poetry" in which he argues for an art which can act as a form of imaginative redress to the polarities and imbalances in political, social, and other spheres.[5]

More directly, Heaney himself has suggested that Philoctetes' position in *The Cure at Troy* could "suit a Sinn Féiner." In *The Cure at Troy*, Philoctetes has been marooned on Lemnos and excluded from his rightful place in Greek society. As the play opens, the Greeks have returned to Lemnos to further their act of dispossession by taking from him the bow and arrows bequeathed to him by Hercules. Dispossession and marginalization are concepts central to the understanding of the Northern Irish, Catholic, nationalist culture from which Seamus Heaney sprang. They were also central to the Jacobean colonization of Ulster. A key moment in the reformulation of colonial attitudes in Northern Ireland came in 1921 when, at the behest of Protestant Unionists, the independence of Ireland from British rule was only partially realized and whole communities of unwilling Northern Irish Catholics found themselves stranded in a Protestant-dominated statelet which proceeded systematically to deprive Catholics of equality in employment and housing through extensive manipulation of constituency boundaries and voting procedures ("gerrymandering"), which left the control of these areas in the hands of Unionist politicians. Deprived, excluded from power both inside and outside the province and denied any means of political redress, Catholic frustration eventually found expression in the form of a peaceful civil rights movement which was violently repressed by Unionists at official and unofficial levels on the pretext that the movement was a cover for militant republican activities. In such conditions, backlash was inevitable and the Unionist pretext soon obtained a basis in fact.

If one imagines an alignment of Philoctetes with a broadly Catholic stance, and Odysseus and Neoptolemus as occupying something akin to a Protestant position, Philoctetes with his bow can easily be regarded as analogous to a pre-ceasefire I.R.A., or militant republican position. His arms are "decommissioned" by deception at first—the promise to take him "home" perhaps signifying the end of partition—and then by force. He is to be coerced into participating in a colonial enterprise which is anathema to him, signaling, in this allegory, a return to the days of unbridled Protestant ascendancy through Stormont rule. On his persistent refusal to join the campaign, he is deserted again. This tallies with traditional republican attitudes towards British initiatives in Northern Ireland which were characterized above all by suspicion and skepticism, always fearing that "perfidious Albion" would act in bad faith. In such a climate, the trust necessary for voluntary disarmament was entirely absent. The fear was that the Protestant state would be content to exclude and deprive them again as soon as they no longer posed a military threat.

But that is not the only possible allegorical reading of *Philoctetes* in relation to modern-day Northern Ireland. One could equally read *Philoctetes* as representing the besieged mentality of 1990s Ulster Unionism, fearing a repeat betrayal at every step, as in the Treaty of Independence of 1921, the Sunningdale Agreement of 1974, or the Anglo-Irish Agreement of 1985. In such a reading, the Neoptolemus–Odysseus partnership would represent the alliance of the perennially distrusted Irish government and the faithless British government who had "sold out" in the past and, given a chance, would do so again. Here, the bow represents the double lines of defense rendered by the Protestant police state and loyalist paramilitarism, ever ready to avenge any attack or betrayal. Their resistance to the assimilation of the two communities was expressed by a point-blank refusal to cooperate in any power-sharing executive or cross-border arrangements; hence the workers' strike of 1974 against the Sunningdale Agreement that marked the end, for twenty years, of the chance of conciliatory, cooperative politics in Northern Ireland, as Heaney recounted in his Nobel address.

When seen in the context of colonial discourse, these divergent but equally plausible allegorical readings illustrate how the version may represent the independence of the south of Ireland as having profoundly affected the colonialist consciousness, with serious ramifications for the colonized. Protestants in Ulster, viewed by nationalists as the historical colonists, themselves feared the "colonizing" consciousness of the South as it was then enshrined in Articles 2 and 3 of the Irish constitution. (These articles have since been repealed by the referendum that ratified the Good Friday Agreement.) The Catholic community in Northern Ireland was therefore perceived as treacherous fifth-columnists. The upshot of this is that both unionists and nationalists were in highly ambivalent positions regarding their own locations in a colonial discourse. Both shared in, or were perceived to share in, elements of a colonizing, as well as colonized, mentality, and this ambivalence is reflected in *The Cure at Troy*. The version is therefore a potentially flexible vehicle through which Heaney could explore the multiple layers of complex relations in Northern Ireland, between past and present, nationalist and unionist.[6]

Heaney's version often realizes the possibility of polyvalent allegorical alignments through a careful and often ingenious reworking of language and imagery. In the Sophoclean play, for instance, Philoctetes comments on the injustice that has been done to him; whereas Philoctetes had joined the expedition against Troy voluntarily, contributing seven ships, Odysseus had been coerced into service. This detail would tend to cast Philoctetes as willing exponent of the colonial project. Heaney omits it. Through such translational operations, Heaney's version of the play continues to remain open to the widest possible range of allegorical readings with regard to its significance for Irish affairs.

The outlines of possible allegorical readings above lead to the conclusion that, in reading the *Philoctetes* in relation to modern-day Northern Ireland, as *The Cure at Troy* does, neither the narrative of the colonist, nor that of the colonized, is exclusively dominant. It does, however, portray colonial discourse itself as a dominant, thus reflecting the primacy in Northern Irish culture of the Catholic–Protestant divide. The most overt evidence of this discursive dominance of colonial attitudes was sustained paramilitary campaign against the perceived colonizing power (a campaign construed by the ideologues of militant republicanism as the tradition of "a rising in every generation"), and in the correspondingly ruthless military and legal means of opposing it. The dominance of colonial discourse further manifested and perpetuated itself by the constructs of "Otherness" represented in the irreconcilable oppositions of Catholic and Protestant, nationalist and unionist cultures.

In any of the allegorical readings offered above, Odysseus and, in the earlier part of the play, Neoptolemus, represent a colonizing mentality—the relation of Odysseus to Philoctetes is always one of colonist to colonized. By definition colonial discourse relies upon the assertion of a fundamental distinction between colonist Self (superior) and colonized Other (inferior); to dissolve that distinction would be to step beyond the bounds of colonial discourse. Yet, in *The Cure at Troy*, Neoptolemus offers Philoctetes the possibility of being assimilated into the colonizing body on the basis of equality. In returning to Philoctetes the ill-gotten bow, and offering to take him home to Greece in good faith, Neoptolemus represents the dissolution of the very distinction upon which not just colonialism, but colonial discourse itself, depends. Furthermore, Heaney's version seems to suggest that the postcolonial condition produces hybrid forms of consciousness in both colonized and colonist. Seen in this light, Heaney's version represents not only a critique of colonialism and colonial attitudes, but also a route-map to a new postcoloniality.

* * *

I will now analyze these structures by examining a common trope of colonial rhetoric which figures largely in *The Cure at Troy*, namely the rhetoric whereby the colonists attempt to assert their "natural superiority" over the colonized through attributing to the colonized subhumanity/animalism. Pursuing this approach, it can be seen that throughout the version, the Greeks systematically construct an image of Philoctetes as subhuman, animalistic (Calibanesque), and one who can therefore legitimately be hunted by them. Ironically, however, it is this very construct which, while it enables them to assume superiority over him, nevertheless also radically undermines those claims to superiority.

The language of Sophocles' *Philoctetes* is laden with references to animals and with terminology associated with hunting.[7] There is an ideological overlap between the "Otherness" of slavery and of animalism. In many cases the colonist seems to make little distinction between the two states:

ODYSSEUS:
Yes.
> This is the place.
> This strand.
This is Lemnos all right.
> Not a creature!

Odysseus's brief first words, establishing the landscape as Lemnos, conclude: "Not a creature!" We may assume that he is referring to the absence of fauna, but this becomes less clear as the Odyssean narrative unfolds and as he describes to Neoptolemus why Philoctetes was marooned on the island:

> We couldn't even get peace at the altar
> Without him breaking out in these howling fits,
> And slabbering and cursing.

Odysseus describes Philoctetes in terms which are half-animal, half-human: "slabbering and cursing." A few lines later, Odysseus imagines Philoctetes to be "out scavenging, likely, / Poking for things to eat."[8] Shortly after that, Neoptolemus refers to Philoctetes as "the creature,"[9] and Odysseus tells Neoptolemus that the use of deceit will result in Philoctetes "eating out of your hand."[10] The association of the colonized with animals commonly occurs as part of the colonist's construction of the "Other" in colonial discourse. Defining the colonized as bestial is a highly useful ruse for the colonist in a number of ways, the most obvious of which is that the colonized "Other" need not be dealt with in terms of equality. It is a norm of Western civilization that it is valid to exploit animals for service and materials; that animals are considered primarily in terms of their value to humans. More precisely, from as early as Roman times the public display and hunting of animals (e.g., in the arena) was an important part of the performance of imperialism, signifying the ascendancy of Rome over nature and foreign lands.[11] According to their usefulness or profitability, animals are tamed, domesticated, or conquered. In *The Cure at Troy*, Philoctetes is physically represented as a "wild man," although he has not a Caliban's fins or fangs to lend credence to the colonists' definitions of him as an animal. Even when Philoctetes supposes that he looks "like a wild animal," he is referring only to his unkempt state.[12] In *The Cure at Troy*, therefore (unlike Shakespeare's *The Tempest*), the audience is physically confronted with the fictionality of the colonists' constructions of the colonized.

As with the colonist/colonized relation, the essential human/animal relation is one of exploitation. The primary relation of Odysseus, and initially Neoptolemus, to Philoctetes is also one of exploitation. Neither is concerned with Philoctetes as a fellow human being, but only that he is the possessor of the magical bow. Odysseus urges Neoptolemus to "Sweet talk him and relieve him / Of a bow and arrows that are actually miraculous," and Neoptolemus agrees that "The weapons are our target." Republican analysis of the Northern Irish crisis is determinedly and self-consciously located within a discourse of colonialism, as this perpetuates a sense of historical grievance: vital fuel for the movement. The classic republican position on British involvement in Northern Ireland is that it is, and always has been, determined by exploitation. Humanitarian considerations, especially regarding Catholics, are perceived to be secondary to the economic, military, and political advantages to Britain's "occupation." The Sinn Féin account of "the nature of the problem" as given to the Forum for Peace and Reconciliation in November 1994 states this position succinctly:

> Even the British Government would acknowledge that ... British policy on Ireland was driven in the past by strategic, military, economic and political imperatives. Partition is the product of that policy. Currently, the British Government have amended their position by disclaiming any military or economic interest. However, they have refused to declare that they have no "political" interest.[13]

Evocative of this interpretation, Heaney represents Odysseus' and Neoptolemus' perception of Philoctetes as so exclusively determined by his potential value that they do not initially even seem to distinguish between the man and the bow; when Neoptolemus hears Philoctetes crying out in pain, his immediate response is excitedly to exclaim: "This is the hour of the bow!" There is no Sophoclean precedent for this comment which turns the cries of Philoctetes, if not Philoctetes himself, into a metonym for the bow—for Neoptolemus, Philoctetes is not a man deserving of pity, but rather an opportunity for his own gain. This view of Philoctetes is contrary to the sense of the oracle which explicitly states that Philoctetes must "leave this island—of his own accord." For Odysseus, therefore, a combination of deception and force are what is required to bring Philoctetes to Troy; he cannot conceive of the relation with Philoctetes as one of equality. Once the bow has been procured, he quickly gives up any attempt to force or persuade Philoctetes to come to Troy in a manner that reveals his motives:

> All we need
> Is Philoctetes' bow. Not him ...
> . . . .
> You should have been the Lord of Fallen Troy
> But that's an honour fallen now to me.

This may be a ruse to provoke Philoctetes to go to Troy, but either way, with or without Philoctetes in the boat, Odysseus cannot lose. In the Sophoclean play, Odysseus persuades the reluctant Neoptolemus to use deceit to get the bow by describing the benefit of such actions to the boy:

> ODYSSEUS:
> You would be said to combine in yourself ability and courage.
> NEOPTOLEMUS:
> So be it. I shall cast aside all shame and do it.[14]

Heaney's Neoptolemus can see that the repute he may gain may be at variance with the truth, but Odysseus' argument based on selfish gain is still sufficient to persuade him:

> ODYSSEUS:
> You'll be praised for courage first.
>   Then for farsightedness.
> NEOPTOLEMUS:
> Duplicity! Complicity!
>   All right.
>   I'll do it.

Another primary relation between human and animal is that of hunter to hunted. When this relation is extended to colonial discourse, the relation between colonist and colonized becomes essentially one of opposition; the "Other" is not only different, the "Other" is an enemy. So long as this relation obtains, the interests of "Self" and "Other" can never coincide. In Sophocles' *Philoctetes*, too, Odysseus' descriptions of Philoctetes as animal free him from the need to treat Philoctetes with either the pity or justice that a full recognition of his humanity, Greekness, or of his heroic status and aristocratic ancestry would demand.[15] As an animal, he can validly be treated as a quarry to be hunted for the gain of the hunters. His accommodation is described as a "den" (*aulion*, lines 954, 1087, and 1149). In Heaney's version, the term is used from the outset of the play:

> Somewhere here he has a sort of den,
> ....
> Go very easy now.

> Study the lie of the land
> And then we'll plan the moves.

Odysseus implicates Neoptolemus in his construction of their relation to Philoctetes as one of hunter to hunted, portraying Philoctetes as a wounded animal who is their quarry. Neoptolemus seems to accept the Odyssean narrative in its entirety, soon afterwards instructing the Chorus to "Be very careful as you go. / Keep on the lookout for the creature." Indeed, Heaney amplifies the Sophoclean hunting imagery when he has Philoctetes ask Odysseus: "Are you going to herd me like a wild animal?"[16] Odysseus affirms that he considers this a valid option: "That's up to you."

In the context of colonialism in Ireland, however, the repercussions of the hunting imagery are somewhat removed from those envisaged by Sophocles, and Heaney has reworked the imagery accordingly. Whereas in the Greek play the relation of hunter to hunted derives from designations of Philoctetes as animal-like, in Heaney's version, hunting images are often supplemented or changed to images of military maneuvers. For Heaney's Greeks, while Philoctetes can be hunted, it is not only as an animal, but also as a human; he is a legitimate military target. "Catching" the bow (*lephthésetai*) in line 68 of *Philoctetes* is rendered by Heaney as "commandeer." Another occurrence of the hunting term in line 107 (*labónta*) is replaced by Heaney with the phrase: "Combat is out." "Leading" or "bringing" (*agein*) in line 90 becomes "Why could we not / Go at him, man to man?" The bow is Neoptolemus' "quarry" (*therate*) in line 116, but in Heaney's version it is "our target." In each case, the hunting references have been phrased in language which carries military connotations. Heaney thus exploits the Sophoclean imagery to represent dimensions of the consequences of colonialism and counter-colonialism in present-day Northern Ireland, drawing his version into a frame of reference which at once looks back to the Sophoclean play and forward to the modern culture to which it is addressed.

The superiority that the Greeks assume over Philoctetes is compromised by their own description of their relation to him as one of hunter to hunted. We have already seen how this stratum of imagery contributes to the depiction of Philoctetes as an animal, but it also serves to call into question the humanity of those who hunt—those who are, supposedly, "civilized."[17] Read in terms of colonial discourse, the hunting theme in *The Cure at Troy* exposes the sub-civilized dimension of the colonialist no less than that of the colonized. Moreover, reading Heaney's version in the context of colonial discourse reveals that such brutal methods of repression through dehumanization, which brutalize the colonist as well as the colonized, are the unavoidable adjuncts to colonialism and colonial attitudes. That the colonial enterprise inflicts psychological wounds upon the colonist can be observed in the character of Neoptolemus. Having successfully deprived Philoctetes of his bow by deceit, Neoptolemus' qualms rise to the surface. He is visibly upset, but Philoctetes does not, as yet, understand that he has been betrayed, asking "what has upset you now? Don't be afflicted." Neoptolemus responds: "I'm an affliction to myself, that's all I am." The word "affliction" is only used on two other occasions in Heaney's version, each time to refer to Philoctetes' wound. Neoptolemus' "wound" is inflicted upon him by his involvement in the colonial project because it requires him to "wound" Philoctetes. Heaney, indeed, often alters the Sophoclean hunting imagery, giving it military connotations so that it can evoke colonial attitudes in modern-day Northern Ireland, such as the following example in which the Merchant describes the scene at Troy:

> So Odysseus organizes a night raid
> And with all his usual old dirty dodges
> He captures Helenus and shows him off
> In front of the Greek army.

By exposing the brutality of the "colonist," this passage also undermines the rhetoric which justifies colonialism on the grounds that it is a "civilizing" force. Here, the supposed civilizer, using "dirty dodges" and showing his prisoner off as a trophy, is portrayed as little short of barbaric.

Highly conscious of the brutality of the Greeks, Philoctetes turns the colonists' terms against them, and defines *them*, rather than himself, as animals—a reversal of the application of the animal stigma which is not present in Sophocles. Philoctetes, betrayed, calls Neoptolemus a "Hard little two-faced crab." That Neoptolemus has indeed two "faces" eventually comes to be Philoctetes' salvation, but at this moment, the sideways scuttling crab seems to Heaney's Philoctetes the perfect image of deceit. He goes on to describe himself as having been "bitten" by Neoptolemus, implicitly likening his betrayer to the snake that wounded him—another reversal of the colonist's animal imagery by the colonized. Philoctetes reiterates this metaphor a little later when he addresses Neoptolemus: "You slithered in like this, / All sincerity till you got the bow." But, in fact, Philoctetes goes even further; in his eyes Neoptolemus is worse than an animal:

> If I shout for sympathy
> To animals and birds, they'll answer me.
> There's more nature in their dens and nests
> Than there is in you, you sacrilegious
> Heartbreaking little coward.

But this semantic reversal signals a disturbing circularity. If the colonial dehumanization of the colonized also signals the dehumanizing effect of colonialism upon its supposedly "civilized" champions, by usurping their language, Philoctetes himself becomes brutalized. While the fate he wishes upon Odysseus is that of an animal ("I'd give the whole agony of my life just to see you cut down in the end, and your tongue ripped out of you like a bleeding ox-tongue," in its acrimonious ferocity it, too, has crossed over into barbarism.

Heaney's version, through amplifying and sharpening aspects of its Sophoclean model, has succeeded in representing the reciprocal barbarity implicit in the colonial project, and in suggesting connections with the effects of colonial discourse in Northern Ireland. The two sides seem doomed "To repeat themselves and their every last mistake, / No matter what" as Heaney's Chorus outlines at the opening of the version. However, that Chorus also speaks of "The voice of Hercules / That Philoctetes is going to have to hear." This voice marks the turning-point, and the awakening of an embryonic alternative consciousness in which colonially conceived, divisive notions of identity might have to give way.

Ultimately, as the Chorus understands, the inexperienced Neoptolemus has more *in*sight than either Odysseus or Philoctetes. His recognition that he himself is an "affliction" may signal that, to some degree, he has been inducted into the counter-colonialist ideology that Philoctetes has pioneered. In retrospect it may be seen that this reverse induction has, perhaps, been germinating in Neoptolemus' consciousness almost from the very start. Early in the play, under the sway of Odyssean colonial ideology, Neoptolemus instructs the

Chorus to "Keep on the lookout for the creature," a designation of
Philoctetes as animal which the Chorus evidently accepts. But in
the course of the following exchange, Neoptolemus appears to move
away from the conception of Philoctetes as beast, exploring instead
a vocabulary which at least opens the possibility of recognizing
Philoctetes as human. As Neoptolemus begins to resist the lure of an
exclusively Odyssean ideology, details begin to emerge which miti-
gate the dehumanization of Philoctetes. The animalistic "scavenging"
describing Philoctetes out hunting for food at the play's start—a direct
echo of Odysseus' use of the word—yields to "proud" in the course
of eight lines. Gradually, Neoptolemus senses that Philoctetes is not
simply "the creature," but also "an archer," "the master bowman, the
great name"; not merely the quarry of Greeks, Philoctetes is now also
recognized as a hunter of "game" in his own right, albeit a pathetic one.
From the outset, then, Neoptolemus had already begun to deconstruct
the colonialist narrative, imagining a Philoctetes who is "Contrary,
hard and proud," and the Chorus's next words: "It's a pity of him too
/ Afflicted like that"—directly evoke the response that will in the end
determine Neoptolemus' behavior towards Philoctetes: pity.

But Neoptolemus has by no means completely extricated himself
from the Odyssean narrative. Despite distancing himself from Odyssean ideology and his recognition of the respect due to Philoctetes as
a man, Neoptolemus also retains the ability to recognize that to some
degree Philoctetes *is* indeed animalistic:

> Your courage has gone wild, you're like a brute
> That can only foam at the mouth. You aren't
> Bearing up, you are bearing down. Anybody
> That ever tries to help you just gets savaged.
> You're a wounded man in terrible need of healing
> But when your friends try, all you do is snarl
> Like some animal protecting cubs.
> So listen now to me, Philoctetes,
> And brand this into your skull.
> You're a sick man.

Odysseus is partially justified in thinking of Philoctetes as "hunted"
because that is in truth the role Philoctetes has assumed in regard to
the world about him—the severe reciprocity of hunter and hunted.

What this suggests is that *The Cure at Troy* represents the route out of colonialism as a hybrid consciousness, shared, though differently experienced, by both "colonist" and "colonized." The mutual brutalization brought about by the colonial project—wounds inflicted and endured—are recognized, but no longer form the basis of identity. Neoptolemus is the first to make the perceptual breakthrough. In coming to recognize the wounds and worth of both Self and Other, his "insight" dissolves the boundaries of prejudice and inequality between the erstwhile "colonist" and "colonized." In attaining this hybrid consciousness, he transcends the bounds of a colonial structuring of "Otherness." In other words, given that colonial discourse relies on the primary distinction between colonist and colonized, Neoptolemus' ultimate assimilation of Philoctetes into a relationship of equality—one which recognizes the ineluctable hybridity of the postcolonial condition—represents nothing less than a breach of colonial discourse itself.

For a moment, then, it appears that a space has opened into which the possibility of a new, *post*-colonial discourse might enter (a fraught concept, admittedly). If this were so, then it would necessitate the reassessment of every facet of life and society which is conditioned by the colonial experience: language, historical narratives of every colonial complexion, constructs of the relation between past and present, the structure of state apparatuses, of political, social, economic and, of course, artistic discourses. Mapping the transition from a colonially determined conception of relations to a hybrid, postcolonial consciousness, Neoptolemus stands in a borderland between the existing order of things, with its predominance of hatred and victimization, and a possible alternative hegemony in which those deathly forces are transcended by life-giving friendship.

But the distance between imagined and real space has not been, and is not now, negligible. Neoptolemus attempts to play a mediating role both between Philoctetes and the Greeks, and between the bestial and human dimensions of Philoctetes' personality—educating him into fuller consciousness. Philoctetes, however, deeply entrenched in his sense of grievance, staunchly resists the mediating force of Neoptolemus' persuasion. As a consequence of his adamant refusal, all the signs are that the old cycle of victimhood and suffering are set to continue indefinitely, with the wound poisoning the future as it has corrupted the past. But then, into these certainties, enters the possibility of the miraculous. The Chorus steps forward and addresses the audience in lines invented for them by Heaney:

> Human beings suffer,
> They torture one another,
> They get hurt and get hard.
> No poem or play or song
> Can fully right a wrong
> Inflicted and endured.

The Chorus proceeds to set out the ethical implications of Philoctetes' crisis for the modern "crisis" in Northern Ireland, culminating in an emphatic series of imperatives:

> So hope for a great sea-change
> On the far side of revenge.
> Believe that a further shore
> Is reachable from here.
> Believe in miracles
> And cures and healing wells.

This sequence functions as a prelude to the epiphany of Hercules, who returns in a volcanic eruption recalling the funeral pyre that Philoctetes once lit for Hercules which enabled the hero's apotheosis. Hercules, portrayed by the Chorus, and *"ritually claimant,"* requires Philoctetes to lay aside his grievance, and to fulfill his heroic destiny, being healed and reincorporated into Greek society at Troy. In *The Cure at Troy*, the *deus ex machina* of the Sophoclean play is portrayed as the emergence of a previously suppressed part of Philoctetes' consciousness. Philoctetes' role is defined as Neoptolemus' "twin in arms and archery," which represents a recognition that Philoctetes will transcend bestial status when he subordinates himself to his function within society, and honors the claims of humanity over the claims of bestiality—of justice over revenge. His victory over bestiality will be signified by the "cure" of the bestial wound.

The Herculean dimension of Philoctetes cannot ignore the years of brutalizing hardship, and the price for assuming his rightful place in society is to undertake labors which, while performed in the service of Greek society, are nevertheless brutalizing. Hence, Hercules enjoins them: "you must be ... Marauding lions on that shore." Dazed, Philoctetes responds: "All that you say / Is like a dream to me and I obey." With the arrival of Hercules, then, Philoctetes undergoes a dual transformation, both from beast to human and from "scavenging" beast to "marauding lion." In *The Cure at Troy*, due to the interiorization of Hercules, the term "marauding lion" signifies that Philoctetes accepts that, to some degree, he has allowed himself to become brutalized by his experience. At the same time, it is paired with the line stipulating his role as Neoptolemus' equal—his "twin." This suggests an emergent dual consciousness about his own ambivalent status, somewhere between the identities of "colonized" and "colonist." Both lines also include Neoptolemus in their referential embrace. This constitutes recognition of the equally hybrid status of the "colonist"—neither fully beast, nor unmarked by the colonial encounter. From the perspective of the colonized, in particular, the inclusion of definitions of the colonist as both human and animal is at once an indictment of the colonial project, and a reluctant acknowledgement of the "civilizing" aspects of the legacy of that project. This signifies that Philoctetes, like Neoptolemus, has become susceptible to the lure of both ideologies and thereby developed the same hybrid, "postcolonial" consciousness as that held by Neoptolemus. Moreover, it was Neoptolemus' preemptive reconciliatory gesture—telling the truth and returning the bow—that precipitated Philoctetes' visionary "self-revealing/Double-take of feeling" at the arrival of Hercules. This suggestion finds support in the way in which the earlier language and symbolism of the transactions of friendship between Neoptolemus and Philoctetes anticipate those between Hercules and Philoctetes. The earlier ritual handings of the bow between Philoctetes and Neoptolemus, for example, recall Hercules' original gift of the bow to Philoctetes for "generous behaviour" and Philoctetes' language in response to Neoptolemus' (seeming) extension of friendship explicitly anticipates that of the subsequent Herculean epiphany. The implication seems to be that, just as hatred breeds hatred, so generosity can multiply in response to generosity, or, as Neoptolemus says: "befriend a friend / And the chance of it's increased and multiplied." But it also enables us to infer that a colonially defined conception of relations between people (or sectors of communities) is fundamentally incompatible with a shared forging of "postcolonial" identity or, now, with those relations mapped out by the Good Friday Agreement.

Yet in the very instant that this rupture of colonial discourse becomes visible, this visionary postcolonialism is also fundamentally compromised. Whereas relations on Lemnos can no longer be accounted for in terms of colonial discourse, relations between Greeks and Trojans are still very much those of colonist to colonized. Philoctetes and Neoptolemus are to go "Into the front line" and "sack" Troy, taking and burning "spoils"—they are to be "Troy's nemesis and last nightmare," which on first impression is hardly language designed to inspire confidence in the *post*-colonial credentials of Heaney's vision. That Philoctetes and Neoptolemus go to Troy to assist in a colonial project represented no ideological contradiction for Sophocles. As General during the Samian Revolt (441–439 B.C.), and State Treasurer for the Athenian empire, Sophocles was not concerned with constructing a critique of colonialism itself, but rather of the kinds of values that must inform colonial enterprises if they were not to become barbaric and self-defeating.

In Heaney's narrative, however, the colonial constructs of Otherness of the Sophoclean play which lead to the sacking of Troy are seen as the way in which hope and history are to "rhyme," in which "a crippled trust might walk." Heaney's own reading of it is, politically speaking, conciliatory, as he said in his Trinity College Dublin seminar in March 1995: "Troy would be, not an United Ireland, as such, but an integrated possibility . . . a possible future. It would be a redemptive. It *might* be the fall of the border or something [laughs], but not necessarily. . . . I didn't mean it to be triumphant—I meant it to be a visionary possibility." In light of comments of this nature floated by the Field Day directorate in the press—designed to ward off potential suspicion of green fingers—the fall of Troy thus aspires to represent some form of pluralistic constitutional settlement or, perhaps, the fall of the amassed prejudices and hatreds that separate people on the island; as Alan Peacock argues in his "Mediations: Poet as Translator, Poet as Seer," "the play is beyond any sectional pleading of a case." Accordingly, the "cure" of the version's title refers to both Philoctetes' wound and to the Trojan war, as Neoptolemus tells the stricken hero: " . . . you're to be / The hero that was healed and then went on / To heal the wound of the Trojan war itself."

Such interpretations all apparently argue that the methods used by the colonial power, and the bestializing effect they have upon both sides in the conflict, are only symptoms of an underlying sickness: the

very existence of colonially defined, and colonially determined relations. In the context of the then intense military conflict in Northern
Ireland, the image of Troy sacked seems an ill-conceived vehicle for a
mode of cultural politics which purports to be reaching towards some
kind of shared cultural ground within Ireland. Here, perhaps, certain
dangers attendant upon the project of Heaney's conservative neoclas-
sicism become apparent: committed to retaining the received structure of the Sophoclean plot, Heaney is here forced to compromise his
postcolonial aspirations.

Other readings, however, are possible. Rather than offering the
anaesthetizing panacea of mere aestheticization, the image of Troy
could signal that the collapse of colonially determined relations are
only the first faltering steps in an unceasing dialectic between tradition and change, history and hope, grievance and tolerance which
must be undergone again and again in order for a postcolonial society
ultimately to emerge.[18] In the political acoustic of 1990—resonant
with cynicism and disbelief—it could be argued that the cautionary
irony of Troy may actually have served to valorize the hard-won optimism of the luminous, visionary, Herculean epiphany.

If we look again with such thoughts in mind at the language with
which the fall of Troy is described, slightly more subtle colorations
than may at first have been apparent begin to catch our attention,
indicating perhaps that Troy does indeed represent a refinement of
consciousness—that the campaign at Troy has penetrated one stage
further into the dialectic of history and hope which we saw played out
into a preliminary form of synthesis upon Lemnos. For example, the
Greek campaign on Lemnos involved, in Neoptolemus' own words,
"a policy of lies." And later, on receiving his bow back from Neoptolemus, Philoctetes' first act is to attempt to kill Odysseus. Yet by
the end of the play their experiences on Lemnos have brought both
Philoctetes and Neoptolemus some distance from relations characterized by either ambition or revenge. Their shared new perspective
is manifest in the words of Hercules that explicitly renounce their
former shortcomings: "Win by fair combat. But know to shun /
Reprisal killings when that's done." Significantly, in order to produce
these lines, Heaney had to diverge from the Sophoclean text in which
Hercules enjoined Philoctetes to kill Paris who began all the troubles.
It is not difficult, in the context of sectarian murders in Northern
Ireland, to see what prompted the departure from this sentiment, but

the new lines may, beyond this, also be indicative of what Heaney has called "a higher consciousness." A further expression of this dialectic of refinement can be identified. On Lemnos, we recall, Neoptolemus had been "sacrilegious," by falsely acquiring sacred objects. The Herculean injunction to sack Troy, however, demonstrates a renunciation of this kind of behavior, saying:

> But when the city's being sacked
> Preserve the shrines. Show gods respect.
> Reverence for the gods survives
> Our individual mortal lives.

This is very close to the sense of the Greek, and entirely accords with the colonial agenda of the Sophoclean text, but in *The Cure at Troy* it is also congruent with an emergent postcolonial discourse. Indeed, the call to respect the pieties of the Other has obvious implications for a society whose colonially derived divisions are principally mapped, and fueled, by divisions in religious discourse.

Hercules' speech also imagines a time when they will "sail at last / Out of the bad dream of your past." There is a self-conscious overlap between Lemnos and Troy in this image, suggesting that the "cure" at Troy should in some way resemble the Lemnian reconciliation of "hope and history." Hercules' injunction to "make sacrifice" also recalls the compromises Philoctetes and Neoptolemus have both had to make to achieve their shared understanding and their partnership of equality. Considered in the context of colonial discourse, these slight apertures are significant, suggesting that despite the violence that saturates the image of Troy, on some levels at least the implications of the reconciliation on Lemnos for the Trojan campaign have been sensed, and may in due course be enacted.

In 1990, at a time when peace and reconciliation seemed merely the barren hopes of a naive few, *The Cure at Troy* voiced the birth-cries of a difficult, halting, yet visionary, *post*-colonial discourse. Straining to supplant the old mythologies of victims and victors with a new post-colonial mythology, Heaney's reworking of Sophoclean tragedy itself entered into the annals of that new mythology. Almost a decade before the 1999 Good Friday Agreement's proposed power-sharing institutions, or their subsequent ratification in referenda north and south of the border, *The Cure at Troy* projected into public view a vision of a radical reconciliatory future for Northern Ireland, one which would require the sacrifice of old pieties and wounds, but which would be sustained by a new sense of shared heritage and shared destiny forged through mutual respect. In the light of the extraordinary reception of Heaney's revision, with which this article began, it is perhaps not too much to assert that for a time *The Cure at Troy* not only portrayed that vision—it indeed *became* that vision.

NOTES

1. Seamus Heaney, *The Cure at Troy: A version of Sophocles's "Philoctetes"* (London: Faber and Faber, 1990), 77.
2. There is no corresponding passage in Sophocles, *Philoctetes,* 1407 ff.
3. Heaney, Trinity College Dublin Seminar, March 2, 1995. The reference is to Ian Paisley, leader of the Democratic Unionist Party in Northern Ireland.
4. Seamus Heaney, *The Government of the Tongue: The 1986 T.S. Eliot Memorial Lectures and Other Critical Writings* (London: Faber and Faber, 1989).
5. Dated October 24, 1989, this was the first of Heaney's lectures as Oxford Professor of Poetry to be published, initially as an Oxford University Press pamphlet in 1990, the same year in which *The Cure at Troy* was first published, and again as the title essay in *The Redress of Poetry: Oxford Lectures* (London: Faber and Faber 1995). Retrospectively we can also note that Neoptolemus' "credit what I'm going to tell you" carries the charge of Heaney's Nobel Lecture, published as *Crediting Poetry* (Loughcrew, Co. Meath: Gallery Press, 1995) which deals with the same kinds of questions. Later in the play, Neoptolemus urges Philoctetes to start "seeing things," which is the title Heaney gave to the next collection he published after *The Cure at Troy: Seeing Things* (London: Faber and Faber, 1991).
6. A consideration of *The Cure at Troy* in regard to the agency of colonial discourse throws up startling correspondences with recent readings of *The Tempest* vis-à-vis the Jacobean colonization of Ulster and the New World. [See Barker, Francis and Peter Hulme, "'Nymphs and Reapers Heavily Vanish': the Discursive Con-texts of *The Tempest*," *Alternative Shakespeares,*

ed. J. Drakakis (London: Methuen, 1985), 191–205; Susan
Bennett, ed., "The Post-Colonial Body?: Thinking Through
*The Tempest," Performing Nostalgia: Shifting Shakespeare and the
Contemporary Past* (London: Routledge, 1996), 119–150; Paul
Brown, "'This Thing of Darkness I Acknowledge Mine': *The
Tempest* and the Discourse of Colonialism," *Political Shakespeare:
Essays in Cultural Materialism*, ed. J. Dollimore and A. Sinfield
(Manchester: Manchester UP, 1994, 48–71.] Heaney, who had
been re-reading *The Tempest* at the time of writing *The Cure at
Troy*, amplifies some of these. The expression "sea-change," in
particular, is a highly charged term in Heaney's version, invoked
by the Chorus at the opening of the play and imagistically
expanded and developed at a pivotal moment towards the end
of the play. The implication is that modern "colonial" relations
in Northern Ireland not only had their historical origins in
the Jacobean colonization of Ulster, but continue to be shaped
by it and/or to shape themselves according to that historical
paradigm.

7. See J. P. Vernant and P. Vidal-Naquet, *Myth and Tragedy in
Ancient Greece* (New York: Zone Books, 1988), 165 ff.

8. Heaney, *Cure* 5, corresponding to Sophocles, *Philoctetes*, 43–4
("gone out to look . . . for food)."

9. Heaney, *Cure* 12, corresponding to Sophocles, *Philoctetes*, 146–7
("terrible settler").

10. Heaney, *Cure* 9, corresponding to Sophocles, *Philoctetes*, 98–9.
There is no comparable sense in the Greek text.

11. For example, see Beacham, Richard, *Spectacle Entertainments of
Early Imperial Rome* (Yale University Press, 1999), 64.

12. Heaney, *Cure* 15, corresponding to Sophocles, *Philoctetes*, 226
("my wild appearance").

13. Forum for Peace and Reconciliation, *Paths to a Political
Settlement in Ireland: policy papers submitted to the Forum for Peace
and Reconciliation* (Belfast: Blackstaff Press, 1995), 36.

14. Sophocles, *Philoctetes* 119–20. All translations from the Greek
unless otherwise stated are taken from Sophocles' *Philoctetes*, ed.
and trans. R. G. Ussher (Warminster: Aris and Phillips, 1990).

15. Segal, *Tragedy and Civilization: An Interpretation of Sophocles*
(Cambridge, Mass.: Harvard UP, 1981), 300–3.

16. Heaney, *Cure* 54. The corresponding lines (984–5) contain no animal imagery: "These men will take me by force, you utter knave and scoundrel?"
17. As Charles Segal comments, "on the scale of civilized values hunting occupies an ambiguous place." Segal, *Tragedy*, 300.
18. For a similar argument, see Henry Hart's discussion of Heaney's poem, "Hercules and Antaeus" in *Seamus Heaney: Poet of Contrary Progressions* (New York: Syracuse UP, 1993), 98.

"THE GUEST"
(ALBERT CAMUS)

"Ambiguity and Colonialism in Albert Camus's 'The Guest'"
by Michael D. Sollars, Texas Southern University

"I rebel—therefore we exist" (Camus, *Rebel*, 22). Albert Camus's pronouncement in his philosophical work *The Rebel* succinctly encapsulates the central dilemma of modernist writers in the middle of the twentieth century. The Frenchman Camus (1913–1960), born in what was then the French colony of Algeria in northern Africa, won the Nobel Prize in Literature in 1957, making him the first African to receive the award. Camus's focus falls on the individual as a rebel, whose choices and actions bring existence, awareness, and newfound identity to what is often referred to as "the other;" a separate group, or even a nation of people. Camus acknowledges the inevitable relationship—one marked by responsibility—between the individual and the other. The other becomes a complex term concerning colonialism and postcolonialism, as seen in Camus's short story "The Guest." This work, perhaps more so than Camus's *The Stranger* or *The Plague*, is centrally concerned with colonialism and its devastating affect on indigenous cultures.

Camus had an ambivalent perspective regarding his homeland of Algeria. Born into a poor European family in the African country, he regarded Algeria, a land under French dominance since 1830, as his home. This dual identity was shared by a great many other Europeans born in Africa under colonial rule. But Camus also recognized the plight of native Algerians who desired political and economic independence from France, their imperial ruler. In his nonfiction writings and political statements, Camus did not favor total Algerian independence, but a limited freedom for the Muslim country. This ambivalence produced an estrangement and a sense of unreality in Camus, according to Mangesh Kalkarni: " ... These contradictions arose from Camus's predicament as a pied-noir consciously frozen in historical immobility and incapable of directly confronting the problem of the European-Arab relation which continued ... to surface in his fiction as an admission of historical guilt" (1528). The author died in 1960, two years before the end of the rebellion that finally brought Algerian independence. Algeria had languished under French dominance since 1830.

Thus, Camus's clarion call—"I rebel—therefore we exist"—carries a heroic tone, very much mimicking his French predecessor René Descartes's assertion of certain knowledge based on the individual's rational faculties: "*cogito ergo sum*" ("*je pense, donc je suis*"; "I think; therefore I am"). The author purposely models Descartes's dictum. Camus notes that "In our daily trials rebellion plays the same role as does the 'cogito' in the realm of thought: it is the first piece of evidence. But this evidence lures the individual from his solitude. It founds its first value on the whole human race" (*Rebel*, 22).

Despite the bravado of Camus's precept, the statement also gives evidence to a personal and philosophical dilemma for the characters portrayed in much of the author's fiction, particularly the short story "The Guest," first published as one of several stories in *Exile and the Kingdom* in 1957. Susan Tarrow comments in her article "Exile from the Kingdom" that "Colonialism constitutes a major motif in the collection" (158). The dilemma involves the question of alienation from an absurd world. This paradox as to how to live separately, even privately, in a public world is also evident in Camus's novel *The Stranger*, in which the protagonist Mersault projects a cold indifference toward the demands and expectations of social conformity. The colonial situation of Algeria under the French flag served as a literary canvas for many of Camus's central works of fiction. In addition to "The Guest" and many of the other short stories in *Exile and the Kingdom*, *The Stranger* and *The Plague* are also set in Algeria.

An ethical dilemma plays out in Camus's "The Guest." The story is set in the author's Algerian homeland, on the eve of a turbulent and armed rebellion against French rule. Camus does not directly describe the broad epic struggle of Algeria's fight against colonialism, but instead takes readers to a remote desert landscape where three men of different backgrounds are facing daunting choices.

Daru, a young schoolmaster, is the enigmatic protagonist; a loner who has chosen to live an isolated existence in an impoverished and remote desert region in the African country. Although a European, he was born in Algeria and lived there his whole life,. He speaks French and Arabic fluently. He finds solace and safety in his solitude and remoteness from the outside world. In addition to teaching the Algerian peasant children French language and culture, Daru is also responsible for disbursing French grain during periods of winter drought. He straddles two cultural identities in many ways and has willingly chosen physical and spiritual isolation from the world.

Daru's home landscape is a rugged and rocky mountain plateau. He appears content in his solitude and freedom from social and political pressures, a predicament many of Camus's characters find themselves in. As Germaine Brée notes, "A major source of Camus' work . . . is [his] understanding of and sensitivity to that part of all lives which is spent in solitude and silence" (6). Strangely, Daru is shaped into Camus's modern Prometheus; a rock-bound, solitary hero, distant from the rest of the world. I say "strangely" because Daru, as a modernist figure, is portrayed as drained of blood, sinew, and a passionate spirit. He appears as empty and barren as his landscape. He has withdrawn from the world to be a school teacher, bringing knowledge that promotes the assimilation of the Muslim population. Camus asks: "Why rebel if there is nothing permanent in oneself worth preserving" (*Rebel* 16)? He goes on to explain that when one finds common ground with the other, then he has formed a landscape on which to rebel (*Rebel* 16). "What is crucial, however, is the conscious *recognition* of the absurd in order then to transcend it. One avenue of reaction, predicated on this recognition, may be rebellion. It may be possible . . . that rebellion is a quest for meaning, a quest to transcend the absurd" (Goodwin 837).

Daru's safe, private world is invaded by Balducci, the second character. He is a French gendarme soldier from El Ameur, who brings with him an unnamed Arab prisoner. Balducci quickly informs Daru that the school teacher must take charge of the prisoner and deliver him to the police authorities in the nearby settlement of

Tinguit. Balducci impresses on the reluctant Daru the importance of official governmental orders, especially in this time of "civil unrest," an allusion to the Algerians' growing rebellion. Daru protests this new responsibility and refuses to comply; however, the Arab is left in his charge. Daru takes the prisoner into his school and finds himself confronted with a moral dilemma of which he wants no part.

The third character, the prisoner, is known only as the Arab. He has been arrested by the French authorities for the murder of his cousin over a dispute about some grain, and now he faces a French government trial. Daru soon learns his charge speaks Arabic but not French. Camus's limited narrator does not reveal any of the Arab's thoughts, leaving the reader a curious outsider.

The thrust of "The Guest" examines the relationship between Daru and the Arab, and the choices they make regarding freedom. Daru desires to be free of the Arab and not responsible for the other man's fate. The two spend an inhospitable evening under the same schoolhouse roof. Daru shares hot tea and a meager meal with the prisoner. They speak little, always in Arabic. Daru is not unfriendly, but he maintains an indifferent, hard tone. He dislikes that he has been placed in this predicament, as he wants no involvement in the other man's fate. During the night, the murderer is neither bound nor confined, as Daru hopes that his "guest" will escape and thus relieve him of his responsibility.

At morning light Daru finds the Arab has not taken advantage of his easy escape. He then reluctantly walks with the Arab some distance to a fork in the road, where he intends to leave the man. He gives the Arab food and money for his journey. But then Daru explains to the prisoner the two choices in front of him. The road to the east leads to the prison in Tinguit, where the French authorities await him. The road to the south leads to pasturelands and groups of nomads. "They will take you in and shelter you according to their law" (108), Daru speaks to the other man in their common language, and then turns away from the prisoner. Feeling relieved, Daru departs and climbs the terrain back to the schoolhouse, where he watches the Arab take the rocky path toward Tinguit.

In the schoolhouse, Daru finds scribbled on the blackboard a threatening message: "You handed over our brother. You will pay for this" ("The Guest" 109). The assumption is that the threat comes from other unseen Arabs. Daru's existential action, leaving the Arab to his own free choice, has been interpreted by his fellow Arabs as a betrayal. The word "brother" can be seen as problematic, perhaps elusive. Does Camus mean the fraternity of Arabs as brothers, or does he imply a universal sense, that the Arab is the brother to Algerian-born Daru as well?

The relationship between the two central characters in "The Guest" is a microcosm for an understanding of the larger world of Arab and European relationships in French colonial Algeria, which at the time of Camus's writing, faced armed rebellion. Daru considers the colonial Algeria his home. The narrator explains: "Daru had been born here. Everywhere else, he felt exiled" (88). At the same time, his chosen isolation from the larger social body suggests his uncomfortable status in what he feels is his homeland. Tarrow adds: "Many of the characters [like Daru] are misfits in their environment, even when they feel they belong there" (158). He is as unlike the French soldier Balducci as he is unlike the Arab. The narrator does not explain why Daru has become a recluse. Edwin P. Grobe offers this insight: " . . . Daru asserts his inability to live within the framework of a society erected upon false concepts of justice . . . a reaffirmation of the decision which brought him to the desert upon his release from military service" (360). Although Daru has taken refuge in the mountain school, he finds that he cannot escape the forces of change, as they inevitably invade his world.

Like Daru, the Arab is not fully described by the narrator. He is poor, perhaps uneducated, and quick to react to what he thinks is an insult, particularly in the way he killed his cousin over some grain. While in the schoolhouse, he remains calm and polite and recognizes the class distinction between Europeans and the Arabs. The Arab asks Daru, "Why do you eat with me?" Daru merely responds, "I'm hungry" (99). There is a mere modicum of fraternity evident between the men, and though they share a meal, they never share a common understanding. They see themselves neither as brothers nor as enemies. Grobe refers to Daru and the Arab as "two spiritual outcasts" or "spiritual doubles" created to offer "a probing study of the solitary man viewed as a contemporary phenomenon" (357). Both are exiles from their respective societies. Daru is marked with the taint of colonialism, and the Arab has sinned through the murder of his cousin. Both have become isolated or marginalized through their own acts. English Showalter, Jr. comments that it is impossible for the reader to add up a firm understanding or judgment of Daru's guest: "The Arab ... explicitly identified with ... impersonal natural reality ... is not a puzzle we are meant to solve but rather a blank ... meaningless [canvas]" (Jones 727). While there exists a kinship of sorts, although unspoken, the men face the ambiguity of inevitable choices, actions, and outcomes.

The ultimate choices of Camus's characters—Daru refuses responsibility in the Arab's fate, and the Arab follows the road to colonial justice—are framed in a world of ambiguity. An overarching point is Camus's title "The Guest." The word "guest" suggests that one of the men is the visitor. The Arab is a guest, albeit prisoner, in Daru's lodgings, but the French Daru can also be seen as a guest in the African country of Algeria, thus making the Arab the host. Donald Lazere comments that Camus chose "The Guest" for the English translation, but "added that it was a pity the ambiguity was lost in translation." Camus points out that the word "host"—another possible translation of the original Frech title "L'Hote"—carries a diverse spectrum of meanings: Eucharist, victim, sacrifice, stranger, and enemy. Lazere asks, "Is 'L'hote' Daru or the Arab, or perhaps both? Each man is at the same time friendly stranger, victim, and enemy" (62).

Daru and the Arab are lightly sketched figures. The reader senses that the two characters have been partially erased by the author. In "The Guest," Daru never speaks of Algerian nationalism, as he sees himself apart from any political movement. His focus falls on the region in front of him and the Arab, whom he treats as a troublesome guest in his humble quarters. But by not providing detailed descriptions of his protagonists or their personal histories, Camus's two characters come to represent the French and the Algerians in general.

Daru's choice of his isolated home and the consequences of this decision also bring him face-to-face with an ambiguous landscape. The terrain is quickly recognized as another powerful dimension in the narrative: "a wasteland peopled only by stones." The landscape is a bleak, barren plateau country. It is filled with silence, with a "muteness of surrounding rocks." "The only plowing here was to harvest rocks," the narrator says. The area is remote from the villages, which are poor and scarcely populated. The rocky hillside is difficult to access. Even the horse the soldier Balducci is riding stumbles in the rough ascent. Winter and cold make the landscape only more inhospitable.

Camus's poor landscape becomes a stark stage for Daru's physical and moral isolation. The desert schoolhouse is the protagonist's chosen escape from not only the people but also the forces of political change. He is described as living in monastic isolation. At first he feels safely bivouacked on his remote plateau, exempt from political involvement in the inevitable conflict between the French and Arabs, although neither the limited omniscient narrator nor Daru speaks about politics. Only Balducci references the Arab rebellion, and these warnings are underestimated and understated by the soldier. But Daru learns that moral solitude eludes him, as the arrival of the Arab disrupts his self-imposed isolation. He cannot escape moral involvement with the other. This focus points the reader to the fact that the French have been the guests of Algeria during the many decades of colonialism. Once again, Camus's meaning is ambiguous, suggesting multiple possibilities.

The existential individual, one estranged from his homeland and self, is clearly recognizable in much of Camus's fiction, like the novels *The Stranger* and *The Plague*, and his essay "The Myth of Sisyphus." Camus's sense of rebellion comes not in the form of overt social or political protest, but as the individual, a private soul, seeking his own authentic existence, one apart from that traditionally defined by the social and political status quo. In *The Stranger*, the enigmatic and complex protagonist Mersault, a French clerk living in Algiers, finds himself caught in an existential world. Soon his actions lead to an absurd outcome. "The Myth of Sisyphus" recreates in modern terms the classical Greek story of Sisyphus, who has been condemned to roll a gigantic boulder up a mountain slope, only to watch it fall back again, where he must eternally repeat his absurd efforts. And *The Plague*, the novel in which rats carry a deadly plague to the Algerian city of Oran, presents an allegory for resistance against Nazi invasion.

Camus's attempt to balance unbounded metaphysical notions of freedom and responsibility with the confinement of sociopolitical restrictions is played out in Daru's decision concerning the Arab. Daru represents the revolt against the absurd condition of the universe, or as Mersault describes in *The Stranger* "the benign indifference of the universe." The absurd can be described as an undeniable sense of meaninglessness in a vast universe that remains indifferent to human reason and actions. There exists a great chasm between our idea of justice, for example, and the reality of it we encounter in the world. The actions of an individual like Daru, despite his moral and ethical intentions, bring an empty outcome. Death becomes the ultimate manifestation of the absurd, in that life seems meaningless, as we must always face our mortality. On the personal level, the school teacher, having escaped moral involvement by his isolation from society, is confronted by the ethical choice between carrying out the government's orders, which will lead to the Arab's death, and releasing the Arab to his fate with his own people, which too will likely end in his death. Daru seeks to remain uninvolved and allows the Arab to choose his destiny. But on a national scale, Daru's choice to remain independent of the Arab's fate captures the moral dilemma posed by Algerian independence. For, as Camus shows us, Daru's absurd predicament is the result of France's exploration and the nightmarish consequences of colonization.

WORKS CITED

Brée, Germaine, ed. *Camus: A Collection of Critical Essays.* Englewood Cliffs, NJ: Prentice-Hall, 1962.

Camus, Albert. *Exile and the Kingdom.* Trans. Justin O'Brien. New York: Knopf, 1958.

———. *The Myth of Sisyphus and Other Essays.* Trans. Justin O'Brien. New York: Knopf, 1964.

———. *The Plague.* Trans. Stuart Gilbert. New York: Vintage, 1975.

———. *The Rebel: An Essay on Man in Revolt.* Trans. Anthony Bower. New York: Vintage, 1991.

———. *The Stranger.* Trans. Matthew Ward. New York: Vintage, 1989.

Goodwin, Glenn A. "On Transcending the Absurd: An Inquiry in the Sociology of Meaning." *The American Journal of Sociology.* 76.5 (1971): 631–846.

Grobe, Edwin P. "The Psychological Structure of Camus's 'L'Hote.'" *The French Review.* 40.3 (1966): 357–367.

Jones, Rosemarie. "A Reading of Camus's Exile and the Kingdom by English Showalter, Jr." *The Modern Language Review.* 80.3 (1985): 727–728.

Kulkarni, Mangesh. "The Ambiguous Fate of a *Pied-Noir*: Albert Camus and Colonialism." *Economic and Political Weekly.* June 28, 1997.

Lazere, Donald. "*The Myth* and *The Rebel*: Diversity and Unity." *Albert Camus.* Ed. Harold Bloom. 61–78.

McGregor, Rob Roy. "Camus's 'Jonasou L'Artiste au Travail': A Statement of the Absurd Human Condition." *South Atlantic Review*. 60. 4 (1995) : 53–68.

Tarrow, Susan. "Exile from the Kingdom." *Albert Camus*. Ed. Harold Bloom. New York: Chelsea House, 1989.

HEART OF DARKNESS
(JOSEPH CONRAD)

"Close Encounters of the Absurd Kind
in Joseph Conrad's *Heart of Darkness*"
by Jonathan Wright, Faulkner University

"absurd. *adj.* Out of harmony with reason or propriety; incongruous, unreasonable, illogical. In modern use, *esp.* plainly opposed to reason, and *hence*, ridiculous, silly. *n.* An unreasonable thing, act, or statement."

—*Oxford English Dictionary* (*OED*)

The frame narrative of Conrad's *Heart of Darkness* begins with five men reflecting on the River Thames's historic role in worldwide exploration, while waiting for the tide to turn onboard the *Nellie*, a sea-bound yacht (1958–59). The frame narrator, swelling with nationalistic pride, recalls the "venerable stream" had launched explorers seeking gold and fame, wielding weapons, bearing torches of "sacred fire," and carrying the dreams and "seeds" of civilization "into the mystery of an unknown earth" since the time of Britain's "great knights-errant of the sea" (1959). In contrast, Charlie Marlow, a seaman known for his "inconclusive experiences" (1961), remembers the Thames itself was once a dark, mysterious destination for Romans to explore. Consequently, when the seaman first breaks his silence, he speaks not of light, but of darkness: "And this also has been one of the dark places of the earth" (1959). Afterwards, Marlow imagines aloud what it must have been like for Roman invaders who "were men

67

enough to face" Britain's uncivilized, wild, mysterious, savage, detestable, incomprehensible, fascinating, abominable darkness (1960) and then segues into an account of his own exploratory journey into the heart of Africa's darkness.

In time, his companions discover that Marlow had met with two kinds of darkness in Africa. He had found beneath the canopies of Africa's "millions of trees" (1983) a literal darkness, the kind of tactile, "thick darkness" that plagued Egypt for three days (Purdy 68). And he had found in the natives and the European explorers and colonists a figurative "darkness" of mystery, ignorance, indifference, and depravity. As Marlow's tale unfolds, he draws his listeners deeper and deeper into nature's and humanity's dense darkness, and then leaves them there by ending on a trailing dark note: "It would have been too dark—too dark altogether ..." (2016). Darkness engulfs Marlow's tale from his first words to his last. One might reasonably assume, then, that the seaman's account continually evokes common reactions to "the dark," such as revulsion, depression, frustration, anxiety, panic, fear, and horror. Surely the seaman's yarn evokes these reactions, but as implausible as it might seem, it also evokes the unexpected—scornful laughter. Marlow's ability to make others laugh in the face of darkness is no small feat. Nevertheless, he accomplishes it by recounting his repeated experiences with absurdity. As Marlow tells one highly descriptive farcical episode after another, he reveals that despite all of the "rot let loose in print and talk" (1965) about the white man's glorious "idea" to shine light into Africa's darkness, to "civilize" the "uncivilized," European exploration and colonization, especially in the Congo, was often tragically, laughably absurd.

Ermien van Pletzen suggests that Marlow's narrative "re-enacts a crisis of witnessing the unspeakable, of confessing and justifying one's own involvement and that of one's associates" (156). Marlow indeed speaks with a confessional air, but the seaman seems more intent on judging than justifying the thoughts and actions of European explorers. Before judging others, Marlow judges himself for the irrational, desperate, and impulsive behavior that he displayed at times as a younger man. The seaman first admits his decision to explore Africa was nothing more than a childish whim. As a boy, Marlow so loved maps that he could "lose [himself] in all the glories of exploration" for hours (1961). He found the "many blank spaces of the earth" fascinating, placed his finger on those that "looked particularly inviting" and announced, "When I grow up I will go there" (1961). As a young adult, Marlow still had such an irrational "hankering after" Africa (1962) that he followed his childhood dream with a vengeance.

Desperate to explore the Congo, Marlow abandoned all reason and gained employment as a steamboat pilot. Driven by the notion that he had to get to Africa "by hook or by crook" (1962), the seaman left his usual path of self-reliance and pestered the men at the Trading Society for a job (1962), and when they failed to deliver, Marlow did the unthinkable. He sought the help of a "dear enthusiastic" aunt who knew the "wife of a very high personage in the Administration" and "[made] no end of fuss to get [him] appointed skipper of a river steamboat" (1962). Marlow reveals that the "notion" also drove him to throw all caution to the wind when he learned that the Trading Society had an opening. Although Marlow knew his predecessor "had been killed in a scuffle with natives" (1962), he asked no questions. He saw the job as his "chance" (an ironic word choice) and became "the more anxious to go" (1962). Consequently, Marlow "flew around like mad to get ready," as if he could not get to the Congo to take charge of the dead captain's boat fast enough, crossed the channel to interview for the job, obligated himself to a company that he knew almost nothing about, and literally placed his life on the line, all within forty-eight hours of learning about the vacancy (1962–63).

As he recounts his experiences in Africa, Marlow confesses other instances when he thought and behaved irrationally. For example, the pilot came to the think of his "battered, twisted, ruined, tinpot steamboat" as an "influential friend" (1978). She was "nothing so solid" and not so "pretty," Marlow recalls, but he "loved" her nonetheless because he had put a lot of work into her and she helped him "find out what [he] could do" (1978). When he could not find a single rivet to fix his "love," Marlow raged "like any actor in a farce" (Pletzen 165):

> "What more did I want? What I really wanted was rivets, by heaven! Rivets. To get on with the work—to stop the hole. Rivets I wanted. There were cases of them down at the coast—cases—piled up—burst—split! You kicked a loose rivet at every second step in that station yard on the hillside. Rivets had rolled into the grove of death. You could fill your pockets with rivets for the trouble of stooping down—and there wasn't one rivet to be found where it was wanted." (1977–78)

Once Marlow learned that rivets should arrive in three weeks, he shared the news with his foreman, and the two began cavorting around the deck. As Marlow recalls the incident, he recognizes that their celebration over the rivets was insane:

> "I slapped him on the back and shouted 'We shall have rivets!' He scrambled to his feet exclaiming 'No! Rivets!' as though he couldn't believe his ears. Then in a low voice, 'You . . . eh?' I don't know why we behaved like a couple of lunatics. I put my finger to the side of my nose and nodded mysteriously. 'Good for you!' he cried, snapped his fingers above his head, lifting one foot. I tried a jig. We capered on the iron deck." (1979)

The men stopped dancing only when they realized that the "frightful clatter" coming from the tinny hulk had echoed in a "thundering roll upon the sleeping station" and had probably frightened men from their sleep (1979).

After the seaman received his rivets, made his repairs, and headed upriver to retrieve Kurtz, a corrupt, diseased agent, Marlow had a crazy and comical thought that he wisely kept to himself. He hoped that the cannibals onboard would continue to exercise restraint in spite of their gnawing hunger, but because of his "fantastic vanity" (1988) he also hoped that he looked more appetizing to them than the other men on board. Farther upriver, Marlow's anxiety over his helmsman's death produced an irrational desire that escalated into more nonsensical behavior. When a native onshore mortally wounded the helmsman with a spear, his blood pooled and filled Marlow's shoes (1992). As the helmsman lay dying, Marlow tried to tend to him and steer the boat. However, upon seeing the man's face contort in death, Marlow became so "morbidly anxious" to change his bloody socks and shoes that he forced the manager, who had no navigating skills, to take the wheel (1992). Marlow then tore at his laces madly and threw his shoes overboard (1992–93).

Marlow confesses that something else absurd happened as he "sacrificed" his shoes to "the devil-god of [the] river" (1993). His thoughts turned to Kurtz. Though Marlow later regretted the loss of his helmsman (1995), at the moment of his death, the seaman regretted that Kurtz was likely dead, too, and that he would not enjoy the opportunity to speak with the agent after all (1992). Upon hearing a sigh at this point, Marlow assumes that he has exasperated someone onboard with "the absurdity of his narrative and its incongruous connections" (Pletzen 166). In response, Marlow passionately acknowledges that such misplaced regret was absurd: "Why do you sigh in this beastly way, somebody? Absurd? Well, absurd. Good Lord! [. . .] Absurd! [. . .] Absurd! Absurd be—exploded! Absurd! My dear boys, what can you expect from a man who out of sheer nervousness had just flung overboard a pair of new shoes? Now I think of it, it is amazing I did not shed tears" (1993). Even though Marlow confesses these absurdities and others as he spins his yarn, his recollections of the absurd European men and women that he encountered on the Continent and in the Congo make him seem surprisingly intelligent, rational, reasonable, and "sound" by comparison.

Though Marlow could see his own absurdity only in hindsight at times, he generally saw others' absurdity with clarity in the moment. Marlow noticed immediately that most of the white-collar employees he met in the Trading Society's offices were quirky in their mannerisms and stupid in their work. The two women dressed in black in the outer office "knitted black wool feverishly" (1964) during work hours, but they did little else. Marlow perceived that they guarded "the door of Darkness" and cared nothing for human life (1964). The young knitting zombie who escorted Marlow into a waiting room without a word (1963) incessantly "introduced" men "to the unknown" (1964), but her old, fat knitting partner only peered over her spectacles and scrutinized "the cheery and foolish faces" of the men leaving for Africa with her "unconcerned eyes" (1964). The squatty, plump "great man" who "had his grip on the handle-end of ever so many millions" (1963) was equally unconcerned about the new hires and wasted no time with them in the interviewing process. Marlow's "interview" lasted all of forty-five seconds, just enough time for the employer to shake hands with Marlow, verify he could speak French sufficiently, mumble something incoherently, and bid him *Bon voyage* (1963). The brevity of the interview suggests that "the great man" was efficient to a fault and not so great after all, regardless of his purse, position, and power. If Marlow was struck by the absurdity of the brief interview at the time, he did not let it stop him from accepting the job and enduring yet another absurd formality: a visit with the company doctor.

The company doctor was the only one in the office who seemed genuinely interested in Marlow, but he turned out to be a self-serving quack. The doctor voiced his approval of the seaman's plan to go to Africa, but the slippered, "unshaven little man" (1964) had an ulterior motive for praising his decision. The "harmless fool" was conducting a "research" project and hoped that Marlow's "going" would support his "scientific" theory that Africa wrought psychological changes in men (1964–65). For this reason, the doctor treated Marlow more like a lab rat than a coworker. After determining Marlow's pulse was "good" for Africa (1964), the doctor took measurements of the seaman's head (with his permission) and recorded his findings. Within moments, Marlow realized the doctor's "research" was actually a futile "triple-blind" study. First, the doctor took *outside* measurements of his subject's skulls, even though he knew the "changes [took] place inside" (1964). Second, the doctor knew that he would never see those he had examined in his office again. Third, he had no plans to go to Africa himself to see the "mental changes" occur "on the spot" (1965). Aware that the doctor's methods were unsound, the seaman became annoyed and impatient (1964–65). At first, the doctor seemed oblivious to Marlow's irritation, but before bidding him adieu, the doctor gave Marlow strict orders to "[a]void irritation more than exposure to the sun" and to "keep calm" (1965). Marlow had no idea at the time how difficult it would be to follow the doctor's orders in the Congo.

Although Marlow knew that the Trading Society cared more about empire-building and making "no end of coin by trade" (1963) than taking care of its employees or "weaning" Africa's "ignorant millions from their horrid ways" (1965), he foolishly pushed ahead with his travel plans. And when the time came for his departure, Marlow did not hesitate. He did, however, have a "startled pause" (1965). Marlow admits that for a brief moment he felt like he was about to embark on a journey into the "centre of the earth" instead of the "centre of a continent" (1965). John W. Griffith asserts that Marlow's imaginative thought "suggests the absurdity of the attempt to define the parameters of his journey" into a place "where maps clearly have no significance" and indicates that Marlow perceived "the gap between the expectation and the reality of travel" (29). Even before Marlow reached the mouth of the Congo River, he began to see that traveling to the center of Africa was much like traveling to the center of the earth. The heat was intense, the land along the shore was steamy, and the wilderness was, by all appearances, "God-forsaken" (1966). Worst of all, most of the white men Marlow met along the way were "red-eyed devils" (1968) who were as absurd as those he had encountered in the Trading Society's offices.

Much to Marlow's dismay, white men of all nationalities made his dream of exploring Africa a nightmare by flaunting their ignorance, engaging in senseless "work," and treating their fellow man with calloused indifference. On a steamer bound for the Congo River, for instance, Marlow saw that France "tackled" Africa's darkness by landing customhouse clerks and soldiers all along the coast. Marlow assumed the soldiers had been sent to protect the clerks (1966), but he realized no one cared for the soldiers. Marlow recalls hearing that some soldiers had drowned in the surf, "but whether they did or not, nobody seemed particularly to care" (1966). The French had no regard for the lives of the natives, either. Marlow witnessed men on a French ship firing six-inch guns into the wilderness, hoping to wipe out a whole camp of natives, and he was awestruck by their futile methods of "warfare" and their perception that the natives were their enemies:

> "There wasn't even a shed there, and she was *shelling the bush* [...] In the empty immensity of earth, sky, and water, there she was, *incomprehensible,* firing into a continent. Pop, would go one of the six-inch guns [...] and nothing happened. Nothing could happen. There was a touch of insanity in the proceeding, a sense of lugubrious drollery in the sight; and it was not dissipated by somebody on board assuring me earnestly there was a camp of natives—he called them enemies!—hidden out of sight *somewhere.*" (1966) [emphasis added]

Marlow's juxtaposition of "lugubrious" and "drollery" in the passage above suggests that the seaman was conflicted; he did not know whether to laugh or cry after seeing how the French were going about the business of "colonization."

Upon arriving at the Central Station, where he was to take command of his boat, Marlow saw in the manager the same kind of stunning absurdity that he had seen in the French. The most obvious example of the manager's stupidity and incompetence left the seaman "thunderstruck" even before the two met (1972). Just inside the station's gate, Marlow learned from an "excitable chap" that his steamer was at the bottom of the river. He later learned the manager was to blame for "the affair," which struck Marlow as "too stupid

[...] to be altogether natural" (1972): "They had started two days before in a sudden hurry up the river with the manager on board, in charge of some volunteer skipper, and before they had been out three hours they tore the bottom out of her on stones, and she sank near the south bank" (1972). Since Marlow had the responsibility of "fishing" his boat out of the river (1972), he did not seem to find the fact that the manager had proven himself incapable of piloting or commanding a boat in almost record time a laughing matter, at least in the moment. Instead, the sunken steamer and the overall "deplorable condition" of the station made Marlow wonder in all seriousness if the inept manager had risen on the corporate ladder simply by resisting disease and surviving in the jungle longer than his competition (1972–73).

Interacting with the manager at work and observing the effects of his decisions only confirmed Marlow's suspicion that the manager had survived his way to the top. Marlow recognized that the "hollow" manager (1973) was filled with an unsettling darkness and that he had one "effective faculty"—the ability to make other men uneasy enough to obey him (1972). Apart from these characteristics, the "flabby devil" was commonplace in almost every way (1972). According to Marlow's estimation, he had no learning or intelligence, and he lacked the "genius for organising, for initiative, for order even" (1972). He could not originate anything on his own; he could only "keep the routine going" (1973). However, the manager did not keep the "routine going" smoothly. An egocentric, the manager ignored the needs, challenges, frustrations, and pains of others in the company—unless another man's struggles had an adverse effect on him personally. For instance, when Marlow arrived after a twenty-mile journey on foot, the manager did not offer him a chair, a small courtesy that any guest, whether rested or weary, would appreciate (1972). But when the white men in the company quarreled at mealtime "about precedence," he became annoyed with them. Consequently, he ordered a massive round table to be built, which required construction of another building just to house it, a useless waste of manpower and resources on both counts (1973). This round table in the jungle bore no semblance to the round table in the court of England's legendary King Arthur. It did not establish equality among those seated, nor did it inspire unity; it only led to more frustration and chaos (1973).

While the manager had little concern for those nearby, he cared a great deal about Kurtz, who was miles away, and he described the corrupt agent in glowing terms—Kurtz was "the best agent he had, an exceptional man, of the greatest importance to the Company" (1973). He also expressed anxiety about the news that Kurtz had fallen ill, hoped it was just a rumor, and exclaimed, "Ah, Mr. Kurtz!" (1973). Marlow's insight into the manager's flaws reveals two reasons why the manager might have had an interest in the health of this so-called "exceptional man." First, the manager might have seen Kurtz as a man after his own heart because the two were very much alike in many respects. The manager, like Kurtz, was driven by greed and self-aggrandizement (e.g., wherever he sat at the table was "the first place—the rest were nowhere" (1973)), and his "methods" resulted in utter chaos. Moreover, he had no internal or external checks on his behavior. Consequently, he turned a blind eye not only to his men's concerns about precedence and orderliness, but also to their suffering, even when their lives were at stake. For example, when a tropical disease had sickened most of the men in the station, the manager remarked coldly, "Men who come out here should have no entrails" (1973). Ironically, Marlow wondered whether the manager himself had anything on the inside, and he surmised that "[p]erhaps there was nothing within him" (1973), unless the same darkness that Kurtz carried inside him counted for something. Second, and perhaps more important, because the manager lacked intelligence and good judgment, he relied on Kurtz's help to "keep the routine going" (1973). Consequently, while he likely did not see it for himself, the manager's feelings of admiration and pity for Kurtz amounted to no more than self-love and self-pity.

The manager's greed and self-pity spread through the station's employees like a virus, and the only way for Marlow to escape it, to keep his "hold on the redeeming facts of life," was to figuratively "turn his back on that station" by working to reclaim his sunken steamer from the river (1973). Whenever Marlow was man enough, he faced the darkness of the station. He watched in wonder at the manager's men wandering aimlessly around "here and there with their absurd long staves in their hands, like a lot of faithless pilgrims bewitched inside a rotten fence" (1973). He heard how "[t]he word 'ivory' rang in the air, was whispered was sighed," as if all the men in the station "were praying to it" (1973–74). He sensed the "air of plotting about [the] station" and the agents' common desire to "get appointed to a trading-post where ivory was to be had, so that they could earn percentages" (1975). He recognized that the plotting was as "unreal as everything else—as the philanthropic pretence of the whole concern, as their talk, as their government, as their show of work" (1975). He realized that the men waiting for an appointment "intrigued and slandered and hated each other" because they all hoped to profit from the ivory (1975). He perceived, though they could not, that "the only thing that ever came to them was disease" (1974). He saw that the "first-class agent," the "young, gentlemanly'" brick maker, who had been waiting idly for over a year for the missing ingredient that he needed to manufacture his first brick (1974), was as greedy and hollow as the manager. Over time, Marlow came to think of him as a "papier-mâché Mephistopheles'" with "nothing inside but a little loose dirt, maybe" (1976), perhaps because he viewed Kurtz as an obstacle to the promotion he had been planning during his period of futile, senseless waiting for materials that were likely to never come (1974), or perhaps because he boasted that "he feared neither God nor devil, let alone any mere man" (1978). Though engulfed in the station's darkness, its inactivity, inefficiency, idolatry, empty talk, unrealistic expectations, and hollow ambition, Marlow could see that beyond the rotting fence the "silent wilderness" surrounding the station was "something great and invincible, like evil or truth, waiting patiently for the passing away of this fantastic invasion" (1974).

Another character who memorably seems to personify the foolishness of European efforts to explore and colonize Africa is a character known only as "the Russian"—a character Marlow met as he made his journey upriver to "save" (2004) Kurtz, the diseased renegade agent who (it turns out) had established his own perverse colony and plundered a vast amount of Africa's ivory (1994) by whatever methods he deemed necessary. Marlow first found a sign scrawled on a piece of board that read, "Wood for you. Hurry up. Approach cautiously" (1985). Marlow recalls how he and others onboard wondered what the message meant and ridiculed the author's style: "Hurry up. Where? Up the river? [. . .] Something was wrong above. But what—and how much? That was the question. We commented adversely upon the imbecility of that telegraphic style" (1985). Marlow next found the Russian's most prized possession: a sixty-year old book entitled *An Inquiry into some Points of Seamanship*. Although the book was "dreary" and filled with "illustrative diagrams and repulsive tables of figures" (1985), Marlow thought it an incredible find:

"Such a book being there was wonderful enough; but still more astounding were the notes pencilled in the margin, and plainly referring to the text. I couldn't believe my eyes! They were in cipher. [...] Fancy a man lugging with him a book of that description into this nowhere and studying it—and making notes—in cipher at that! It was an extravagant mystery." (1985)

Marlow soon discovered that the cipher was actually Russian (1998) and that the book's owner was also an "extravagant mystery" in his dress, his convictions, and his methods of exploration. When the seaman saw the Russian for the first time, he knew that there was "something funny" about his appearance; he realized suddenly the youth's patchwork clothing made him look like a harlequin. By likening the man to a harlequin and referring to him as "[t]he harlequin" (1997), Marlow subtly suggests that the clownish, foolish, motley clothing (1998) not only "made the man," but it reflected the man. Within moments, the Russian revealed to Marlow that he was indeed a fool. He spoke incessantly (1997), laughed frequently (1997–98), grabbed and shook both of Marlow's hands constantly (1998), praised Kurtz, a man blinded by greed and ambition, for making him "see things" (1998), and demonstrated repeatedly how much Kurtz had "enlarged [his] mind" (1998–99; 2005) with his outstretched arms (1998–99).

During their discourse, Marlow learned the Russian's mind had been in need of enlarging for some time. Calmed by a pipe and English tobacco, the young man revealed that he had begun his journey into the Congo's interior with little thought or preparation. The explorer set out by himself with only a few provisions, "a light heart, and no more idea of what would happen to him than a baby," and he went thoughtlessly deeper and deeper into the jungle until he lost his way (1998). Lost and alone, he wandered along the river for almost two years before he found "civilization" at Kurtz's station (1998). Marlow admits he found it difficult to believe that the Russian had survived such an exploration:

"His very existence was improbable, inexplicable, and altogether bewildering. [...] For months—for years—his life hadn't been worth a day's purchase; and there he was gallantly, thoughtlessly

alive, to all appearance indestructible solely by the virtue of his
few years and of his unreflecting audacity." (1998–99)

While Marlow marveled at the Russian's ability to stay alive during his
"futile wanderings" and "almost envied" the "be-patched youth" for his
"absolutely pure, uncalculating, unpractical spirit of adventure" (1999),
he held the youth in contempt because he was just as thoughtless in
his devotion to Kurtz.

The seaman accurately perceived that the Russian's mind still
needed enlarging when it came to Kurtz, "the most dangerous thing"
the adventurous youth had encountered in his wanderings (1999).
"The harlequin" idolized Kurtz to the point that "[t]he man filled his
life, occupied his thoughts, swayed his emotions" (2000). In his slavish
devotion, the Russian also refused to "judge" Kurtz "as an ordinary
man" (2000), even though the agent was the quintessence of flesh
and carnality as an invader (2001), raider (1999), swindler (1993),
thief (1993, 2000), manipulator (2000), murderer (2001), and deceiver
(2003, 2007–09). Moreover, Kurtz's devotee did not want others to
judge his false idol. He was stunned by Marlow's refusal to hear how
the natives had approached Kurtz on their knees and shocked by
the seaman's laughing at Kurtz's absurd notion that the natives were
"rebels ' worthy of death'" (2001). The Russian defended Kurtz "almost
passionately" when Marlow became amused that the dying agent had
once talked to the youth of "everything," including love (1999). And
he plead with his "brother seaman" not to share what he had seen and
heard of Kurtz's behavior with others so that Kurtz's reputation would
not suffer (2005).

Because the Russian thought Kurtz an extraordinary man and
thought himself "a simple man" with "no great thoughts" (2002), the
youth seemed to value the vile agent's life and reputation more than
his own. He put his own life in danger to nurse Kurtz through two
bouts of grave illness (1999), sacrificed ten nights of sleep trying to
sustain the agent's life (2002), and fled from the manager, who planned
to hang him, only after Marlow assured him that Kurtz's reputation
would be safe with him (2005). Moreover, when the Russian fled
back into the jungle, he put his life in jeopardy once again by failing
to take adequate provisions for the journey ahead. This time, he had
only a few gun cartridges, a handful of tobacco, a pair of used shoes,
and his beloved book; nevertheless, Marlow recalls that he "seemed

to think himself excellently equipped for a renewed encounter with the wilderness" (2005). Marlow's observation reveals that "Kurtz's last disciple" (2002) had not learned much over the years, which makes the thoughtless youth's parting words, "Oh, he enlarged my mind!'" (2005), seem questionable and the "disciple" himself seem as laughably absurd as his teacher.

Griffith contends that the Russian is "almost" a parody or a comic exaggeration of the agent (47); if so, he parodies other Europeans as well because Kurtz himself serves as a tragicomic character whose absurd ideas and actions exaggerate, slightly or grossly, those of other European colonists and explorers. Prior to his experience in the Congo, the "original Kurtz" (1994) had embraced the widely held notion that Europeans could and should help civilize Africa's inhabitants (Griffith 89–91). He had even written an eloquent, inspiring seventeen-page report on the subject under the direction of the International Society for the Suppression of Savage Customs (1995). He left for the Congo to serve as a "cultural emissary" (Griffith 91), a torch bearer who ostensibly believed that "[e]ach station should be like a beacon on the road towards better things, a centre for trade of course, but also for humanising, improving, instructing" (1981).

Tragically, Kurtz followed the plan he laid out so eloquently in his report. Upon his arrival at the Inner Station, he "necessarily" demonstrated to the "savages" through the firing of his guns that he was a supernatural being (1995) who wielded in his hands the power of thunder and lightning (2000) with hopes that he might, through "the simple exercise of [his] will," be able to "exert a power for good practically unbounded" (1995). Ironically, Kurtz's exertion of power resulted not in unbounded good, but in the agent's unrestrained "gratification of his various lusts" (2001). Though Kurtz was filled with lofty ideas, he was "hollow at the core" (2001), which made him vulnerable to his unbridled lust (2001) for power, success, wealth, and fame (2009). And though Kurtz was supposedly a light bearer and "the voice" of one crying in the wilderness, Marlow suggests that the light within the idealist and his message was intermingled, paradoxically, with a great darkness:

> "[O]f all his gifts the one that stood out pre-eminently, that carried with it a real presence, was his ability to talk, his words—the gifts of expression, the bewildering, the

> illuminating, the most exalted and the most contemptible, the pulsating stream of light, or the deceitful flow from the heart of an impenetrable darkness." (1993)

Because the hollow idealist was filled with darkness, he eventually adopted "the vehemently racist notion of the irreclaimable nature of 'savages,' an idea that was still prominent in Conrad's time" (Griffith 91–92). Even worse, Kurtz eventually "concentrated" his intelligence "upon himself with horrible intensity" (2008) and concluded that in order to achieve "unbounded good" for himself, he would need to fight darkness with darkness and utterly destroy those he had come to save, one "rebel" at a time if necessary.

Because Kurtz's going to the Congo results in a tragic loss of his own high ideals and human life (his own and others), some might find it difficult to see Kurtz as both a tragic and a comic figure. However, Kurtz deserves to be a target of scornful laughter because as much as Kurtz claims to know, in the end he does not know much. "Exterminate all the brutes!" (1995), the postscript that the new and unimproved idealist "scrawled" on his report after "his nerves went wrong" (1995), amuses not because of the message, but because of the ironic juxtaposition that Kurtz unwittingly created. The detailed, thoughtful, altruistic report promised elevation and hope. In contrast, the sweeping, irrational, hateful postscript beneath it threatened annihilation and doom. Within seconds, Kurtz contradicted and undermined his own carefully crafted argument (1995) and lost his readers in the process. If Kurtz's seventeen pages of "close writing" about civilizing the "savages" made Marlow "tingle with enthusiasm" (1995), his one hastily written four-word sentence jolted the seaman like a lightning bolt (1995).

Tragically, Kurtz followed (but only in an absurdly ironic fashion) the plan he laid out so eloquently in his report. Upon his arrival at the Inner Station, he "necessarily" demonstrated to the "savages" through the firing of his guns that he was a supernatural being (1995) who wielded the power of thunder and lightning (2000) with hopes that he might, through "the simple exercise of [his] will," be able to "exert a power for good practically unbounded" (1995). Unfortunately, however, Kurtz's exertion of power resulted not in unbounded good, but in the agent's unrestrained "gratification of his various lusts" (2001). Though Kurtz was filled with lofty ideas, he was "hollow at the core" (2001), which made him vulnerable to his unbridled lust (2001) for power, success, wealth, and fame (2009). And though Kurtz was supposedly a light bearer and, "the voice" of one crying in the wilderness, Marlow suggests that the light within the idealist and his message was intermingled, paradoxically, with a great darkness:

> "[O]f all his gifts the one that stood out pre-eminently, that carried with it a real presence, was his ability to talk, his words—the gifts of expression, the bewildering, the illuminating, the most exalted and the most contemptible, the pulsating stream of light, or the deceitful flow from the heart of an impenetrable darkness." (1993)

Because the hollow idealist was filled with darkness, he eventually adopted "the vehemently racist notion of the irreclaimable nature of 'savages,' an idea that was still prominent in Conrad's time" (Griffith 91–92). Even worse, Kurtz eventually focused his intelligence "upon himself with horrible intensity" (2008) and concluded that in order to achieve "unbounded good" for himself, he would need to fight darkness with darkness and utterly destroy those he had come to save, one "rebel" native (2001) at a time if necessary. What could be more absurd than this impulse to enslave and exterminate the very persons he had originally hoped to help?

Some critics argue that Marlow's thinly veiled criticisms of Continental Europeans (1962) and his praise of the British (1963) suggest that he thought British exploration and colonization superior to that of the ancient Romans and the Continental Europeans (Ramogale 315; Atkinson 8). Whether or not Marlow is, in fact, "an apologist for the 'civilising mission' of British imperial ideology" and the "lofty ideals of British colonialism," as Marcus Ramogale contends (315), is debatable. Without question Marlow casts the Romans and the Continental Europeans in a negative light, but as Marlow spins his yarn, he reveals that "civilized" man's method of exploring the darkness of a foreign continent had not changed much in nineteen hundred years. Those who were "men enough" to face the Congo's darkness, including Marlow himself, were in no way immune to "the growing regrets, the longing to escape, the powerless disgust, the surrender, the hate" that might have plagued the Romans. Many of the explorers and "colonists" in the Congo were of "no account"; few were devoted to efficiency, and even fewer were capable of efficiency. Finally, and most importantly, as Marlow relates the many instances of European absurdity that he encountered during his journey to the heart of darkness, he demonstrates that many of his contemporaries were capable of tackling Africa's darkness as blindly as any Roman conqueror, which suggests that no nation of people can explore and colonize a "dark" continent without entering into or creating a surreal, fantastically absurd world.

Works Cited

Conrad, Joseph. *The Collected Works of Joseph Conrad: Medallion Edition 1925–28*. New York: Routledge, 1995.

Griffith, John. W. *Joseph Conrad and the Anthropological Dilemma*. Oxford: Oxford University Press, 1995.

THE ILIAD
(HOMER)

The Iliad
by Charles Moorman, in *Kings and Captains:*
Variations on a Heroic Theme (1971)

INTRODUCTION

Charles Moorman, in this excerpt from his book *Kings and Captains: Variations on a Heroic Theme*, examines Homer's *Iliad* in terms of the conflict within the Achaean camp, as well as Homer's refashioning of heroic myth and ancient history. As Moorman writes, "Homer, looking back from the point of view of a romanticized tradition, saw the great legend of the Trojan War not merely, like Hesiod, as the record of an adventurous and golden time[. . . but] as raw material for a commentary on the life of both ages, gold and iron alike, and on the great problem common to both—the individual's relation to the state, and the values involved in the conflict between ruler and ruled, between loyalty to the state and the rights of the individual." Thus the *Iliad*, for Moorman, not only expounds upon the just relation of people to their rulers, but also comments upon the era of Aegean colonization in which Homer wrote.

Moorman, Charles. "The Iliad." *Kings and Captains: Variations on a Heroic Theme.* Lexington, KY: UP of Kentucky, 1971. 1–29.

It is clear that three kinds of source material were involved in the tradition of the Trojan War inherited by Homer: history—the remnants of actual persons, places, and events of the struggle, doubtless distorted by time but still in the main discernible, if not wholly accurate; legend—"primitive history . . . unconsciously transformed and simplified" beyond recognition by an accretion of folktales and wonders; and myth—the stories of the gods, ultimately derived from ritual-expressing in its simplest, though most illusive, form "primitive philosophy, . . . a series of attempts to understand the world, to explain life and death, fate and nature, gods and cults."[1] There was doubtless an actual Trojan War involving allied Greek forces, but in the centuries during which this unusual war was talked and sung about, its leaders and events became aggrandized by the natural tendency of primitive people to glorify and magnify their past heroes and history, and its causes and meaning came to be attributed to supernatural forces, the gods who continually oversee and in the long run control human history.

Unfortunately for the critic, the *Iliad* itself is, like *Beowulf,* our chief historical document for the period it represents, though indeed it contains even less "pure" history than does *Beowulf.*[2] Avoiding for the moment the tangle of technical arguments surrounding the time of composition, it seems clear that the *Iliad* was put into very nearly its present form in the eighth or ninth century B.C. and that its dramatic date, according to Greek tradition, is the late twelfth century, 1184 to be precise, some three to four hundred years earlier. There can be very little doubt that there was a siege of Troy; certainly the Greeks themselves regarded Homer's account as based on historical fact, and the archaeological work at Troy corroborates the possibility that an engagement took place somewhere around 1230.[3] On the other hand, our knowledge of Bronze Age chronology is so scanty as to make any speculation about the actual circumstances of the war extremely risky. Since there are no early Greek accounts of the period, no one can say whether the war was caused by the abduction of a Greek queen, whether it resulted from the colonizing expeditions of the Aeolian tribes into Asia, or whether it was an attempt to break Troy's economic stranglehold on Greek shipping in the Hellespont.

Even so, some general conclusions about the period of the late twelfth century are possible. Whatever the relationship between Crete and the cities of the Greek mainland had been in earlier years, the Achaean stronghold of Mycenae had been from the time of the fall of

Knossos in 1400, and probably for 150 years before, the greatest of the Greek kingdoms and remained so until well into the twelfth century. Her art, which shows during the early centuries of her dominance a strong Cretan influence, her tombs, fortifications, and palaces all evidence that Mycenae was the center of a great commercial empire which extended throughout the Peloponnesus and spread outward into Asia Minor and Cyprus and even into Egypt and Sicily. It was probably also the chief military power of the period, dominating its neighbors by "an elaborate system of gift-giving, which imposed reciprocal obligations without formal alliances or the necessity for a hierarchy of states.⁴ As the tablets which have survived from Pylos and Mycenae show,⁵ the social and economic life of the early Mycenaean period was organized minutely; the scrupulously kept accounts show a tightly controlled, though cumbrous, system of economic control over a vast area.

In time, however, a kind of decadence at home and aggressive restlessness abroad set in as Mycenae's trading empire was threatened by political and trading difficulties in Asia Minor and Egypt and by the decreasing wealth of Crete, from which she had long drawn a great part of her income. Egyptian and Hittite records dating from the late fourteenth century downward record a change in the relations between the Achaeans and their overseas neighbors. At first the allies of the Hittites, to whom they may have been related, against the Egyptians, by the middle thirteenth century Achaeans had become "sea raiders" fighting for the economic life of their empire against the Hittite colonies in Asia Minor as well as against Egypt. There are records of broken treaties and coastal raids, all evidencing the vigor with which the Mycenaeans pursued new trade routes and areas for colonization. In 1225 and 1194, together with other tribes, the Achaeans attacked Egypt unsuccessfully, but the cumulative effect of these campaigns was the destruction of the Hittite empire in Asia Minor and the beginning of political divisions among the Greeks. The wealth and influence of Mycenae apparently continued to decline until the great waves of Dorians in the twelfth century put an end to a civilization already crippled by economic failures, dynastic feuds and internal struggles, and a long and costly series of wars. The centuries following were in every way the "dark ages" of Greece.

It is during the last period of Mycenaean domination, the period of aggression and the struggle to survive, that Greek tradition placed

Greece's "heroic age." Hesiod interposes an age of heroes between the age of bronze of early Mycenae and the prosaic age of iron in which he considered himself to live. The two great events of the heroic age, he tells us, were the sieges of Thebes and Troy. The Greeks themselves envisioned the heroic age as closing with the Doric invasions, and Homer's genealogies indicate that he thought of the period as encompassing some two hundred years, a period roughly coinciding with the restless, aggressive activities of the Achaeans, a time in which the whole Mediterranean world was marked by wars and confusion and the restless migration of its peoples.

It seems probable that while the epics of Homer reflect the warlike spirit of these later centuries, they occasionally in spirit if not in fact look back even farther, to the tradition of the power and influence of early Mycenae. Certainly Homer had no accurate knowledge of life in the Mycenaean ages nor of the historical causes or conduct of the Trojan War; his picture of the period was likely a distorted one shaped by a long and probably at times a weak oral tradition. Almost every element in Homer is thus an amalgam. His geography, his language, his poetic technique, his descriptions of armor, of battle procedures, architecture, customs, and beliefs—all derive both from the Ionic uses of the dark ages and of his own time and from the Mycenaean period, remnants of which were retained, though distorted, in the historical and poetic tradition which survived, probably through the descendants of Achaean refugees in Asia Minor. But the Achaean Confederacy is seen in the poem not as a desperate and decaying civilization, nor as one fighting for trade and colonization opportunities, but as the world's greatest established power in its heyday of unification and influence. The great catalog of ships demonstrates the range and might of its domain; the power of Agamemnon to keep a united expeditionary force in the field for ten years, the dominance of Mycenae in its organization.

The use of the term *Achaean* in Homer as a general name for the Greek force gathered at Troy is in itself puzzling. Certainly we are not to gather from it that there was ever anything resembling a single Mycenaean kingdom, much less a single people; but considered along with the Hittite records, the use of the term in Homer demonstrates that the Mycenaeans were indeed the dominant military group as well as the most prosperous people of the age. This fact throws considerable light on the position of Agamemnon and hence on his role in the poem. He is clearly commander in chief: he has the sole power to continue or abandon the siege, and the strategy and tactics of the war are his; he has in his power the disposition of the booty; he presides at council by virtue of the scepter; and he has, as Nestor says, a divine commission to command. But it is clearly the power to command rather than to rule absolutely. He may rebuke the stormy Achilles but not punish him, and although his decisions are final, he is constantly open to the criticisms of his officers and even of the common Thersites. His real power lies in his scepter rather than his person: Achilles can also use the scepter to call together a council, the purpose of which is to condemn an action of Agamemnon; and Odysseus can restrain the Greeks from leaving Troy only because he holds the scepter.

Agamemnon's position in the field as military commander of a conglomerate, though unified, expeditionary force seems to indicate the limits and degree of his authority as well as the place of Mycenae in the Achaean empire. Nestor clearly states that Agamemnon's authority is based on the wide extent of his kingdom. And not only does his kingdom, joined with that of Menelaus, encompass almost the whole Peloponnesus, but he is clearly the political overlord of some of his subordinates as well as their military superior. Yet, as the catalog makes clear, the Achaean leaders are for the most part kings in their own right and have merely delegated to Agamemnon the military authority necessary for efficient command. Like the Hittite commands of the same period, the Mycenaean military force was a confederacy of kings organized for efficient military action.

Such a position as that held by Agamemnon thus seems to be based on a confederacy of kings in the Mycenaean period rather than on the disposition of the Ionian aristocracy in Homer's own time. Homer is portraying a historical reality, a portrait of military king-ship drawn from the past. Whether or not an actual Agamemnon directed the operations at Troy is outside the sphere of debate; there is historical evidence neither for nor against his existence. Yet certain names appearing in the Hittite records may verify the existence of an Eteocles and an Atreus, and certainly some Achaean king directed the siege of Troy, whatever his name was.

To summarize briefly, the figure of Agamemnon is drawn from history, and his position reflects the extensive, though in some ways limited, power held by the Achaean commander in chief at Troy. The mixed nature of the authority delegated by the Achaean kings, moreover, does much to explain Agamemnon's dramatic role in the poem. According to the legend, the Greek rulers were called into service because of an agreement among them, made years before during their courtship of Helen, to protect the marriage of Menelaus and Helen should it be threatened. Having with some difficulty gathered the army at the port of Aulis, Agamemnon was unable to launch the expedition because of the enmity of the goddess Artemis, Apollo's sister. In desperation he agreed to sacrifice his daughter Iphigenia in return for favorable winds and so finally set sail.

But nine long years of frustration and deprivation have gone by. The Achaean kings, who were never eager to leave their homes to honor a long-forgotten, boyish agreement to protect Menelaus's wife, have become testy; a hoax designed by Agamemnon to test their loyalty reveals their eagerness to abandon the expedition. It is little wonder, therefore, that Agamemnon both resents and reacts hotly against any challenge to his authority, even one by the god Apollo. The general council of the Greeks clearly wishes him to return Chryseis; Achilles calls a meeting of the council without his consent; he is accused of personal cowardice; even the army soothsayer speaks against him. He is clearly in the wrong and probably knows it, but the circumstances are such that a proud man, pushed to the limits of his patience and fearful of his position, can react in no way except to bully his way through.

It should be remarked also that no question of romance or of a lady's honor is involved. Indeed Homer, especially in the *Odyssey*, creates a striking number of intelligent, sympathetic women, but Chryseis and Briseis have no real personalities in the poem, and it is clear that their captors care little for them. The captured girls are thus only the excuse for the quarrel among the chieftains. The real issue is *aidos*, the relationship between the commander in chief and his best warrior, and it is an issue which has presumably been simmering for a long time, needing only a catalyst to set it boiling.

Although Agamemnon reflects in his position, if not necessarily in his personality (which is almost purely the invention of Homer and/or an inherited tradition), a historical situation, Achilles does not seem to have been drawn at all from history but instead from myth. There is, in the first place, some confusion regarding his inclusion in the expedition at all.[6] He is not really an Achaean but is said to come from Phthia in Thessaly rather than from any of the Peloponnesian centers from which the other heroes are called. His people, the Myrmidons, are unknown to historians. He is thus to some degree an outlander, distinguished even by his speech from his compatriots. Throughout the *Iliad* he is a lonely figure; we never see him in close association with the other Greek leaders. He is, moreover, the only major hero to be killed during the war.

There are also an unusual number of tales associated with his birth and *enfance*. He is of semidivine origin; according to myth, his mother, Thetis, attempts to secure immortality for him by dipping him either in the river Styx or in fire. He is reared by Cheiron the centaur on Mount Pelion, and his weapons and horses are miraculous. He is, moreover, doomed either to live a long, though pedestrian, life or to fall in glory at Troy.

His actions and powers also are different not only in degree but also in kind from those of the other heroes: his armor is forged by the god Hephaestus; a magical fire blazes about his head on the eve of battle; in his ire he fights the swollen Xanthus. Homer throws about Achilles, as about none of the other characters, an aura of the superhuman and the mythical. Even the gods seem to respect and shun him; unlike the other heroes, he is free from their tricks and deceits.

[...]

Certainly, however, his unrelenting fury and the aura which surrounds his head seem vestiges of his mythic past, as does his appearance at dawn on the last day of battle after his long sojourn in his tent. I would not insist on this point, but it may well be that Achilles' retreat in isolation reflects also, at least in part, the withdrawal–return pattern which is an essential part of the myth of the questing hero.[7] For although most of the familiar stages in the withdrawal–return— the call to adventure, the crossing of the threshold, etc.—are not to be found in the *Iliad*, Achilles does indeed return to his people to bring victory out of defeat.

But my central point is that the figure of Achilles is the only one derived from myth and that his mythic origin explains his individuality, his isolation from others, and from their common cause. Never after the initial quarrel with Agamemnon does he exhibit the slightest interest in an Achaean victory. He is perfectly willing, therefore, to sacrifice the whole mission to justify his own position and to salve the wound of a personal assault. All the efforts of Odysseus and Phoenix to appeal to his sense of duty or his responsibility to their common cause fail simply because he has no conception of such a role. When he finally does emerge, it is to avenge a personal wrong, the death of Patroclus, and even here he fights as an individual; his killing of Hector is prompted not by Hector's position as leader of the enemy forces but by the fact that Hector killed Patroclus. When at last his fury is abated and his wrath assuaged, it is not because he realizes that his actions have been irresponsible and his brutality unreasonable but because Priam's grief moves him to think of his own father and his father's sorrows.

Thus the *Iliad* poses as antagonists king and captain: the historical Agamemnon, whose sense of the responsibility, of leadership steadily grows until it overcomes the egotism and personal pride that originally inspired his quarrel with Achilles; and the mythical Achilles, whom fury and pride send raving into alienation until he becomes more beast than man. The other characters of the poem, moreover, illuminate various aspects of this central clash in authority. As C. M. Bowra has pointed out, the minor characters tend to "fall into two classes, the soldiers and the statesmen. In the first class are Aias, Diomedes, and Menelaus, and in the second are Nestor and Odysseus."[8] Like Achilles, Aias and Diomedes are essentially individualistic warriors, fierce and aggressive in combat; neither has any use for the councils of the wise. Diomedes, in fact, will not accept Agamemnon's grief-stricken decision to abandon the siege and deplores Agamemnon's having humbled himself in attempting to make amends to Achilles.

But neither Aias nor Diomedes can match Achilles. Aias is compared by Homer to both a lion and an ass; he has a stubborn natural courage, but he is essentially slow-witted, a great, hulking brute whose ultimate fate is frustration, dumb rage, and suicide. He thus differs from Achilles, whose intelligence immediately pierces Priam's flattery. Diomedes has a good deal of Achilles' dash and brilliance in the field, but he lacks the fury that makes Achilles "godlike" in battle. The scene in which Diomedes and Glaucus courteously exchange armor on the battlefield sharply contrasts with Achilles' refusal to spare the unarmed and suppliant Lycaon. Both Aias and Diomedes, however, help to define the essential quality that sets Achilles apart from the others: an unswerving and unalterable faith in the rightness of his own conduct, a prideful self-assurance capable of destroying an army for the sake of personal honor.

The true foil to Achilles is, of course, Hector, his Trojan counterpart and, at least to modern readers, the most sympathetic of the heroes. Unlike Achilles he fights only to protect his home and country, and his prowess and heroism stem from necessity rather than, as with Achilles, the fury of personal insult. The famous scenes with Andromache show him at his best, kind and loving, yet thoroughly responsible, a conscientious soldier and a wise leader. Yet the fire of the gods never burns about his head, nor in the end can he understand the nature of the man whose ire he has incurred. He decides to press the Trojans' hard-won military advantage by opposing Achilles and later to stand alone against his fury. But at the sight of Achilles brandishing the spear of Pelion, his armor glowing "like a blazing fire or the rising sun, he no longer had the heart to stand his ground; he left the gate, and ran away in terror."[9] In the end Hector is duped by Athene into fighting and dies charging into Achilles' lance. Deliberate courage and prowess and a cause to defend have failed to stand against the wrath of the godlike Achilles.

The characters of Nestor and Odysseus throw light in much the same way upon that of Agamemnon. For if Agamemnon struggles to understand the nature of authority and command, Nestor is surely past understanding it. A man of great experience, he has come to live only in the past and its glories, and therefore his experience is of little use to the Greeks. His advice is nearly always ineffective and at times almost disastrous. It is he who on the basis of a false dream counsels the building of the wall, which soon crumbles under the Trojan assault, without offering the necessary sacrifices to Poseidon. The futile embassy to Achilles is his idea as is the plan to have Patroclus appear on the battlefield dressed in Achilles' armor. In Nestor Homer portrays the uselessness of mere experience as a basis for authority and wise decision, and though Nestor can in his interminable yarns suggest a heroic standard of conduct, the appeals to valor by the high-spirited Diomedes are much more effective in rallying the army.

Odysseus, on the other hand, is (in the *Iliad*, at least) so totally involved in the affairs of the moment that he lacks the breadth of judgment great authority demands. He operates always at the level of device and stratagem and is thus always the man called upon to deal with the immediate problem by the most practicable means. He can be trusted to return Chryseis to her father with perfect tact; he manages to cope with the panic that follows Agamemnon's announcement that the army will embark for home; he can worm information from the unsuspecting Dolon; he wins the wrestling contest with Aias by a trick; and he even talks the bloodthirsty Achilles into allowing his soldiers to eat before battle. But he fails in the greatest, the only crucial mission assigned him: he cannot dent Achilles' determination to refrain from battle; his subtlest arguments cannot match Achilles' prideful determination. He is in every way a man of the greatest intelligence and charm, but he lacks Agamemnon's stature and honesty and, ultimately, his sense of the responsibilities of power.

The gods also reflect, in their eternal bickering, the theme of the nature of authority that so occupies the heroes below. Zeus rules by sheer power rather than intelligence and is reduced all too often to shouting and threatening. The other gods, wary of his thunderbolts, must take advantage of their father in whatever devious ways they can: Here by nagging and eventually by seduction, Athene by argument, Aphrodite by flattery; Thetis (not even a close relative) by wheedling. Whatever Homer may have thought of the gods, it is clear that they present no proper model for government among men.

Because of the scantiness of biographical and historical information, it is difficult to ascertain with any hope of exactitude Homer's ultimate purposes in the poem. He almost certainly lived in the late ninth or early eighth century, apparently in Ionia in Asia Minor, and was thoroughly trained in the usages of formulaic poetry. He was, moreover, an inheritor of a long tradition of lays concerning the Trojan War, a tradition which he might well fabricate into a single brilliantly conceived and executed poem but which he could not basically change. The major causes, events, and characters of the tradition were beyond alteration; similarly, one could not today write a poem, however heroic, in which the South won the Civil War and Lincoln appeared as a drunken scoundrel. But Homer, by selection and emphasis, might well use his tradition to shape a theme. He might not alter a received character, but he might, by the addition of detail, shape that character to fit his own purpose.[10]

It is this sense of purpose that everywhere distinguishes the *Iliad* from the imitations and continuations of the so-called epic cycle that follow it. Obviously Homer did not recount the ancient stories simply for their own sakes; in fact he leaves out the most exciting among them, that of the Trojan Horse. Nor are they told historically; the full chronology of the war is not only ignored but often, as in the engagement of Menelaus and Paris in Book 3, actually violated.[11] Nor are they told, as men often tell stories of the past, either reminiscently or, despite Robert Graves's interpretation, satirically;[12] the poet is neither a Nestor nor a Mark Twain.

Some help in determining Homer's attitude toward the past, and hence in defining his purpose, may be gleaned from the bits of history that have come down to us. The Greek world of Homer's own time was emerging from over two hundred years of civil chaos and cultural disruption, the so-called dark ages. Undeniably, however, the Ionian colonies had prospered as a result of the new trade and maritime ventures that followed the dark ages, and by Homer's time they must have enjoyed considerable social stability. More important, Ionia had by then completed, as had most of the Greek kingdoms, the shift from a monarchic to an aristocratic, and federal form of government, a change caused primarily by the shift in population from the land to well-defined cities, what are later to emerge as the great city-states of the golden ages. These new aristocratic republics such as that under which Homer must have lived were governed for the most part efficiently, though rather narrowly. The governing class was trained in the business of ruling, and they passed their knowledge and skill along from generation to generation.

There is little doubt that the new form of government rescued the Greek cities from the anarchy and poverty which followed the collapse of the Mycenaean empire. Colonization began anew throughout the Aegean area and eventually beyond, and under the careful direction of the new republics it became systematic and profitable. The colonies had to be supplied both with agricultural goods such as wool and with manufactured articles and so provided the republics with new markets as well as sources of raw materials. The new age might well have been, as Hesiod complained, an age of iron in which the practices of the ages of silver and gold had fallen into disuse, but it also created social conditions in which a poetry celebrating the glories of those former ages might be composed; furthermore, it provided through its commerce with Phoenicia an instrument, the alphabet, which could preserve those glories forever.

I would maintain that Homer, looking back from the point of view of a romanticized tradition, saw the great legend of the Trojan War not merely, like Hesiod, as the record of an adventurous and golden time; more important, he saw it as raw material for a commentary on the life of both ages, gold and iron alike, and on the great problem common to both—the individual's relation to the state, and the values involved in the conflict between ruler and ruled, between loyalty to the state and the rights of the individual.

To frame this great commentary Homer selected from the oral tradition of history and legend and myth which had kept alive the memory of the war at Troy a single incident, the quarrel of Agamemnon and Achilles, and by arrangement and emphasis built into his account of that incident all his reflections upon his own time and the heroic past. Not that the poem is a personal judgment and commentary in the sense that a Romantic poem is, for Homer observes scrupulously the objectivity of the great classical artist. He narrates and shapes the action, but he never imposes his own voice on it. To do so would have been to sacrifice universality and to reduce the poem to something less than heroic in scope. But a judgment is there, nevertheless, implicit in the actions and speeches of the characters and in the development of the conflict between the two great antagonists.

We too often read the *Iliad* as though it were only an *Achilliad*, as though Achilles were the only person of interest. He is, as I have said, the thematic center of the poem; everything depends upon his actions. Yet opposed to him stands the rest of the *dramatis personae*, the Greek force led by Agamemnon. One man thus stands against a whole state, and by an odd whim of destiny this person holds in his hands the fate of the nation. Victory or defeat is his to give, and for a few days in the midst of a raging battle the representatives of state and the individual stand opposed.

The resolution of this opposition is the substance of the *Iliad*. Agamemnon must learn that authority entails responsibility, that he cannot rule by prideful whim, and that he cannot jeopardize the safety of his command or the success of his expedition merely to demonstrate publicly the extent of his power. In the end his values are those of the organization which he both commands and serves. If in order to assure the success of the group he must conquer his natural inclination to despair, subdue his haughty spirit and imperious attitude, humble himself before his subordinate, and even refuse to snatch a trivial moment of glory in the javelin-throwing contest, then these things he must do. Originally drawn from history, he must in the poem develop within himself a sense of history and of his place in it. The greatest values of the leader in any age, golden or iron, are those of responsibility and loyalty to his cause and to his command.

Opposed to these values are those of Achilles—personal honor and the integrity of the individual. At first identified with and subject to the common welfare, Achilles' honor, once slighted (over however trivial a matter), turns sour; growing like a tumor within the hero, it becomes *hubris* and comes to dominate his personality. His mythic origins are far older than the historical origins of the king; like the sun, he rules alone, subject in his blazing pride to no laws beyond his own, loyal only to the dictates of his own honor. But unchecked *hubris* can lead only to irresponsibility and disaster. Achilles' motives in allowing Patroclus to appear in his armor are essentially egocentric. In granting permission to Patroclus he reiterates, rather pathetically now, his long list of grievances, expresses his delight at the Trojan victories, and cautions Patroclus not to perform too brilliantly lest he cheapen his own eventual reappearance as ultimate savior of the Greek force. In short he is delighted at the opportunity to demonstrate, as Patroclus has suggested, that his armor alone can rout the Trojan host.

After the death of Patroclus Achilles' high-minded *hubris* becomes simply animal rage and his atrocities mount; he kills indiscriminately everyone who opposes him on the battlefield, mutilates the dead body of Hector, and burns twelve young Trojans on Patroclus's pyre. But just before he begins the bloodbath which will culminate in Hector's death, he becomes reconciled with Agamemnon; admits his error in withdrawing from the common effort, an action from which only Hector and the Trojans profited; and urges that Agamemnon order an attack. Agamemnon, insisting that the whole army listen, apologizes in turn and the breach is healed. However, Achilles' wrath, now turned upon the Trojans, continues until the visit of Priam, and it is clear from his rebuffs of Priam's attempts at flattery that his ire still lies very close to the surface.

Homer thus reaches no solution to the dilemma he has faced. Agamemnon, it is true, comes to understand his kingly responsibility, but in doing so he must sacrifice the pride and personal integrity that so distinguishes Achilles. Achilles, on the other hand, maintains the sense of honor and fierce individualism that mark the hero, but they lead only to tragedy and in the end to quiet resignation. Yet paradoxically, Agamemnon appears at his best in apologizing publicly to Achilles and in graciously agreeing to share the prize with Meriones—in short, when he is most humble and least heroic; and Achilles is most impressive when, at the height of his ungoverned rage, he stands upon the beach, Athene's light upon his head, and three times howls his defiance at the Trojans.

Nearly everyone has remarked upon Homer's sense of the futility and waste of war, but no one has seriously questioned his approval of what are usually designated as the chief values of the heroic age: a sense of honor so great that it cannot brook the slightest affront; loyalty and fidelity to one's comrades—what is later to be called the *comitatus* code; and generosity.[13] Yet it is obvious that in the *Iliad* these heroic values are contradictory. What indeed happens when the value of honor crosses that of loyalty, when the rights of the individual conflict with those of society? Both values are rightful parts of the heroic code; because Hector and Diomedes can observe both, they are the most admirable of the warriors. Yet these values do conflict, and it is in their opposition that one finds, I think, the real strength of heroic literature. For all their bravery and intelligence, Hector and Diomedes cannot reach the glorious heights which Achilles reaches in his raging, wrongheaded, but nonetheless heroic, fury. Conscious always of the fate which hangs over him, he is willing to sacrifice his own welfare and that of his companions to satisfy a point of honor. And Agamemnon, despite his almost schizophrenic moodiness and, in the end, his most unheroic humility, is always a more responsible, because more concerned, leader than either the garrulous Nestor or the crafty Odysseus. The very opposite of Achilles, Agamemnon is willing to reduce himself to what must seem to be, by heroic standards, abject obsequiousness in order to further the Greek cause which he leads and for which he is responsible.

I would maintain that this carefully sustained ambivalence represents the considered point of view of a writer, perhaps the wisest who ever lived, looking back, from a highly structured commercial society toward a heroic age—to use David Riesman's terms, from an other-directed to an inner-directed society. That Homer recognizes the virtues of the former age is certain; his love of its dignity and strength is apparent in every line. But that does not mean that "this code of behavior seems to have been accepted by Homer without limitations."[14] Certainly the more prosaic values of the newer age are everywhere seen to balance the excesses of the older code. Both individual heroism and corporate authority are ideals worthy to be upheld, but they may well conflict and their opposition may bring about the destruction of both the individual and his society. Homer is able to view the great Bronze Age heroes with the rationalism and objectivity of a man who lives just outside the era of which he writes and who is able because of an unusual critical intelligence to escape its sentimental appeal.

[. . .]

NOTES

1. Erich Bethe, quoted by Susanne Langer, *Philosophy in a New Key* (Cambridge, Mass.: Harvard University Press, 1942), p. 177 n.
2. The best and most up-to-date summary of the historical background is probably that of Denys Page, *History and the Homeric Iliad* (Berkeley: University of California Press, 1966).
3. Like all questions of early Greek chronology, the date of the fall of Troy is much disputed. The best account of the problems concerning the period for the general reader is probably Joseph Alsop's *From the Silent Earth* (New York: Harper and Row, 1962), a gifted amateur's synthesis of the technical arguments of the specialists.
4. S. Kirk, *The Songs of Homer* (Cambridge: Cambridge University Press, 1962), p. 14.
5. These are the famous Linear B tablets first translated in the early 1950s by Michael Ventris. An account of this exciting discovery is given in Alsop, *From the Silent Earth*, pp. 30–37.
6. Kirk, *The Songs of Homer*, pp. 152–53.
7. Cf. Joseph Campbell, *The Hero with a Thousand Faces* (New York: Pantheon Books, 1949).
8. Bowra, *Tradition and Design*, p. 204.
9. E. V. Rieu, trans., *The Iliad* (Harmondsworth, Middlesex: Penguin Books, 1950), p. 400.
10. There is of course a good deal of dissension as to whether Homer could actually have written the poem, that is, composed it in writing rather than totally in his head. It seems to me that although Homer's style is based almost entirely on the oral formulas, genealogies, and other devices of orally composed poetry (as they quite naturally would be, given his training), the balanced structure and unity of the whole poem, in short the internal evidence, points to the kind of composition possible

only with a written, and hence manageable, text. The fact that Webster (*From Mycenae to Homer*, p. 272) and Bowra (*Homer and his Forerunners* [Edinburgh: Nelson, 1955], pp. 10–14) believe that the poem was composed in writing while Denys Page calls such an opinion "impossible" (*History and the Homeric Iliad*, p. 158) demonstrates the controversial nature of the external evidence.

11. It would seem that this incident, in which Menelaus and Paris fight a duel for Helen, would fall most naturally in the first days of the war.

12. Graves's eccentric theory is set forth in his introduction to his translation of the *Iliad, The Anger of Achilles* (New York: Doubleday, 1959).

13. Both Bowra (*Tradition and Design*, pp. 234–50) and H. M. Chadwick (*The Growth of Literature*, 3 vols. [Cambridge: Cambridge University Press, 1932–1940], 1:74) agree on these qualities as distinguishing the heroic temperament.

14. Bowra, *Tradition and Design*, p. 244.

THE NOVELS OF TONI MORRISON

"Periodizing Toni Morrison's work from *The Bluest Eye* to *Jazz*: the importance of *Tar Baby*" by Malin Walther Pereira, in *MELUS* (1997)

INTRODUCTION

While describing how "Morrison's complex relationship to colonization is radically transformed from her early to more recent work," Malin Walther Pereira finds that *Tar Baby* plays a central role in Morrison's *oeuvre*. Arguing that "one of the central concerns throughout Morrison's work is colonization," Pereira details how *Tar Baby* represents a turn away from "the effects of colonization on African American individuals and community," toward "an exploration of decolonized African American culture and history."

It is a mark of an author's status as "major" when we begin to periodize their work. William Faulkner, Adrienne Rich, William Butler Yeats, Gwendolyn Brooks, and T.S. Eliot are among the major authors for whose ouevres periods have been suggested. Toni Morrison's body of work is large enough, and her achievements notable enough, that it seems appropriate to periodize her work. While literary criticism

Pereira, Malin Walther. "Periodizing Toni Morrison's work from *The Bluest Eye* to *Jazz*: the importance of *Tar Baby*." *MELUS* 22.3 (Autumn 1997): 71–83.

of Toni Morrison's novels has generally acknowledged differences between her early and more recent work, there is a more radical shift in her oeuvre than has been articulated. Morrison's complex relationship to colonization is radically transformed from her early to more recent work. Periodizing Morrison's work in relationship to her process of decolonization clarifies differences between her early and more recent periods and stresses her development across her oeuvre. This approach also gives a central role to *Tar Baby*, a role not accessible within current frames.

Such a project—periodizing Morrison—has profound implications for both teaching and research. When Morrison's work is taught as a whole, as in a major author's course, periodization will affect the way in which the novels are grouped conceptually, the selection of themes and literary techniques to be investigated, even determining which novels would not be taught once her body of work expands further. When one of her novels is taught as part of a survey course in American fiction, women's writing, or African American literature, periodization will affect which one of her novels would be selected as representative. In terms of research, periodization will provide a focus to the discourse and encourage a shared vocabulary instead of the disparate theoretical discourses now in place.[1]

What I want to begin here is a call/response dynamic on the issue of Morrison's canon and its periods, and I hope my call generates many responses. The conversation on periodizing Morrison should be exciting and multi-voiced; I do not intend the periodization I propose here as a final product.[2]

One of the central concerns throughout Morrison's work is colonization.[3] Her early work struggles with the effects of colonization on African American individuals and the community, while her later work moves into an exploration of decolonized African American culture and history. In this context, her fourth novel, *Tar Baby*, assumes a rich significance. Understanding the importance of *Tar Baby* to Morrison's distancing from the colonizing effects of Euro-American culture is central to understanding how the novel divides her early and later works.

Tar Baby seems an unlikely choice for pre-eminence in the Morrison canon. It is, after all, the least admired, least researched, and least taught of her novels. It has been called her "most problematic and unresolved novel" (Peterson 471) and has received little critical attention generally, and virtually no critical attention in the past five years.[4] Few of us teach it, choosing the shorter, "woman-oriented" *Sula*, or the richer, male quest patterned *Song of Solomon*, or the current favorite, the cathartic *Beloved*. Yet perhaps *Tar Baby* seems problematic and unsatisfying to many of us precisely because it functions as a transitional text in Morrison's oeuvre. Viewed in this light, *Tar Baby*'s ambivalences, refusal of answers, and weaknesses in plot and characterization reveal tensions in Morrison's process as a writer; the novel offers maximum insight into both her periods.

Tar Baby's central concern is colonization.[5] The island hierarchy at the beginning of the novel reinscribes the classic colonial schema, with the white colonizer, Philadelphia exile Valerian Street, presiding over a household empire that includes a beautiful wife, Margaret, a black "assistant," Jadine, black servants, Ondine and Sydney, and occasional employees from the island, Gideon and Therese. The arrival of a black American drifter, Son, disrupts the household hierarchy and challenges Jadine's uncritical acceptance of white European culture and values. *Tar Baby* thus constitutes a working through for Morrison of issues of colonization and culture and provides a key focal point in understanding Morrison's relationship to colonization in both her early and later periods.

Focusing on Morrison's struggle with the colonizing effects of Euro-American culture, on African Americans might seem to eclipse other themes, such as African American folklore [see Harris] or double-consciousness [see Heinz]. Yet a decolonizing frame for Morrison's oeuvre provides a way of connecting concerns that at first seem more central; such a frame can account for both the double-consciousness in *The Bluest Eye* and *Song of Solomon*, as well as the African American folklore and musical emphases of *Beloved* and *Jazz*. Likewise, focusing on Morrison's decolonizing process also integrates an understanding of her emergence as a writer during the Black Arts Movement (approximately 1964–1974) and its concern with decolonizing the black psyche. Her first novel, *The Bluest Eye*, published in 1970, focuses intently on the colonizing effects of white female beauty on a black girl and her community. In her 1993 Afterword to the novel, Morrison explicitly ties the issue of beauty in *The Bluest Eye* to the politics of racial beauty and identity in the 1960s. She writes:

the reclamation of racial beauty in the sixties stirred these thoughts [about beauty], made me think about the necessity for the claim. Why, although reviled by others, could this beauty not be taken for granted within the community?.... The assertion of racial beauty [in the novel] was . . . against the damaging internalization of immutable inferiority originating in an outside gaze. (210)

Rejecting that internalization of the (white) outside gaze was part of the project of the Black Arts Movement. Essays such as Ron Karenga's "Black Cultural Nationalism," Larry Neal's "The Black Arts Movement," and Morrison's own "What the Black Woman Thinks About Women's Lib"—all written during this period—each discuss the black struggle to be free of white ideas, aesthetic or otherwise. A representative poem of the period, Don L. Lee's "The Primitive," illustrates the dominant Black Arts theme of rejecting colonization in the lines,

[whites]
christianized us.
raped our minds with:
T.V. & straight hair
Reader's Digest & bleaching creams,
tarzan & jungle jim,
. . .
european history & promises.
Those alien concepts
of whi-teness (297)

During the Black Arts Movement writers delineated the impact of the cultural colonization of the black community by Euro-American culture and values and actively pursued a black aesthetic. Using a decolonization framework for periodizing Morrison's work thus embraces both her recurring concerns as well as her literary origins during the Black Arts period.

Morrison's first four books, *The Bluest Eye, Sula, Song of Solomon,* and *Tar Baby*, constitute Morrison's struggle with colonization, both for her characters and their communities, as well as in her own writing. We can see this pattern in the dialogical way in which Morrison frames her early novels: *The Bluest Eye* is framed with a deconstructive dialogue with the Dick and Jane children's books; *Sula*, with the Bible; *Song of Solomon*, with the American capitalist success myth. With *Tar Baby*'s explicit identification of colonization as a central issue, Morrison finally breaks free from the need to focus primarily on white ideas, aesthetic or otherwise; following *Tar Baby*, Morrison begins publishing a trilogy, of which we now have seen *Beloved* and *Jazz* published, a trilogy focused on black history and written primarily within an African American cultural perspective. In contrast to the concern with white frames in the early novels, both *Beloved* and *Jazz* take as their frames historically documented events in black lives: *Beloved*, on the case of Margaret Garner; *Jazz*, on a photo taken by James Van Der Zee that appears in *The Harlem Book of the Dead*.

One of the many thematic concerns that can be clarified by a periodization of Morrison's work based on her struggle with colonization is her treatment of beauty throughout her work.[6] In the novels before *Tar Baby*, Morrison repeatedly depicts black female characters engulfed by white ideals of beauty. In *The Bluest Eye*, Pecola's desire for blue eyes reflects a community absorbed by white ideas of what is beautiful. References to idols of white female beauty, Greta Garbo, Ginger Rogers, Jean Harlow, and to the child icon of beauty, Shirley Temple, bespeak an obsession with a standard of white female beauty that, in turn, renders black women and girls invisible. Pecola's insanity at the end of the novel mirrors, Morrison suggests, a cultural insanity that threatens the black community's identity and strength. Likewise, in *Sula*, Nel is raised in accordance with white ideas of beauty. She is told to pull on her nose to make it "nice," and endures the hot comb in her mother's pursuit of smooth hair for her (55). In *Song of Solomon*, the Hagar subplot revisits the maddening effects of internalized white standards of female beauty on black women. When Hagar sees the new object of Milkman's affections, a girl with light skin and smooth, long hair, she begins an obsessive downward spiral, attempting to buy and "put on" those markers of beauty more in accordance with received notions of white-identified beauty. Part of Milkman's quest in the novel is to come to an appreciation and acceptance of a beauty based on black ideals, as reflected in his taking a lock of Hagar's hair with him upon returning to Not Doctor Street.

In *Tar Baby*, Morrison's struggle with the colonization of African American beauty by white notions of beauty comes to a head in her portrait of a colonized black beauty, Jadine. Unlike the previous three female characters, who are hurt by, struggle with, and ultimately succumb to internalized views of beauty, Jadine is thoroughly happy with a definition of beauty based on white standards, because she fits it. In fact, Jadine struggles not against a white-defined standard of female beauty, but against a black-defined beauty, as represented by the woman in yellow who haunts her dreams, because it reminds her of her inauthenticity. The character in *Tar Baby* who is personally hurt by white standards of beauty, Alma Estee, as exemplified in her grotesque russet wig, is a marginal character. Thus, Morrison makes an important shift in her handling of the ideas of beauty and colonization in *Tar Baby*, for by moving away from focusing on the personal devastation caused in black women by internalized ideas of white female beauty to instead concentrating on a black woman who fully identifies with and achieves those internalized standards, Morrison shifts her concern away from the personal toward the cultural. Jadine represents the cultural costs to the African American community of blacks who identify with white culture to the extent that they reject their own. Jadine is not absorbed only by white culture's definition of beauty, she fully identifies with European cultural values about art, nature, family, and money.

Tar Baby also represents a departure from Morrison's earlier depictions of beauty in its plurality of beauty ideals. While in the earlier novels the idea of beauty seems to be dominated by white standards, in *Tar Baby* Morrison represents and elaborates on alternatives. First, several types of female beauty are represented: a white female beauty, Margaret; a white-identified black female beauty, Jadine; and a black-identified black female beauty, the woman in yellow. Second, characters discuss differing aesthetic values throughout the novel, with Jadine favoring Picasso and hating the swamp, with Valerian preferring his hothouse blooms to the tropical vegetation outdoors, and with the emperor butterflies deploring the sealskin coat Jadine adores. There are aesthetic and cultural *choices* available to the characters in this novel, even for the white beauty, Margaret, who by the end of the novel chooses natural beauty over her previous high-class, artificial beauty object persona. Jadine *chooses* to reject the swamp women and Son, and decides to return to her life in Europe, and thus chooses to remain colonized.

By placing this issue of beauty and aesthetic value in the context of colonization, and by making colonization a choice rather than an inescapable fact (once your options are made available), Morrison is then free in *Tar Baby* to reject colonization by white ideas and choose a decolonized stance. When Jadine's plane takes off and she leaves the novel, Morrison in effect says goodbye to colonization in her work and turns the novel's attention to the black cultural mythos of the blind horsemen and the tar baby folktale. Morrison's work after *Tar Baby* continues this decolonized focus on black history and culture. Morrison's primary dialogue with and critique of white culture becomes tertiary with *Tar Baby*.

Paralleling this general shift in emphasis between Morrison's early and later periods, *Beloved* departs from Morrison's first four novels in its complete disinterest in the colonization of black female beauty by white ideals. The main female characters simply don't think about whether they fit prescribed notions of beauty, nor are they held to a beauty standard within or without the community. The two instances where beauty becomes an issue are minor, and unrelated to colonization. First, Paul D, who had initially found the scars on Sethe's back beautiful, reacts negatively after having sex with her and thinks her back is a "revolting clump of scars" (21). Both he and Sethe are having doubts and thinking of how little the other measures up. Second, *Beloved* is described as beautiful, which is part of her magical effect on others. Both of these are quite unlike the trap of white-identified female beauty elaborated on in the early novels. Thus, the lack of the female beauty issue in *Beloved* supports reading Morrison's post-*Tar Baby* work as decolonized.

However, it could be argued that *Beloved* does not reflect a post-*Tar Baby* decolonized stance because it constitutes Morrison's dialogue with and critique of white versions of the history of slavery. *Beloved* certainly offers an alternative version of the slavery experience, written as it is from the perspective of African Americans, both free and enslaved. But *Beloved* is not focused on correcting white versions of slavery, of Margaret Garner, or even on depicting the horrors of slavery, although it does, in effect, do these; instead, the central focus in the novel is on the inner realities and interpersonal relationships of the central black characters, while the white characters remain marginal. Furthermore, *Beloved*'s (and *Jazz*'s) focus on primary philosophical issues such as memory, identity, time, and love, issues that are not circumscribed by any dominant cultural frame, suggests a turning away in her later work from a primary focus on cultural colonization.

In *Jazz*, Morrison picks up the theme of beauty but treats it from a decolonized perspective by signifying on it.[7] In many ways, *Jazz* is about signification. The epigraph, "I am the name of the sound / and the sound of the name. / I am the sign of the letter / and the designation of the division," from The Nag Hammadi, frames the novel's playing on the division between signs and their referents. Joe and Violet's last name is Trace, taken by Joe after being told his parents "disappeared without a trace" (124), surely signifying on Jacques Derrida's concept of the trace left by the absent sign in the process of signification.[8] Signs proliferate throughout the novel: Dorcas's photo on the mantel is a sign of the dead girl, a sign which in its différance (to differ and defer) marks the trace of her presence in Joe's and Violet's minds as well as her absence in death, and which signifies differently depending on the beholder (12); Joe tells of waiting to learn his mother's identity, asking that "All she had to do was give him a sign" and he would know it was the wild woman who was his mother. Morrison has fun in *Jazz* with the proliferation of meanings offered by the process of signification, as in the case of Malvonne, who, upon discovering the sack of mail her nephew had stolen, reads the letters and makes additions that alter the senders' intended significance (40–44). Under signification, meaning, while multiple, cannot finally be determined. Cause and effect, *arche* and *telos*, become separated when signs are at play. While indeterminacy can be disorienting, there is a freedom and lightheartedness associated with signifying. One is free of oppressive meanings; one escapes being determined by a final, transcendental signified.

From this postmodern, decolonized stance, the novels of Morrison's later period revoice and revise those of her earlier period. For example, Morrison signifies in *Jazz* on the meanings of female beauty in her first novel, *The Bluest Eye*, in which the white ideals of beauty were oppressive determinants of Pecola's identity. We can say of *The Bluest Eye* that signs of white beauty throughout the culture were internalized by the black community. We can say that, according to that discourse of signs, Pecola was rendered invisible. We can even say that the sign system of beauty (along with the rape by her father) drove her mad. We cannot make such statements about beauty in *Jazz*. In *Jazz*, Morrison signifies on the signs from *The Bluest Eye*, but her characters and the novel escape being determined by them. They remain at play, never resting with a final signified. And that breaks their power.

The first sign in *Jazz* that Morrison is signifying on *The Bluest Eye* from a decolonized position comes in Morrison's repetition and revised use of the narrator Claudia's opening comment, "Quiet as it's kept, there were no marigolds in the fall of 1941" (5). In *Jazz*, this phrase reappears in the first section in the narrator's disclosure about Violet: "but quiet as it's kept, she did try to steal that baby although there is no way to prove it" (17). Such repetition of a phrase might seem coincidental, were it not for Morrison's newly published Afterword to the 1993 edition of *The Bluest Eye*, in which she discusses at length her use of that opening sentence in *The Bluest Eye* as representative of her writing at that time (211–214). As the Afterword makes clear, Morrison is looking back with a critical eye at her early work, noting its limitations, and, in *Jazz*, playing with its possibilities.

Morrison also signifies in *Jazz* on the color and musical motifs of *The Bluest Eye.* The blue eyes Pecola longs for are not only blue because they represent a white, Aryan ideal, but because her desire for them and the madness that brings is a theme suitable for a blues song. As Ralph Ellison defines it, the blues

> is an impulse to keep the painful details and episodes of a brutal experience alive in one's aching consciousness, to finger its jagged grain, and to transcend it, not by the consolation of philosophy but by squeezing from it a near-tragic, near-comic lyricism. As a form, the blues is an autobiographical chronicle of personal catastrophe expressed lyrically. (78–79)

Pecola has the blues and cannot sing them away. She is "the bluest I." In *Jazz*, however, the blues is transposed into jazz, which, while grounded in the "blues impulse" that acknowledges the painful realities of a complex experience, transforms blues materials into something different. As Craig Werner explains the relationship between the blues and jazz impulses, "the jazz impulse provides a way of exploring implications, of realizing the relational possibilities of the (blues) self, and of expanding the consciousness of self and community through a process of continual improvisation" (xxi-xxii). In *Jazz*, Morrison, like any jazz artist, whose work is, according to Ellison, "an endless improvisation upon traditional materials" (234), takes her earlier, blues materials and improvisationally explores their implications and envisions alternative possibilities. While the tragedy of Joe and Violet's love triangle is the stuff of a classic blues song, it becomes a far more complex, freewheeling jazz piece. Violet, unlike Pecola, is not "the bluest I," although she has the blues; instead, she is violet, a color suggesting a more nuanced understanding of the complex realities before her.[9]

Morrison signifies directly on the issues of beauty and colorism in *Jazz* in her depictions of Joe, Violet, Golden Gray, and Dorcas and adopts a decolonized stance toward their involvement with beauty ideals. Joe and Violet are both purveyors of beauty ideals: he, with his case of "Cleopatra" beauty products for black women; she, as the neighborhood hairdresser who presses, trims, and curls black hair. Both are haunted, in a sense, by a past involving Golden Gray, the white-appearing mulatto offspring of Miss Vera, who Violet's grandmother True Belle helped raise and adored and whose encounter with Joe's probable mother, Wild, has been passed on to Joe by Hunter's Hunter. Beautiful, blond, elegant Golden Gray is a trace in the novel, a trace of the allure of white-identified beauty ideals, as well as a trace of plantation mythology in American literature that plays out in Faulkner's work.[10] Having rejected the colonizing plantation frame in *Tar Baby*, Morrison in *Jazz* takes a decolonized position and jams on the myth.[11] Golden Gray, like Faulkner for Morrison, still has influence and is a predecessor for Violet, but no longer colonizes Violet's mind. Near the end of *Jazz*, Violet tries to explain to Felice what had gone wrong in her life; how she had wished she were "White. Light. Young again" (208). Violet traces this to the stories True Belle had told her about Golden Gray: "He lived inside my mind. But I didn't know it till I got here. The two of us. Had to get rid of it" (208). Felice asks how she did that, and Violet replies, "Killed her. Then I killed the me that killed her." Felice asks, "Who's left?" Violet answers, "Me" (209). Morrison describes here a process of decolonization in which Violet must destroy the internalized white beauty ideal that's in her mind, as well as the destructive part of her that killed it.[12] What's left is a decolonized self.

The depiction of Dorcas also signifies on the traces of white beauty ideals in the black community from a decolonized perspective in which those standards ultimately lack power. Dorcas has the right signs of "beauty": "creamy" skin tone and hair the narrator suspects she "didn't need to straighten" (5). And Dorcas is very involved in beauty as something valuable. Felice relates how Dorcas's reaction to the photo of her dead parents was that "Dorcas couldn't get over how good looking they both were" (200). In fact, according to Felice, "She was always talking about who was good looking and who wasn't" (200). But Dorcas's signs of and involvement with beauty don't, finally, signify that she is beautiful, Morrison points out. As Felice muses, "Dorcas should have been prettier than she was. She just missed. She had all the ingredients of pretty too. Long hair, wavy, half good, half bad. Light skinned. Never used skin bleach. Nice shape. But it missed somehow. If you looked at each thing, you would admire that thing— the hair, the color, the shape. All together it didn't fit" (201). Just as blue eyes won't make Pecola beautiful according to a white-infused beauty ideal, neither will having all the signs of it make Dorcas pretty. Dorcas, as her name implies, is a dorky schoolgirl with pimples.[13] Furthermore, the power of the white-identified beauty attributes Dorcas does have is substantially diminished in *Jazz*, as compared to *The Bluest Eye*, because Dorcas is dead.

The signifying on beauty in *Jazz* breaks the power of beauty over the characters and their community because of their self-reflexiveness and sense of having choices, two markers of a decolonized self exemplary of Morrison's recent work to date. Ultimately, Joe and Violet become aware of their issues and choose not to remain stuck on them. Joe, for example, when Felice asks if he is still stuck on Dorcas, responds, "Stuck? Well, if you mean did I like about what I felt about her. I guess I'm stuck to that" (212). Joe explicitly states it is not Dorcas and her signs of beauty he is stuck on; rather, he now understands it is the issues from his past he projected onto her that he must handle. By the end of the novel Joe chooses Violet, although he had not done so before. Making choices is a motif the novel returns to again and again: Violet chooses Joe (23), although Joe didn't choose Violet (30); Joe chooses Dorcas (135), although when Acton chooses her (216), she dumps Joe. And Golden Gray, when he meets his father, Hunters Hunter, hears him demand, "Be what you want—white or black. Choose. But if you choose black, you got to act black, meaning draw your manhood up" (173). In *Jazz*, Morrison's characters choose their affinities.

Morrison's central concern in her later work with self-reflexive African American characters focused on issues of identity, memory, and love differs radically from her focus in her early work with black characters' struggles with the effects of psychological and cultural colonization. Tracing Morrison's treatment of beauty makes the differences between her early and later work salient; *Tar Baby* marks a key shift in her oeuvre between these two periods. Such a periodization of Morrison's work recommends we begin teaching *Tar Baby* as a central novel in her canon, a novel that functions as the hinge high-lighting the transition between periods. Likewise, further research on *Tar Baby* could profitably trace how other concerns shift between Morrison's early and more recent work.

NOTES

1. While periodization may seem a rather traditional endeavor, in light of how post-structuralism and ideas of intertextuality have broken down the specific locations of texts (author, date of publication, nationality, etc.), it seems to me a worthwhile means of engaging the complexity of major authors who have written a body of diverse texts. By foregrounding a key framework, periodization can account for seemingly radical differences among an author's works. Of course, one possible limitation is that a marginal thread may be over-emphasized, but such claims are usually corrected in the critical debate.

2. Philip Page's excellent book on Morrison, *Dangerous Freedom* (1995), published in the interval between this essay's creation and publication, has already answered an earlier call of mine in which I argue *Tar Baby* is a key transitional text in Morrison's *ouvre*. See Walther, "Toni Morrison's *Tar Baby*: Re-Figuring the Colonizer's Aesthetics" and Page's chapter on *Tar Baby*, in which he agrees it is pivotal.

3. Although Morrison herself has not used a post-colonial theoretical vocabulary in her interviews or essays about her work, much of her non-fictional work concerns issues of colonization for African Americans. Early essays such as "What the Black Woman Thinks About Women's Lib" and "Behind the Making of The Black Book" center on her belief in the importance of black resistance to internalizing white culture and, instead, focusing on African American cultural values. Such a concern also appears in her later non-fiction, such as the essay "City Limits, Village Values," thereby indicating the issue of colonization as an on-going thread throughout her work. A

recent application of postcolonial theory to Morrison's fiction is found in Homi K. Bhabha's *The Location of Culture.*

4. In Debbie Mix's bibliography of Morrison criticism, *Tar Baby* has a mere sixteen articles, only three of which have been published in the past five years.

5. See Walther, "Toni Morrison's *Tar Baby*: Re-Figuring the Colonizer's Aesthetics," for a fuller discussion of the novel's treatment of colonization.

6. For a fuller explanation of Morrison's treatment of beauty in *The Bluest Eye, Song of Solomon,* and *Tar Baby* see Walther, "Out of Sight: Toni Morrison's Revision of Beauty" and "Toni Morrison's Tar Baby: Re-Figuring the Colonizer's Aesthetics."

7. For a full definition of the term signifyin(g) see Gates. Eckard's essay offers a basic discussion of signifying in *Jazz.*

8. While this essay was under consideration at *MELUS*, Philip Page's fine article on *Jazz*'s affinities with Derridean concepts appeared in *African American Review.* See it for a detailed discussion of différance, the trace, and the breach in *Jazz.* A slightly different version appears in his book.

9. Such a signifying on the color blue—and the blues—also occurs in Duke Ellington's "Mood Indigo." Thanks to Craig Werner for pointing out this echo to me.

10. In *Playing the Changes,* Werner asserts that the Golden Gray section of *Jazz* functions as a "Faulknerian fable" (301).

11. Mbalia suggests that the Golden Gray section of the novel is the "jam session" of the novel (640).

12. Violet's killing-off of an ideologically-infected self echoes Virginia Woolf's essay "Professions for Women," where she describes killing the Victorian ideal of womanhood—the "angel in the house"—that was in her head and kept her from writing. Note, too, the shift in pronouns in Violet's statement, in which she first refers to "him" (Golden Gray) and then refers to killing "her," more closely echoing Woolf's figuration. This conflation of Faulkner and Woolf in Violet's psychological killing of the colonized self is especially interesting in light of Morrison's master's thesis on the two authors.

13. Thanks to Lucinda Ramsey for pointing out this slang parallel in Dorcas's name to me.

WORKS CITED

Bhabha, Homi K. *The Location of Culture*. London: Routledge, 1994.

Eckard, Paula Gallant. "The Interplay of Music, Language, and Narrative in Toni Morrison's *Jazz*." *CLA Journal* 38.1 (1994): 11–19.

Ellison, Ralph. "Richard Wright's Blues." *Shadow and Act*. N.Y.: Random House, 1964. 77–94.

Gates, Henry Louis, Jr. *The Signifying Monkey: A Theory of African American Literary Criticism*. New York: Oxford UP, 1988.

Harris, Trudier. *Fiction and Folklore: The Novels of Toni Morrison*. Knoxville: U of Tennessee P, 1991.

Heinze, Denise. *The Dilemma of "Double-Consciousness": Toni Morrison's Novels*. Athens: U of Georgia P, 1993.

Karenga, Ron. "Black Cultural Nationalism." *The Black Aesthetic*. Ed. Addison Gayle, Jr. Garden City, N.Y. Anchor Books, 1971. 31–37.

Lee, Don L. "The Primitive." *The Back Poets*. Ed. Dudley Randall. New York: Bantam Books, 1971. 297.

Mbalia, Doreatha Drummond. "Women Who Run With Wild." *Modern Fiction Studies: Toni Morrison Double Issue* 39.3&4 (1994): 623–646.

Mix, Debbie. "Toni Morrison: A Selected Bibliography." *Modern Fiction Studies: Toni Morrison Double Issue*. 39.3&4 (1994): 795–817.

Morrison, Toni. Afterword. *The Bluest Eye*. New York: Plume, 1993. 209–216.

———. "Behind the Making of The Black Book." *Black World*. Feb. 1974: 86–90.

———. *Beloved*. New York: Plume, 1987.

———. *The Bluest Eye*. 1970. New York: Plume, 1993.

———. "City Limits, Village Values: Concepts of the Neighborhood in Black Fiction." *Literature and the Urban Experience*. Ed. Michael C. Jaye and Ann Chalmers Watts. New Brunswick, N.J.: Rutgers UP, 1981. 35–43.

———. *Jazz*. New York: Plume, 1992.

———. *Song of Solomon*. New York: Plume, 1981.

———. *Sula*. New York: Plume, 1973.

———. *Tar Baby*. New York: Plume, 1981.

———. "What the Black Woman Thinks About Women's Lib." *New York Times Magazine* 22 Aug. 1971: 14–15, 63–66.

Neal, Larry. "The Black Arts Movement." *The Black Aesthetic*. Ed. Addison Gayle, Jr. Garden City, New York: Anchor Books, 1971. 257–274.

Page, Phillip. "Traces of Derrida in Toni Morrison's *Jazz*." *African American Review* 29.1 (1995): 55–66.

Peterson, Nancy J. "Introduction: Canonizing Toni Morrison." *Modern Fiction Studies: Double Issue on Toni Morrison* 39.3&4 (1994): 461–479.

Walther, Mahn LaVon. "Out of Sight: Toni Morrison's Revision of Beauty." *Black American Literature Forum* 24 (1990): 775–789.

———. "Toni Morrison's Tar Baby: Re-Figuring the Colonizer's Aesthetics." *Cross-Cultural Performances: Differences in Women's Revisions of Shakespeare.* Ed. Marianne Novy. Urbana: U of Illinois P, 1993. 137–149.

Werner, Craig Hansen. *Playing the Changes: From Afro-Modernism to the Jazz Impulse.* Urbana: U of Illinois P, 1994.

Woolf, Virginia. "Professions for Women." Orig. published in *The Death of the Moth and Other Essays*, 1942. Rptd. in *Virginia Woolf: Woman and Writing.* Ed. Michele Barrett. New York: Harcourt Brace & World, 1979. 57–63.

"My Kinsman, Major Molineux"
(Nathaniel Hawthorne)

"'That Evening of Ambiguity and Weariness': Readerly Exploration in Hawthorne's 'My Kinsman, Major Molineux'"
by Robert C. Evans,
Auburn University at Montgomery

Exploration and colonization are two of the most prominent themes of Nathaniel Hawthorne's famous short story "My Kinsman, Major Molineux," and both themes have been the subject of frequent discussion by commentators. In her invaluable *Reader's Guide to the Short Stories of Nathaniel Hawthorne*, which summarizes commentary produced up until the mid-1970s, Lea Bertani Vozar Newman reports the responses of many analysts who have commented on the colonial background of the work. Newman notes the many parallels between Robin's journey of exploration in "Major Molineux" and the journeys of numerous other literary figures, including "Odysseus, Heracles, Aeneas, and Dante" (221), to mention just a few. Commentary produced in the decades following the publication of Newman's book has continued to emphasize these themes (see, for instance, the annual reviews in *American Literary Scholarship*), with special interest in the colonial aspects of the story, but with little agreement on whether the story offers a positive or negative depiction of the revolutionists who tar and feather the title figure in the story's final pages.

Hawthorne himself calls prominent attention to the two themes, emphasizing the colonial and political background of the story,

especially in the opening paragraph (68) and in the final pages of
the tale (84–87). Much of the rest of the text is given over to two
converging journeys: the exploratory journey of Robin as he searches
for his mysterious kinsman, and the humiliating journey of the
Major. In Hawthorne's story, the journey motif is given far more
explicit emphasis than the colonial or political dimensions; one has
only to contrast Hawthorne's telling of the events with the later
dramatic adaptation by the twentieth-century poet Robert Lowell to
see the differences. Lowell is much more obviously concerned with
the political aspects of the story; his play is far less mysterious and
provocative than Hawthorne's narrative. Hawthorne leaves much to
the reader's imagination, in some ways allowing readers to acutely
feel Robin's confusion as their own. Lowell, in contrast, spells out the
political dimensions of the tale almost immediately and stresses them
throughout his play.

In Lowell's play, Robin already knows much more about his
cousin's British allegiances and status as a colonial administrator than
he does in Hawthorne's tale. Robin explicitly states about Molineux,
a mere two pages into the play's dialogue, "He cares for England.
Rule Britannia, / that's the tune he taught me" (67), to which another
character replies, "He wished / to teach us *Rule Britannia,* but / we
couldn't get it through our heads" (68). Lowell immediately empha-
sizes the political tensions that dominate his play, particularly the
conflict between the rebellious colonists and Molineux, who is clearly
and quickly depicted as the unwelcome representative of the British
monarchy. British soldiers appear blatantly and repeatedly in Lowell's
play (68); Whigs and Tories are openly mentioned (72); Molineux's
official position is constantly stressed (83); and British and Colonial
flags are continually paraded onstage. Lowell's Robin openly aligns
himself with the British side, at least for most of the play (96), and
Hawthorne's mysterious anonymous man, whose face seems both red
and black (78), is in Lowell's version given an actual name (Colonel
Greenough) and made an admired leader of the Colonial rebellion
(103). Lowell is explicitly and consistently interested in the tensions
between the colonists and the British, while for Hawthorne, the main
interest of the story is Robin's exploratory journey. Even when the
political tensions between the British and the Americans do take
center stage in Hawthorne's story—particularly at the very end of
the tale—Robin's response is highlighted more than the tensions. For

Hawthorne, the interest is in the personal and private dimensions of the story; for Lowell, politics are obviously front and center.

Hawthorne's story, then, is much more plainly about exploration than is Lowell's play, and Hawthorne has constructed the tale in such a way that the exploration is as much a metaphorical process undertaken by the reader as it is a literal journey undertaken by Robin. Hawthorne forces his readers to confront and feel many of the same uncertainties, fears, puzzlements, and apprehensions as Robin endures, so that the stress in Hawthorne's tale is not only on the physical movement of Robin through the streets of a strange city, but also on the mental journey of the reader. Hawthorne's story helps remind us that a work of literature is less an object (like a painting that can be seen whole and all at once) than a process (like a work of music, which unfolds in time and whose next moment can never be absolutely predicted). Lowell, in his play, creates a companion for Robin in the form of a much-younger brother (called merely "Boy"), but in Hawthorne's story the only real companion Robin has is the reader, to whom the unfolding events often seem as mysterious and unnerving as they do to Robin himself. Much of the tension and suspense built up and sustained in Hawthorne's story is experienced not only by Robin but by the reader, and Hawthorne's tale is an effective work of art largely to the extent that it manages to put the reader, metaphorically, in Robin's shoes.

Hawthorne's story takes place, appropriately enough, during a "moonlight evening" (68), a time of day that already suggests ambiguity, mystery, and the inability to perceive with absolute clarity. Robin is literally in unfamiliar territory, and the fact that he is "a youth of barely eighteen years" (68) puts him, significantly, at an in-between age: old enough so that he is no longer a mere boy, but still too young to have had much experience in the ways of the world. His journey (as practically every commentator notes) will amount to a kind of initiation into adulthood, but, unlike formalized rites or rituals of initiation, his experiences will have no prescribed or set pattern, nor will Robin himself even be consciously aware that he is undergoing an initiatory process. His journey of exploration will seem to him (and be felt by the reader) as haphazard, disordered, disorienting, and even dangerous, nor will there be any clear and unambiguous sense, at the end of the process, that Robin has learned a definite or valuable lesson, or profited in any definite and certain way. The story, in short, is ambiguous from start to finish; Hawthorne seems less interested in teaching any simple lesson than in stirring up uncertainties in the mind of Robin and in the minds of the tale's readers, as well.

The fact that Robin is on his very "first visit to town" (69) makes his journey all the more significant, but also all the more disorienting, both for him and for us. He has no previous experiences of urban life on which to draw as he tries to make sense of the events he is about to undergo. He cannot interpret his experiences by comparing them to familiar experiences of the past, and so he spends most of the story puzzled and perplexed, as do Hawthorne's readers. Once arriving in town, for instance, it occurs to Robin "that he knew not whither to direct his steps" (69), and so, in that respect, his movement through the streets of the city is literally a journey of exploration. Although he has a definite destination in mind (the Major's home), he has no idea how to get there. His movement through the town consists of a series of misadventures, false starts, and uncomfortable encounters with mostly forbidding strangers who usually react to him with a mysterious hostility that they never bother to explain. Robin cannot comprehend what his experiences mean, and, for the most part, neither can readers. The narrator rarely intervenes in any obvious way to explain the significance of what is happening to Robin; forcing us to suffer through the same kinds of confusion, and to engage in the same kind of guesswork, as Robin himself. Readers are rarely given a superior perspective on the events or characters depicted, for although Robin sometimes seems the target of the narrator's irony (especially during his encounter with the lady of the evening and in the frequent references to his supposed shrewdness), it is hard to feel that we, as readers, know much more than he does or have any better sense than he has of what is going on or of what his experiences finally amount to. We do not simply sit back and observe Robin; instead, we experience his perplexities as our own.

Consider, for example, Robin's initial encounter with a citizen of the town—the "man in years, with a full periwig of grey hair" (69). This person is at first described simply as a distant "figure," an "it" (69), and even after Robin gets a closer and fuller view of the figure's appearance, the man remains a mystery, particularly because of his oddly "excessive anger and annoyance" and his strange and unexplained threat to have Robin put into the "stocks" (70). This threat provokes an equally mysterious "roar of laughter" from other strangers in a nearby barber shop, and although Robin, "being a shrewd youth, soon thought himself able to account for the mystery" by attributing it to the old man's lack of breeding, this encounter is simply the first of many in which neither Robin nor the reader can feel sure of having any clear sense of precisely what is happening, or why. Robin moves through "a succession of crooked and narrow streets, which crossed each other, and meandered" (69)—phrasing that might almost be taken as a metaphorical description of the way Hawthorne's own plot develops. The overall structure of the story consists of one puzzling and inexplicable encounter after another. That structure, however, is never predictable, and each encounter is mysterious (both to Robin and the reader) in its own peculiar way. The effect, both for the main character and for Hawthorne's readers, is one of suspense, frustration, and even a certain annoyance, as the narrator denies both the protagonist and the audience any clear sense that Robin's journey is leading anywhere or amounting to anything. The story's narrative method is one of continual postponement and deferment, a constant putting-off (both of Robin and of the reader's hopes for understanding) that deliberately runs the risk of being off-putting and exasperating. This is a journey with no clear sense of progress and no definite end in sight. Its structure is rambling and repetitive, as both Robin and the reader wander in circles and encounter many of the same characters over and over again. The story conveys a sense of entrapment, offering no clear sense of progress and no obvious exit.

The most memorable characters Robin encounters during the course of his journey are also the most mysterious. This is particularly true of the unnamed stranger with the odd-looking face, whom Robin first glimpses while the stranger is engaged in "whispered conversation with a group of ill-dressed associates" (72). The fact that the man and his associates are whispering suggests that they have something to hide; by calling attention to their "whispered conversation," Hawthorne alerts us to their talk while also—quite typically—denying us (and Robin) any clear understanding of its significance. The stranger himself, meanwhile, is described in ways that make an indelible impact while conveying no clear or unambiguous significance: "His features were separately striking almost to grotesqueness, and the whole face left a deep impression on the memory. The forehead bulged out into a double prominence, with a vale between; the nose came boldly forth in an irregular curve, and its bridge was of more than a finger's breadth; the eyebrows were deep and shaggy, and the eyes glowed beneath them like fire in a cave" (72). Who is this man? What does he represent? What are he and his "associates" discussing? Why is his appearance so strange? As usual, Hawthorne raises numerous questions without offering any clear answers. His method in this tale is to provoke uncertainty, both in his protagonist and in his audience. It is not until the end of the story that the identity and significance of this mysterious stranger become clear, and even then the ambiguities are far from being erased or eliminated.

In the meantime, Hawthorne piles uncertainty upon uncertainty, creating an overwhelming sense of frustration and perplexity both in Robin and in the reader. At one point the narrator mentions Robin's "fatigue" and notes that his "patience now was wearing low" (74). The effect of the story on the reader might be described in similar terms. By continually postponing the outcome of Robin's quest, Hawthorne makes us long for that outcome all the more strongly. Robin's journey is literally exploratory, since the word "explore" derives from Latin roots that imply a calling or crying out, as if engaging in a hunt or pursuit. Robin repeatedly calls out to people for answers to what seems an utterly simple question, but repeatedly he—and we—are refused any simple or definitive answer. It would be easy (and charitable) enough for any of Robin's interlocutors to plainly tell him the political identity and present location of Major Molineux, but by delaying this information, Hawthorne builds an ever-increasing sense of epistemological insecurity both in Robin and in the reader. We can never feel entirely sure what, if anything, either we or Robin know for certain, and nothing quite makes sense.

Typical of the story's style is the paragraph that begins, "He now *roamed desperately*" (i.e., without hope) "and *at random*, through the town, *almost* ready to believe that a *spell* was on him, like that by which a *wizard* of his country had once kept three pursuers *wandering*, a whole winter night, within twenty paces of the cottage they sought" (77; emphasis added). The italicized words exemplify some of the means by which Hawthorne builds and sustains an overwhelming sense of uncertainty and strangeness, both here and throughout the tale as a whole. The atmosphere, here and elsewhere, is almost Gothic, and that effect is heightened when Hawthorne adds such additional details as the following:

The streets lay before him, *strange* and *desolate*, and the *lights were extinguished* in almost every house. Twice, however, little parties of men, among whom Robin distinguished men *in outlandish attire*, came hurrying along; but, though on both occasions they paused to address him, such intercourse *did not at all enlighten his perplexity*. They did but utter *a few words* in *some language* of which Robin *knew nothing*, and perceiving *his inability to answer*, bestowed a *curse* upon him in plain English, and hastened away. (77; emphasis added)

Ironically, the only thing "plain" in this passage is a mysterious and unexplained curse, and even when explanations seem promised in this story (as when the grotesque double-faced stranger tells Robin, "'Watch here an hour, and Major Molineux will pass by'" [78]), they almost inevitably lead (as the one just cited does) to further mystery and further delay.

By the time Robin reaches the end of the story, the reader has been inundated with a flood of ambiguous phrasing, including terms such as "partly remembered" (77), "[s]trange things," "philosophical speculations," "beautiful strangeness" (78), "ghostly indistinctness," "a murmur," "scarcely audible," " a low, dull, dreamy sound," "a distant shout, apparently loud," and an "evening of ambiguity and weariness" (79), to mention just a few. Questions are repeatedly asked but left unanswered (e.g., 79), and the effect of all the terms just quoted is to name things without precisely describing them. Robin's mind is said to have "kept vibrating between fancy and reality" (80), and, in phrasing such as that, Hawthorne not only describes Robin's experience but also calls attention to the dominant method of his own story. Robin is in search of the location of his relative, and the reader is in search of the meaning of the narrative. Both the protagonist and his audience, however, remain perplexed and confused during most of the tale.

Even (or perhaps especially) when the narrative ends with the eventual appearance of the Major as he is pulled, "in tar-and-feathery dignity," in a cart in the midst of a howling, hooting mob (85), ambiguities abound. How much sympathy (if any) should we feel for the Major? What, precisely, has he done (if anything) to deserve this kind of treatment? What specific political issues are at stake in this scene of insurrection? What should we make of Robin's own "shout of laughter" (86) as he witnesses the painful humiliation of his kinsman? All these issues have been endlessly debated, with commentators staking out multiple and often strongly opposed positions and offering masses of often contradictory data in support of their claims. Hawthorne, of course, could have prevented much of this debate by making the "point" of the story clearer, especially its political implications. Is the story pro-revolutionary, skeptical about the revolutionists, or does it stake out some sort of middle position? Does Robin profit from his experiences in the city, or are they merely disillusioning? Does he eventually return to his country home, or does he stay in the city and "'rise in the world without the help of [his] kinsman, Major Molineux'" (87)? And what, precisely, should we make of these famous final words to the story?

Throughout the tale, Hawthorne's main purpose seems to be to raise questions rather than to answer them. The point of the story has been—and will probably continue to be—endlessly debated in part because Hawthorne deliberately refused to make its point (or points) clear. He seems to have been less interested in communicating a political or moral message than in creating an aesthetic or psychological effect, and that effect is continually provoking, intriguing, frustrating, and puzzling to both his protagonist and his reader. By the end of the story, we know little more about Robin or the Major than we did at the beginning, but by that point we have been made—through Hawthorne's skillful artistry—not simply the witnesses to Robin's journey of exploration but also its co-participants.

WORKS CITED OR CONSULTED

American Literary Scholarship. Durham, NC: Duke University Press, 1965.

Hawthorne, Nathaniel. *Tales and Sketches.* New York: Literary Classics of the United States, 1982.

Lowell, Robert. "My Kinsman, Major Molineux." *The Old Glory.* New York: Farrar, Straus & Giroux, 1965. 63–114.

Newman, Lea Bertani Vozar. *A Reader's Guide to the Short Stories of Nathaniel Hawthorne.* Boston: G.K. Hall, 1979.

ONE HUNDRED YEARS OF SOLITUDE
(GABRIEL GARCÍA MÁRQUEZ)

"History, Erasure, and Magic Realism:
Exploration, Colonization, and
One Hundred Years of Solitude"
by Jeffrey Gray, Seton Hall University

One Hundred Years of Solitude (*Cien Años de Soledad*), published in 1967, remains the most important novel in Latin American history. It has been translated into more than thirty languages and has won four international prizes; it is also the work most responsible for winning Gabriel García Márquez the Nobel Prize in Literature in 1982. The exuberant style and technique that made it the exemplar of "magic realism"—a genre still predominant today in the contemporary novels of Toni Morrison, Salman Rushdie, and Isabel Allende—was as impressive as its epic historical narrative, which traces the decline of the Buendía family through several generations, from the founding of the town of Macondo to the whirlwind that finally erases the town and its remaining two inhabitants from the face of the earth. Though Márquez's novel gained international recognition for its innovations and historical sweep, the story especially resonates with Latin American readers. Indeed, *One Hundred Years* at times seems a parable of and for Latin America. The novel represented a stylistic and conceptual revolution, but also an engagement—if not always direct—with the history of Latin America, notably its history of neocolonialism at the hands of the United States. The quality and degree of that engagement has been a problem, however, for activist critics who have found fault with the novel (as also with Márquez's later works) for its purported lack of political commitment. There is a complex tension between the imaginative element of the novel and its apparent representations of material history.

The title of *One Hundred Years of Solitude* suggests a history and a chronology. One hundred years is a coherent, round number, the domain of an apocalyptic narrative that begins in a prehistoric utopia and ends when the text is finally deciphered. The moment of deciphering, the moment of understanding, marks the closure of the story as well as the end of the universe of Macondo and everyone in it. Between these two points, the reader follows a succession of fascinating characters and events. Yet, since there are no dates, and since the novel is not set in a specific period or real geographical place, the ahistorical "magic realist" aspect can be said to undercut its representation of material history, so that, for example, the banana strike and subsequent massacre (which did really occur, in Santa Marta, in 1928, though neither place nor date are mentioned in *One Hundred Years*) is presented in the same way as purely magical events, such as the ascension into heaven of Remedios the Beauty, trailing the family bedsheets. Fictive events and historical fact are both presented as fantasy or hallucination.

Much of the discussion about *One Hundred Years* revolves around this tug-of-war between magic realism and the representation of actual history. Márquez once remarked that his "most important problem was destroying the line of demarcation that separates what seems real from what seems fantastic" ("Interview" 52). Critics who claim that the novel is not politically engaged enough often assume, first, that material history is something accessible prior to representation, and that magic realism is merely a literary technique. But what if magic realism is, rather, a way of perceiving, or a particular mode of being in the world? Alejo Carpentier, in the introduction to his novel *The Kingdom of This World*, has argued that historical events themselves in Latin America partake of magic realism, or what he alternatively called *lo real maravilloso*. The problem, then, is not that magic realism undermines the sense of history, but that history is so bizarre in its bare facts as to seem fantastic.

When, for example, the banana company in *One Hundred Years* pronounces that "The workers did not exist" (324), this is not fantasy but historical fact. The Colombian court actually ruled, in 1928, having heard the arguments of the United Fruit Company's lawyers, that because labor on plantations was temporary and seasonal, the company *had* no workers, and therefore nothing could have happened to them. True machinations of companies and governments may thus exhibit fantastic dimensions.

Neocolonialism—a term used to describe corporate exploitation of nations in the postcolonial world—is critiqued in literary works such as Miguel Ángel Asturias's *Banana Trilogy*, Álvaro Cepeda Samudio's *La Casa Grande*, and Pablo Neruda's *Canto General*. It shares one key feature with the classic colonialism of the Spanish in the New World or the Japanese in Southeast Asia: it constructs the memory and history of the colonized, eclipsing or erasing indigenous ways of knowing history. The picture of neocolonial history in *One Hundred Years* is complicated (some might say, defeated) chiefly by two factors: first, the fact that the novel's paradigm is Borgesian and postmodern; and, second, that the novel presents time as simultaneous, the future implicated in past and vice-versa, and ultimately that all events are literally already *written*, as we discover at the end of the novel.

Let us consider first the extent to which *One Hundred Years* does or does not evoke actual Latin American history. Oscar Collazos writes, "The historical period of the wars is perfectly credible, and the history of Colombia, in its large anecdotal outlines, confirms that García Márquez did nothing less than draw from it the facts of his fiction. Introduced into the immense world of fiction, these facts acquire a clear and tragic significance" (139–140; my translation). The events most referred to in the novel are the fights between Colombian political parties, the civil wars of the nineteenth century, "la violencia" of the twentieth century, and the incursions of the United Fruit Company (called the "banana company" in the novel), leading to the banana strike of 1928 and its bloody suppression. The early colonial period of Colombia is scarcely mentioned (but for the reference to Sir Francis Drake's attack on Riohacha in 1568 at the beginning and the end of the novel), while the neocolonial period constitutes the most important part of the novel. Márquez himself has commented that the passages on the banana company are intentional references to the strike against the United Fruit Company, which paralyzed the banana zone on Colombia's Atlantic coast (*La Novela* 23–24). When the strike broke out, General Carlos Cortés Vargas authorized the army to intervene. The strikers were machine-gunned in the Ciénaga railroad station; the deaths were estimated in the hundreds. (This becomes thousands in *One Hundred Years*.)

But the novel covers not only the major crises, but the whole process and method of the banana company: the first arrival of the North Americans, the tests conducted, the compound built, the company's techniques of subjugation, its power, and its brutality. At first, the villagers don't know what to make of the gringos' observing and measuring. Why are they moving the river? Rather late, they discover that the gold of these conquistadors is bananas. In one episode, because of a careless remark by Colonel Aureliano Buendía, the banana company hunts down and kills all seventeen of his sons. The colonel's subsequent attempts to foment resistance to the invaders are unsuccessful.

After the massacre in Macondo, one person lives to tell the story. José Arcadio Segundo, having escaped by concealing himself among a trainload of corpses, holes up in the laboratory of Melquíades and doesn't come out for six months. He alone knows the truth, but no one believes him. Instead,

> The official version, repeated a thousand times and mangled out all over the country by every means of communication the government found at hand, was finally accepted: there were no dead, the satisfied workers had gone back to their families, and the banana company was suspending all activity until the rains stopped. (333)

But the rains do not stop: *"It rained for four years, eleven months, and two days"* (339). The North Americans, of unlimited power and wile, had unleashed the weather itself. When families ask the whereabouts of their missing sons and fathers, they are told, "'You must have been dreaming.... Nothing has happened in Macondo, nothing has ever happened, and nothing ever will happen. This is a happy town.' In that way they were finally able to wipe out the union leaders" (333).

José Arcadio Segundo's knowledge of what really happened is passed down, so that, eventually, Aureliano, son of Renata Remedios, great-great-grandson of Pilar Ternera, is the last repository of the truth. But

> [e]very time that Aureliano mentioned the matter, not only the proprietress but some people older than she would repudiate

the myth of the workers hemmed in at the station and the
train with two hundred cars loaded with dead people, and they
would even insist that, after all, everything had been set forth in
judicial documents and in primary-school textbooks: that the
banana company had never existed. (419)

Aureliano finds himself "off course in the tide of a world that had
ended and of which only the nostalgia remained" (419). Trying to
establish his lineage, he consults a priest about the name José Arcadio
Segundo. The priest replies,

> "Many years ago there used to be a street here with that
> name and in those days people had the custom of naming their
> children after streets."
> Aureliano trembled with rage.
> "So!" he said. "You don't believe it either."
> "Believe what?"
> "That Colonel Aureliano Buendía fought thirty-two civil
> wars and lost them all," Aureliano answered. "That the army
> hemmed in and machine-gunned three thousand workers and
> that their bodies were carried off to be thrown into the sea on
> a train with two hundred cars."
> The priest measured him with a pitying look.
> "Oh, my son," he sighed. "It's enough for me to be sure that
> you and I exist at this moment." (440)

The colonial and economic hegemony of the banana company is
so absolute that it seems to come from the same imaginative sources
as the ascension into heaven of Remedios the Beauty, the potions
of Melquíades, the proliferation of Aureliano Segundo's livestock,
or the rain that lasts for five years. Such a conflation of reality and
imagination is a problem for readers who read novels not as aesthetic
fantasies, but as depictions of the material struggles of actual people
in actual places. But in fact Márquez is showing the shape that power
takes among the powerless—that is, constructed power presented
as unconstructed, culture presented as "nature." Such a depiction of
power invokes the Borgesian realm familiar from stories such as "The
Lottery in Babylon." Toward the end of that story, Borges' narrator
describes the indistinguishability of the company and the universe:

> The company, with divine modesty, avoids all publicity. Its agents, as is natural, are secret.... That silent functioning, comparable to God's, gives rise to all kinds of conjectures. One abominably suggests that the Company has not existed for centuries and that the sacred disorder of our lives is purely hereditary, traditional. Another judges it eternal and teaches that it will last until the last night, when the last god annihilates the world. Another declares that the Company is omnipotent, but that it only has influence in tiny things: in a bird's call, in the shadings of rust and of dust, in the half dreams of dawn. Another, in the words of masked heresiarchs, *that it has never existed and will not exist.* Another, no less vile, reasons that it is indifferent to affirm or deny the reality of the shadowy corporation, because Babylon is nothing else than an infinite game of chance. (35)

This perception, at the heart of many postmodern novels and films that claim our understanding of reality is determined by powerful, all-pervading conspiracies (*The Matrix, The Truman Show, Sixth Sense, White Noise,* among others), gives readers and audiences a sense of the fantastic and bizarre realities experienced by the colonized.

The presence of neocolonialism's history in *One Hundred Years* is made problematic, secondly, by the fact that—in spite of the Buendia family's genealogical narrative—past, present, and future are simultaneous in the novel, which presents a history that is, as the first sentence suggests, both remembered and foreseen: "Many years later, facing the firing squad, Colonel Aureliano Buendía was to remember that distant afternoon when his father took him to see ice." The presumed presence of the firing squad, while foreshadowing the apocalyptic closing of the novel, soon gives place to the narrative of events that precede that moment, i.e., the foundation of Macondo and even earlier. The remote past and the remote future invade the present.

Márquez's breakdown of linear time—the substitution of a vision of simultaneity and timelessness for conventional, linear storytelling—undermines *One Hundred Years* as a reliable account of Colombian history or an indictment of the forces that subjugated parts of Latin America during the twentieth century. If the story is already written, then the illusion of linearity cannot be sustained. In this view, though we see only a slice of history at any given time, the whole history is already there—which is the view we are left with at the end of *One*

Hundred Years, when we learn that the gypsy Melquíades has written out the whole story of the family in detail, one hundred years prior to the events themselves. In this light, all events in the novel are simultaneous, given, and foreordained.

This idea confounds historical representation, just as the repetition of names confounds linear genealogy, as Úrsula in *One Hundred Years* realizes. As the names and patterns repeat, they confuse "present time with remote periods" (353). When José Arcadio Segundo gives up his position in the banana company to organize a strike, Úrsula says, "'Just like Aureliano, as if the world were repeating itself'" (360). Úrsula finally refuses to continue naming children by the two recurring names of José Aureliano and José Arcadio. She "shuddered with the evidence that time was not passing" but just turning in a circle. (361) Repetition, she knows, destroys linear time. The twins—José Arcadio Segundo and Aureliano Segundo—whose identities slip back and forth between bodies, confusing those around them as well as themselves, embody this danger. The incorrigible repetitions of the family are known best to Pilar Ternera, for whom there are no surprises in the Buendía men: "the history of the family was a machine with unavoidable repetitions, a turning wheel that would have gone on spinning into eternity were it not for the progressive and irremediable wearing of the axle" (334).

Rhetorical repetition in *One Hundred Years* reinforces this temporal repetition, breaking down linear time, just as meter, rhyme, and refrain do in poetry and song. Some of the repetitions in *One Hundred Years* are structural, spaced at intervals throughout the book. The first sentence of the book, for example, which begins "Many years later, facing the firing squad, Colonel Aureliano Buendía would remember ..." is repeated with variations twenty times throughout the book; six of those times are explicit variations on the sense of the first sentence, while the other fourteen relate to other characters in similar situations, as for example, "Years later on his deathbed, Aureliano Segundo would remember ..." (197). The echoes indicate new cycles that are not progressive but, by repetition, static. Beginning with "Arcadio Buendía," evoking sunrise in Eden, the repetition of names is a way of preventing progress, of freezing time, in contrast to the modern and "progressive" depredations of the banana company.

Ironically, the company, its operations complete, creates nonlinear time with its five-year-long rainfall. During the rains, "unbroken time passes, relentless time, because it was useless to divide it into months and years, and the days into hours, when one could do nothing but contemplate the rain" (346–7). When finally the rain ceases, the people and affairs of the town would seem to normalize, but it is not so. Their energy, along with their memory, has been permanently sapped. "The indolence of the people was in contrast to the voracity of oblivion, which little by little was undermining memories in a pitiless way" (371). When the gypsies return, they are shocked to find the people utterly defeated.

Such ideas of nonlinear, simultaneous, or cyclical time provide part of the basis for the accusations leveled against Márquez that his work is unengaged and quietistic: if all is fated, if nothing can be done, then what is the point of even calling attention to evil, much less contesting it? Shouldn't one be true, as Aureliano Segundo says, to the memory of the victims of injustice at the hands of the banana companies? In response to the charge of quietism, one should note that the narrator of *One Hundred Years* (Melquíades, as it turns out) is not resigned to what has happened (and certainly the male Buendía characters strenuously resist evil—when they're not embodying it). The tone of the book—inextricable from its joy and ebullience—is sadness. *One Hundred Years* is an elegy for several vanished generations, for a region weakened by its own politics but destroyed finally by neocolonialism. One of the implicit lessons of *One Hundred Years* is that literacy and dissemination of knowledge will save history from those who would erase it. The problem is that those who would erase history use the same techniques as those who would preserve it, but they have more power at their disposal—more money and more printing presses, but also more government officials and more armed forces.

Márquez begins his Nobel Prize acceptance speech, "The Solitude of Latin America," by citing the early sixteenth-century writer Antonio Pigafetta, whose narrative of Magellan's voyage around the world he describes as "a strictly accurate account that nonetheless resembles a venture into fantasy" (Robles 196). Márquez follows this with an account of the long series of massacres, invasions, dictatorships, and disappearances suffered by Latin America, remarking that "We [Latin Americans] have had to ask but little of the imagination, for our crucial problem has been the lack of conventional means to render our lives believable. . . ." Reality in Latin America has long outpaced the imagination, according to Márquez, and any tall tales among the

Chronicles of the Indies (hogs with navels on their haunches, men with heads below their shoulders, and so on) can scarcely match the improbable events that actually occurred.

WORKS CITED

Bell-Villada, Gene H. "Banana Strike and Military Massacre: *One Hundred Years of Solitude* and What Happened in 1928." *Gabriel García Márquez: A Casebook*. Oxford: OUP, 2002. 127–128.

———. "Conversation with Gabriel García Márquez." [as above] 17–24.

Borges, Jorge Luis. "The Lottery in Babylon." Trans. John M. Fein. *Labyrinths*. Ed. Donald A. Yates and James E. Irby. New York: New Directions, 1962. 30–35.

Collazos, Oscar. *García Márquez: La soledad y la Gloria (su vida y su obra)*. Barcelona: Plaza & Janés, 1983.

Jane, Regina. "Liberals, Conservatives, and Bananas: Colombian Politics in the Fictions of Gabriel García Márquez. *Bloom's Modern Critical Views: Gabriel García Márquez*. Ed. Harold Bloom. New York: Chelsea, 1989. 125–146.

Márquez, Gabriel García. *Cien Años de Soledad*. Madrid: Catedra, 1999.

———. "Interview." *Revista Primera Plana* 234 (Buenos Aires, June 20–26, 1967). 52–55.

———. *One Hundred Years of Solitude*. Trans. Gregory Rabassa. New York: Perennial, 1998. Rama, Ángel.

Márquez, Gabriel García, and Mario Vargas Llosa. *La Novela en América Latina: Diálogo*. Lima: Carlos Milla Batres, 1968.

Robles, Humberto E. "The First Voyage Around the World: from Pigafetta to García Márquez." *Bloom's Modern Critical Views: Gabriel García Márquez*. Ed. Harold Bloom. New York: Chelsea, 1989. 183–202.

A PASSAGE TO INDIA
(E.M. FORSTER)

"Forster's Critique of Imperialism
in *A Passage to India*"
by Hunt Hawkins, in
South Atlantic Review (1983)

INTRODUCTION

Reading *A Passage to India* as a scathing critique of the British colonial government in India and the inequality and mistrust it created, Hunt Hawkins sees the novel's portrayal of friendship and its failure as a representation of colonization and the alienation that it caused. Ultimately, Hawkins concludes that Forster's critique is marred by the "echo" of the Malabar caves, which makes true understanding between peoples and nations impossible.

The chief argument against imperialism in E. M. Forster's *A Passage to India* is that it prevents personal relationships. The central question of the novel is posed at the very beginning when Mahmoud Ali and Hamidullah ask each other "whether or no it is possible to be friends with an Englishman."[1] The answer, given by Forster himself on the

---

Hawkins, Hunt. "Forster's Critique of Imperialism in *A Passage to India*." *South Atlantic Review* 48.1 (Jan. 1983): 54–65.

last page, is "No, not yet.... No, not there" (p. 322). Such friendship is made impossible, on a political level, by the existence of the British Raj. While having several important drawbacks, Forster's anti-imperial argument has the advantage of being concrete, clear, moving, and presumably persuasive. It is also particularly well suited to pursuit in the novel form, which traditionally has focused on interactions among individuals.

Forster's most obvious target is the unfriendly bigotry of the English in India, or the Anglo-Indians as they were called. At times he scores them for their pure malice, as when Mrs. Callendar says, "The kindest thing one can do to a native is to let him die" (p. 27). More tellingly, Forster shows up their bigotry as prejudice in the literal sense of pre-judgment. The Anglo-Indians, as Forster presents them, act on emotional preconceptions rather than rational and open-minded examination of facts. They therefore fall into logical inconsistencies which the author exposes with his favorite weapon: irony. For example, at the hysterical Club meeting following Dr. Aziz's arrest for allegedly molesting Adela Quested, the subaltern defends an anonymous native with whom he had played polo the previous month: "Any native who plays polo is all right. What you've got to stamp on is these educated classes" (pp. 184–85). The reader knows, as the subaltern doesn't, that the native was Aziz himself. A more extended example concerns Aziz's collar stud. When Fielding loses a stud just before his tea party, Aziz, in an impulsive gesture of friendship, hands over his own, pretending it is a spare. Ronny Heaslop, when he arrives to retrieve Adela and Mrs. Moore, notices Aziz's collar riding up his neck. He later comments to the women, "Aziz was exquisitely dressed, from tie-pin to spats, but he had forgotten his back collar-stud, and there you have the Indian all over: inattention to detail; the fundamental slackness that reveals the race" (p. 82). Some pages further on, Ronny again uses his misobservation to condemn all Indians: "Incredible, aren't they, even the best of them? ... They all forget their back collar studs sooner or later" (p. 96). In this ironic example, Forster's clear implication is that if Ronny did not pre-judge, if he were more open-minded and learned the true facts, then he would not despise the Indians, and friendship would be possible. In an article published two years before *Passage*, Forster argued more broadly that even if the Indian did indeed forget such things as collar studs, it was still wrong to despise him: "He has never been introduced to the West in the social sense, as to a possible friend. We have thrown grammars and neckties at him, and smiled when he put them on wrongly—that is all."[2] Against the bigotry of the Anglo-Indians, Forster urged tolerance and understanding in the widest sense.

Several critics have asserted that Forster's attack on the bigotry of the imperialists is not necessarily an attack on imperialism itself. Presumably these Anglo-Indians could repair their attitudes, or they could be replaced by Englishmen who were more open-minded. Forster himself seems to sanction such a view in the text. Fielding, his apparent spokesman, says, "Indians know whether they are liked or not—they cannot be fooled here. . . . That is why the British Empire rests on sand" (p. 260). And Mrs. Moore, regarding her son Ronny while he excuses any unpleasantness of the Raj on grounds that it administers justice, thinks, "One touch of regret—not the canny substitute but the true regret from the heart—would have made him a different man, and the British Empire a different institution" (p. 51). These statements have led Lionel Trilling, among other critics, to conclude that: "A Passage to India is not a radical novel. . . . It is not concerned to show that the English should not be in India at all. . . . The novel proceeds on an imperialistic premise."[3]

Forster does much more in his book, however, than simply deride the intolerance of a few accidental individuals. He carefully shows how this intolerance results from the unequal power relationship between English and Indians, from the imperialistic relationship itself. Thus the numerous complaints by Englishmen in India that Forster had failed to show the "good" Anglo-Indians were beside the point. For example, H. H. Shipley, an India veteran of thirty years, wrote the author, "You have treated the English officials very unfairly. Not one among them is even a decent fellow."[4] Shipley did not see that Forster intended to show how officialism worked to corrupt the English, whether they began as decent fellows or not. The process is best shown in the book in the case of Ronny, who has only recently come out from England to be City Magistrate of Chandrapore.

Ronny was at first friendly toward the Indians, but he soon found that his position prevented such friendship. Shortly after his arrival he invited the lawyer Mahmoud Ali to have a smoke with him, only to learn later that clients began flocking to Ali in the belief that he had an in with the Magistrate. Ronny subsequently "dropped on him in Court as hard as I could. It's taught me a lesson, and I hope him" (p. 29). In this instance, it is clearly Ronny's official position rather than any prior defect of the heart which disrupts the potential friendship. And it is his position in the imperial structure which causes his later defect, his lack of true regret when he tells his mother that now "I prefer my smoke at the club amongst my own sort, I'm afraid" (p. 29).

Forster tells us that "every human act in the East is tainted with officialism" (p. 188) and that "where there is officialism every human relationship suffers" (p. 212). People cannot establish a friendship of equals when the Raj is based on an inequality of power. All relationships are ultimately subordinated to the political reality. This truth is demonstrated when Mrs. Moore tells Ronny how Aziz privately criticized the Callendars to her at the mosque. She is shocked when Ronny says he will report the conversation to Major Callendar. He justifies himself by saying, "If the Major heard I was disliked by any native subordinate of mine, I should expect him to pass it on to me" (p. 33). The final relationship between England and India is that of ruler to subordinate; and in order to maintain their status, the English must betray any friendship with Indians and pool their information.

When Mahmoud Ali raises the question at the beginning of the novel of "whether or no it is possible to be friends with an Englishman," he is thinking most immediately of Ronny Heaslop, who has insulted him in court that day. Ali says, "I do not blame him. He was told that he ought to insult me. Until lately he was quite a nice boy, but the others have got hold of him" (p. 10). Hamidullah gives any Englishman two years for all his initial impulses toward friendship to be destroyed. The process of corruption results not only from the newcomer absorbing the prejudices of the Ango-Indians on the spot, but, as we have seen, from his realization that his official position demands it. In time Ronny becomes almost a caricature of the racist. He decides of the Indians, "They all hate us" (p. 214), and he announces, "I am out here to work, mind, to hold this wretched country by force" (p. 50). When there is concerted agitation against British rule, Ronny has such a low opinion of the Indians that he can't believe they have organized it: "My personal opinion is, it's the Jews" (p. 308).

The one possible exception to this process of corruption among Englishmen is Fielding. He is partially immune to the influence of the imperialistic power relationship because he works in education rather than government, and because, as he puts it, he "travels light"—he has no hostages to fortune. Fielding establishes a friendship with Aziz and maintains it in defiance of all the other Ango-Indians. There is some doubt, however, whether he can maintain this course and still remain in imperial India. He is obliged to quit the Club and says he will leave India altogether should Aziz be convicted. After Fielding marries Stella, thereby ceasing to travel light, and after he becomes associated with the government as a school inspector, he undergoes a marked change of attitude toward the Raj. It would surely be a mistake to continue, as several critics do, to identify Forster with Fielding past this point. The omniscient narrator pulls back and summarizes Fielding's situation: "He had thrown in his lot with Anglo-India by marrying a countrywoman, and he was acquiring some of its limitations" (p. 319). Like Ronny and the other English officials, Fielding begins to be corrupted by his position. Thinking of how Godbole's school has degenerated into a granary, the new school inspector asserts that "Indians go to seed at once" away from the British. Fielding almost exactly echoes Ronny's defense of the Raj to his mother when he excuses unpleasantness in the supposedly neces- sary imperial presence: he had "no further use for politeness,' he said, meaning that the British Empire really can't be abolished because it's rude" (p. 320). Fielding certainly did not start with a defect of the heart, but, as a result of his new position in the imperial structure, he is acquiring one.

The English, of course, aren't the only ones corrupted by impe- rialism. Although most of the Indians in the book have a nearly unbelievable desire to befriend Englishmen, they are ultimately turned from it by the political reality. Some succumb to self-interest. Mahmoud Ali, for example, seems to have been the first to subvert his budding friendship with Ronny by advertising their smoke to potential litigants (see p. 29). More often the Indians succumb to the fear, largely justified but occasionally erroneous, that they will be scorned and betrayed. The prime example is Aziz. He makes the horrible mistake of assuming that Fielding back in England has married his enemy Adela and further that Fielding had urged him not to press damages against his false accuser so Fielding himself could enjoy Adela's money. Aziz, of course, has been conditioned to expect betrayal from his experience with other Anglo-Indians, and this expectation provides an undercurrent to the friendship from the very beginning. After Fielding returns to India, and Aziz learns he really married Stella Moore, their relationship is partially retrieved, but the damage has been done. The new school inspector has shifted toward the Raj, and Aziz, now leery of all Englishmen, has become a nationalist, saying of India, "Not until she is a nation will her sons be treated with respect" (p. 268).

Some critics have complained that Forster did not make his Indian characters sufficiently anti-British from the start. Andrew Shonfield has said, "Forster had little understanding and no sympathy for the complicated and courageous politics of the Indian independence movement."[5] And the Indian commentator Nirad C. Chaudhuri has written, "If we can at all speak of having driven the 'blasted Englishman into the sea,' as Aziz puts it, it was not men of his type who accomplished the feat.... Aziz and his friends belong to the servile section and are all inverted toadies."[6] But these complaints seem to miss Forster's premise. Given his line of argument that imperialism is wrong because it prevents personal relationships, then he can make his case most strongly by presenting friendly, rather than hostile, Indians. Even with the best of will, friendship is made impossible by the Raj; therefore the Raj must end.

In 1924, when *Passage* appeared, the Indian movement led by Mahatma Gandhi was still not yet agitating for independence. They said they wished to achieve dominion status and remain within the empire. Forster took what was at the time a more radical position by declaring that India inevitably had to become free. In an article in *The Nation and the Athenaeum* in 1922, Forster stated that "ten years ago" Indians had looked to Englishmen for social support, but now it was "too late," and he anticipated "the dissolution of an Empire."[7] These phrases are repeated at the end of the novel when Aziz cries, "Clear out, all you Turtons and Burtons. We wanted to know you ten years back—now it's too late" (p. 321).

Forster's novel does not explicitly spell out what has happened in the previous ten years, apart from Aziz's own trial and his blow-up with Fielding. However, the book is full of muted references to recent events.[8] The most important among these was the 1919 uprising in the Punjab which the British brutally suppressed. At the town of Amritsar, General Dwyer ordered his troops to fire on an unarmed crowd, killing nearly four hundred. Later he issued an order requiring Indians to crawl through a street where an English girl, Miss

Marcella Sherwood, had been attacked. In *Passage* Mrs. Turton, after the supposed attack on Adela, says of the Indians, "They ought to crawl from here to the caves on their hands and knees whenever an Englishwoman's in sight" (p. 216). After Amritsar, General Campbell issued an order obliging Indians to approach the houses of Europeans on foot. Thus Aziz, when he goes to visit Major Callendar, has to get out of his tonga before he reaches the verandah (see p. 16). In response to Amritsar, Gandhi launched the Non-cooperation Movement. Among other actions, Indians were to surrender their British titles, withdraw from Government-controlled schools, and go on fasts. These steps are obliquely referred to in the novel when, during Aziz's trial, the Nawab Bahadur abandons his title to become plain Mr. Zulfiqar, the students at Government College go on strike, and the Mohammedan ladies swear "to take no food until the prisoner was acquitted" (p. 214). The Non-cooperation Movement stopped short of demanding independence, but in the novel Aziz's experience makes him a nationalist. On the last page he shouts: "India shall be a nation! No foreigners of any sort!" And Forster, with friendship his goal, surely approves when Aziz tells Fielding, "We shall drive every blasted Englishman into the sea, and then . . . and then . . . you and I shall be friends" (p. 322). Thus five years before the Indian National Congress called for it, and twenty-three years before it actually happened, E. M. Forster called for Indian independence.

There are two important drawbacks in Forster's argument for independence on the grounds that it is necessary for friendship. The first is that his argument takes little account of the less personal, more abstract issues of imperialism, particularly the economic issues. Apart from a passing reference to "the wealth of India" allowed "to escape overseas" (p. 281), there is no mention of England's economic exploitation of India. We see no plantations or mines in British India. Collector Turton presumably takes in tax, but we never see him doing so. And, with the exception of the punkah wallah, we never see an Indian performing physical labor. Thus we have little sense of why the English are in India in the first place. Historians have argued over the economic basis of imperialism, particularly in the African colonies taken in the late nineteenth century where political and psychological motives may have played dominant roles. But there is little dispute over why the English came to India. From 1600 to 1858 the English were represented in the subcontinent not by their government but by a commercial organization, the East India Company. The wealth of India helped to fuel England's industrial revolution, and England's later expansion in Africa, starting with Egypt, was probably governed in large part by the need to maintain access to India.[9] The importance of recognizing economic exploitation is that it puts the issue of friendship in perspective. There are much larger, if less personal, reasons for opposing imperialism. To take another literary work which is in many ways more abstract than *Passage*, when Marlow in Conrad's *Heart of Darkness* objects to the chain gang building the railway line in the Congo, it is not because he is prevented from becoming friends with them. He could hardly expect to establish meaningful friendships with laborers who don't even speak his language. Rather he is moved by the simple desire to stop their exploitation and pain.[10]

Forster may have omitted the economics of the Raj because he was ignorant of them or didn't see their significance.[11] Or possibly he did so because he was following the Bloomsbury aesthetic of starting with characters and bringing in the material world only secondarily. In any case, he left out an important aspect of the Raj, and this omission has led the Marxist critic Derek S. Savage to attack him fiercely: "The ugly realities underlying the presence of the British in India are not even glanced at, and the issues raised are handled as though they could be solved on the surface level of personal intercourse and individual behavior."[12] This criticism may be justified, but in defence of Forster it should be noted that his particular argument against the Raj, its disruption of friendship, was shared by the Indian leaders of his day. In a 1921 letter explaining the purpose of the Non-cooperation Movement, Gandhi wrote: "We desire to live on terms of friendship with Englishmen, but that friendship must be friendship of equals both in theory and practice, and we must continue to non-cooperate till ... the goal is achieved."[13]

The second drawback to Forster's anti-imperial argument is perhaps more damaging. It is that even if the political barriers are overcome, Forster is still sceptical that friendship can be achieved. This scepticism has the effect of undermining the entire political argument and making us say, "Why bother?" *A Passage to India* suggests a number of nonpolitical barriers to friendship: the selfishness inherent in human nature, cultural differences which cannot be bridged, and the human potential for insanity. The most important barrier, though, is the echo. There have been many interpretations of the echo in the

Marabar caves, and it is difficult to explain in words since the echo intrinsically resists language, but it seems first of all to indicate the meaninglessness of the universe. For Mrs. Moore, the echo reduces all human expressions to the same dull "boum," and it says, "Everything exists, nothing has value" (p. 149). Forster told Santha Rama Rau that in *Passage* he tried to "indicate the human predicament in a universe which is not, so far, comprehensible to our minds."[14] Reason cannot penetrate existence to discover any meaning. The universe is a confused muddle, a "frustration of reason and form" (p. 285), rather than a mystery which conceals an intelligible purpose. In the political aspect of the novel, Forster attacked the prejudice of the Anglo-Indians by appealing to a reason which would find the true facts; but in the metaphysical aspect, he tells us that reason is useless.

The effect of the echo on Mrs. Moore is to make her abandon all attempts at human connection. After hearing it, she realizes she "didn't want to communicate with anyone.... She lost all interest, even in Aziz" (p. 150). Mrs. Moore withdraws into herself, leaves India without any further significant interaction with anyone, and finally dies. For her, the echo makes friendship impossible. Later, of course, the figure of Mrs. Moore undergoes a sort of apotheosis in which she is imagined as a benefactress of India. She becomes the Hindu demi-deity Esmiss Esmoor; Professor Godbole makes her part of his ecstatic devotion; and Aziz tells Ralph, "Your mother was my best friend in all the world" (p. 312). There is no objective basis, however, for this exaltation of her by the Indians, and Reuben Brower seems right in saying, "We can hardly accept this about-face in Mrs. Moore's role and its symbolic value. We cannot at the end of the novel regard Mrs. Moore as in tune with the infinite and conveniently forget the mocking denial of her echo."[15] Whatever her effect on others, she seems irretrievably isolated by the echo. Although she senses that Aziz is innocent, she is indifferent to his plight and does nothing at all to help him. When asked to testify, she says irritably, "When shall I be free from your fuss? Was he in the cave and were you in the cave and on and on ... and ending everything the echo." She decides of all people, including Aziz, "They do not exist, they were a dream" (p. 205). Mrs. Moore's friendship for Aziz thus comes to an end. The disruption in this case has nothing to do with the Raj or any other political barrier; rather it is caused by something much more powerful and overriding: the echo.

A Passage to India does suggest a solution to the echo, of course. There is some doubt, however, whether Forster himself subscribed to this solution. And the solution contributes nothing to the argument against the Raj since it transcends politics and all other worldly concerns. The solution is Hinduism, which is shown countering the echo by abandoning reason and embracing the muddle of the universe with irrational joy. The negative echo "boum" is thus transposed into the affirmative chant "OM," representing the Hindu trinity of Brahma, Vishnu, and Siva.

While Hinduism may provide a metaphysical solution, it does not, at least according to Forster's novel, provide a political one. Hinduism is shown embracing everything, including the British empire, with equal mindless affirmation. Professor Godbole points out that good and evil "are both of them aspects of my Lord" (p. 178). There are no villains: everyone attacked Adela. When Shri Krishna is born in the festival of Gokul Ashtami, he saves foreigners as well as Indians (see p. 287). The ecstasy of Hinduism, "flinging down . . . history" (p. 288), attains a union which is heedless of political distinctions and realities. The main Hindu character, Godbole, dislikes Aziz's poems about "the motherland" and instead professes "inter-nationality" (p. 293). He takes up residence in one of the Native States, which, even though they were physically separate from the Raj, were notorious for their support of it. And Godbole even names his high school, King-Emperor George Fifth. [16]

Quite apart from the apolitical, or even reactionary, character of Hinduism as portrayed by Forster, it is doubtful that he believed in it as a solution to the echo. When G.K. Das interviewed Forster in 1968, the novelist said that although he liked "things about Krishna worship," apparently its playfulness and inclusiveness, he was not inclined to believe in the god. He firmly described himself as a "non-believer."[17] In *Passage* Fielding notes that the Hindus have found "something in religion that . . . has not yet been sung," but which "may not be true" (p. 277). And when the omniscient narrator himself describes how at the end of Gokul Ashtami the image of Krishna is thrown in the tank as an "emblem of passage" to a higher unity, he comments, "A passage not easy, not now, not here, not to be apprehended except when it is unattainable" (p. 315).

At the very end of the novel when Aziz tells Fielding, "We shall drive every blasted Englishman into the sea, and then . . . and then . . .

you and I shall be friends," the Englishman asks him, "Why can't we be friends now? It's what I want. It's what you want." The question is never answered by either man because their horses swerve apart. In a beautifully ambiguous closing paragraph, Forster says of their friendship:

> The earth didn't want it, sending up rocks through which riders must pass in single file; the temples, the tank, the jail, the palace, the birds, the carrion, the Guest House, that came into view as they issued from the gap and saw Mau beneath: they didn't want it, they said in their hundred voices, "No, not yet," and the sky said, "No, not there." (p. 322)

One interpretation of this closing paragraph is that Fielding and Aziz cannot be friends until India becomes a nation, but another interpretation, a far more chilling one, is that they can never be friends. Not only politics keep them apart. The very earth and sky do. All of existence and the echo prevent human connection.

This conclusion might seem very depressing, and would be, but for the fact that Forster possessed the characteristics of the secret aristocracy he described in his essay, "What I Believe." He was "plucky." He continued to struggle for friendship, and against all the barriers to friendship, whether political or metaphysical, even though the struggle might have seemed futile. One of the barriers was the British Raj, and Forster conceived *A Passage to India*, at least in part, as an attack against it: "the political side of it was an aspect I wanted to express."[18] Forster did not have much confidence in the political effectiveness of literature. In *Passage* the Anglo-Indians leave literature alone: "The men had no time for it, the women did nothing that they could not share with the men" (p. 40). And Ronny even proclaims that he is not "a vague sentimental sympathetic literary man" (p. 50). Still Forster felt his book made a difference. He said, "It had some political influence—it caused people to think of the link between India and Britain and to doubt if that link was altogether of a healthy nature."[19] Forster even went so far as to send copies to Anglo-Indian officials who caught his eye, including the judge in a case involving Sir Michael O'Dwyer, the man in charge of the Punjab at the time of the Amritsar massacre.[20] And when Forster was told in an interview of the rumor that many British civil servants on the voyage to India had thrown his novel into the sea, he was immensely pleased. He laughed and exclaimed, "Did they indeed! How good for the sea!"[21]

NOTES

1. E.M. Forster, *A Passage to India* (New York: Harcourt, Brace and Company, 1924), p. 10. All future references are to this edition and are given in the text.
2. E.M. Forster, "Reflections in India, I: Too Late?" *The Nation and the Athenaeum*, 21 January 1922, p. 614.
3. Lionel Trilling, *E.M. Forster* (Norfolk, Connecticut: New Directions), p. 150. Shamsul Islam in *Chronicles of the Raj: A Study of Literary Reaction to the Imperial Idea towards the End of the Raj* (Totowa, N.J.: Rowman and Littlefield, 1979), similarly maintains that "Forster is not really interested in granting freedom to India," p. 43.
4. Quoted in P. N. Furbank, *E. M. Forster: A Life* (London: Seeker and Warburg, 1977), II, 126.
5. Andrew Shonfield, "The Politics of Forster's India," *Encounter*, 30 (January 1968), 68. 6. Nirad C. Chaudhuri, "Passage To and From India," *Encounter*, 2 (June 1954), 20 and 22.
7. Forster, "Reflections in India, I," p. 615. See also E. M. Forster, *The Hill of Devi* (New York: Harcourt, Brace and Company, 1953) where he says in a 1921 letter from Hyderabad, "English manners out here have improved wonderfully in the last eight years.... But it's too late. Indians don't long for social intercourse with Englishmen any longer," p. 237.
8. The historical background of *A Passage to India* has been studied most thoroughly by G. K. Das, *E. M. Forster's India* (Totowa, N.J.: Rowman and Littlefield, 1977) from which the observations in this paragraph have been drawn. See especially Das, pp. 47–67.
9. For England's economic exploitation of India, see Vera Anstey, *The Economic Development of India* (London: Longmans Green, 1957); A.K. Cairncross, *Home and Foreign Investment, 1870–1913: Studies in Capital Accumulation* (Cambridge: Cambridge University Press, 1953); and Michael Kidron, *Foreign Investment in India* (Oxford: Oxford University Press, 1965). This exploitation included the city of Patna, upon which Forster

based his fictional Chandrapore. Patna was a major center of the opium trade from 1761 to 1910; it was also an important producer of saltpetre and rice. See Sir John Houlton, *Bihar: the Heart of India* (Bombay: Orient Longsmans Ltd., 1949), pp. 18–19.

10. For Conrad's position, see my article "Conrad's Critique of Imperialism in *Heart of Darkness*," *PMLA*, 94, 2, (1979), pp. 286–99.

11. Forster's obliviousness to the importance of economics is indicated in his "Reflections in India, I" when he says, "The decent Anglo-Indian of to-day realizes that the great blunder of the past is neither political nor economic nor educational, but social," p. 614.

12. Derek S. Savage, *The Withered Branch: Six Studies in the Modern Novel* (New York: Pellegrini and Cudahy, 1950), p. 47.

13. M. Gandhi, *Amrit Bazar Patrika*, 2 February 1921. Quoted in Das, p. 23.

14. See K. Natwar-Singh, ed., *E.M. Forster: A Tribute* (New York: Harcourt, Brace and World, 1964), p. 50.

15. Reuben Brower, *The Fields of Light: An Experiment in Critical Reading* (New York: Oxford University Press, 1951), p. 197. Frederick Crews in *E.M. Forster: The Perils of Humanism* (Princeton: Princeton University Press, 1962) offers a similar interpretation. See pp. 155–59.

16. On the other hand, the state of Mau does harrass its British political agent (see p. 294). And the anti-British lawyer from Calcutta, Amritrao, seems to be Hindu.

17. Das, p. 119.

18. "E.M. Forster on His Life and Books," *Listener*, 61 (1 January 1959), 11.

19. K. Natwar-Singh, p. xiii.

20. See Furbank, II, 122.

21. Das, p. 118.

ROBINSON CRUSOE
(DANIEL DEFOE)

"The Fetishism of Commodities and the Secret Thereof"
by Karl Marx, in *Capital: A Critique of Political Economy* (1867)

INTRODUCTION

In his seminal critique of capitalism, Karl Marx uses *Robinson Crusoe* to elucidate the entrepreneurial spirit of capitalism. Marx's critique explores the intimate connections between exploration, colonization, and profit-making, and the way Crusoe's values reflect contemporary economic theory.

Since Robinson Crusoe's experiences are a favorite theme with political economists,[1] let us take a look at him on his island. Moderate though he be, yet some few wants he has to satisfy, and must therefore do a little useful work of various sorts, such as making tools and furniture, taming goats, fishing and hunting. Of his prayers and the like we take no account, since they are a source of pleasure to him, and he looks upon them as so much recreation. In spite of the variety of his work, he knows that his labour, whatever its form, is but the activity of one

---

Marx, Karl. "The Fetishism of Commodities and the Secret Thereof." *Capital: A Critique of Political Economy*. 1867. Ed. Frederick Engels. Trans. Samuel Moore and Edward Aveling. New York: The Modern Library, 1906. 88–90.

and the same Robinson, and consequently, that it consists of nothing but different modes of human labour. Necessity itself compels him to apportion his time accurately between his different kinds of work. Whether one kind occupies a greater space in his general activity than another, depends on the difficulties, greater or less as the case may be, to be overcome in attaining the useful effect aimed at. This our friend Robinson soon learns by experience, and having rescued a watch, ledger, and pen and ink from the wreck, commences, like a true-born Briton, to keep a set of books. His stock-book contains a list of the objects of utility that belong to him, of the operations necessary for their production; and lastly, of the labour time that definite quantities of those objects have, on an average, cost him. All the relations between Robinson and the objects that form this wealth of his own creation are here so simple and clear as to be intelligible without exertion, even to Mr. Sedley Taylor. And yet those relations contain all that is essential to the determination of value.

Let us now transport ourselves from Robinson's island bathed in light to the European middle ages shrouded in darkness. Here, instead of the independent man, we find everyone dependent, serfs and lords, vassals and suzerains, laymen and clergy. Personal dependence here characterises the social relations of production just as much as it does the other spheres of life organized on the basis of that production. But for the very reason that personal dependence forms the groundwork of society, there is no necessity for labour and its products to assume a fantastic form different from their reality. They take the shape, in the transactions of society, of services in kind and payments in kind. Here the particular and natural form of labour, and not, as in a society based on production of commodities, its general abstract form is the immediate social form of labour. Compulsory labour is just as properly measured by time, as commodity-producing labour; but every serf knows that what he expends in the service of his lord, is a definite quantity of his own personal labour-power. The tithe to be rendered to the priest is more matter of fact than his blessing. No matter, then, what we may think of those parts played by the different classes of people themselves in this society, the social relations between individuals in the performance of their labour, appear at all events as their own mutual personal relations, and are not disguised under the shape of social relations between the products of labour.

For an example of labour in common or directly associated labour, we have no occasion to go back to that spontaneously developed form which we find on the threshold of the history of all civilized races.[2] We have one close at hand in the patriarchal industries of a peasant family, that produces corn, cattle, yarn, linen, and clothing for home use. These different articles are, as regards the family, so many products of its labour, but as between themselves, they are not commodities. The different kinds of labour, such as tillage, cattle tending, spinning, weaving and making clothes, which result in the various products, are in themselves, and such as they are, direct social functions, because functions of the family, which just as much as a society based on the production of commodities, possesses a spontaneously developed system of division of labour. The distribution of the work within the family, and the regulation of the labour-time of the several members, depend as well upon differences of age and sex as upon natural conditions varying with the seasons. The labour-power of each individual, by its very nature, operates in this case merely as a definite portion of the whole labour-power of the family, and therefore, the measure of the expenditure of individual labour-power by its duration, appears here by its very nature as a social character of their labour.

Let us now picture to ourselves, by way of change, a community of free individuals, carrying on their work with the means of production in common, in which the labour-power of all the different individuals is consciously applied as the combined labour-power of the community. All the characteristics of Robinson's labour are here repeated, but with this difference, that they are social, instead of individual. Everything produced by him was exclusively the result of his own personal labour, and therefore simply an object of use for himself. The total product of our community is a social product. One portion serves as fresh means of production and remains social. But another portion is consumed by the members as means of subsistence. A distribution of this portion amongst them is consequently necessary. The mode of this distribution will vary with the productive organization of the community, and the degree of historical development attained by the producers. We will assume, but merely for the sake of a parallel with the production of commodities, that the share of each individual producer in the means of subsistence is determined by his labour-time. Labour-time would, in that case, play a double part. Its apportionment in accordance with a definite social plan maintains the proper proportion between the different kinds of work to be done and the various wants of the community. On the other hand, it also serves as a measure of the portion of the common labour borne by each individual and of his share in the part of the total product destined for individual consumption. The social relations of the individual producers, with regard both to their labour and to its products, are in this case perfectly simple and intelligible, and that with regard not only to production but also to distribution.

NOTES

1. Even Ricardo has his stories à la Robinson. "He makes the primitive hunter and the primitive fisher straightway, as owners of commodities, exchange fish and game in the proportion in which labour-time is incorporated in these exchange values. On this occasion he commits the anachronism of making these men apply to the calculation, so far as their implements have to be taken into account, the annuity tables in current use on the London Exchange in the year 1817. 'The parallelograms of Mr. Owen' appear to be the only form of society, besides the bourgeois form, with which he was acquainted." (Karl Marx: "Critique," &c., p. 69–70.)

2. "A ridiculous presumption has latterly got abroad that common property in its primitive form is specifically a Slavonian, or even exclusively Russian form. It is the primitive form that we can prove to have existed amongst Romans, Teutons, and Celts, and even to this day we find numerous examples, ruins though they be, in India. A more exhaustive study of Asiatic, and especially of Indian forms of common property, would show how from the different form of primitive common property, different forms of its dissolution have been developed. Thus, for instance, the various original types of Roman and Teutonic private property are deducible from different forms of Indian common property." (Karl Marx. "Critique," &c., p. 29, footnote.)

THE PLAYS OF WOLE SOYINKA

"Wole Soyinka and the Nobel Prize for Literature"
by Bruce King, in *Sewanee Review* (1988)

INTRODUCTION

In his introduction to Soyinka's works, Bruce King argues that the Yoruba writer is a mythmaker; one who, like James Joyce and T. S. Eliot, provides "rich layers of imagery, the grounding of myth in ritual and harvest cycles, the creative imitation of literary classics, the organizing of the discontinuous by analogy to myth, and the creation of a private cosmology." Seeing "Soyinka's assertion of Yoruba cosmology as a later, more sophisticated response to colonialism," King concludes, "Soyinka's mythology is part of an active, dynamic, liberating African cultural and political assertion."

The cultural map of the world is changing radically, and recognition of Soyinka's writings constitutes part of our increased awareness of modern Africa, including its popular music, its contemporary art, and the impressive body of literature that the continent is now producing in response to rapid political, social, and economic changes. One

King, Bruce. "Wole Soyinka and the Nobel Prize for Literature." *Sewanee Review* 96.2 (Spring 1988): 339–45.

of the best dramatists of our time, Wole Soyinka blends African with European cultural traditions, the high seriousness of modernist elite literature, and the topicality of African popular theater. He is a modern who writes from an African-centered worldview without nostalgia for an idealized past, and his attitude is sophisticated, cosmopolitan, and international in awareness, reference, and relevance. Rather than protesting against the continuing effects of colonialism, he has tried to overcome fragmented, secularized Western thought with an integrated vision of life derived from his own Yoruba culture. Unlike European writers who, claiming a dissociation of sensibility in the modern world, turn toward various forms of authority, Soyinka is actively committed to social justice and the preservation of individual freedom, in defiance of the various repressive regimes, black and white, that Africa has produced. Despite the complexity of his writing he has a popular following in Nigeria as a dramatist and as an outspoken, daring public figure, deeply engaged in the main political issues of his country and Africa. His periods of imprisonment, especially the long detention during the Nigerian civil war, make him a symbol for humane values throughout the continent.

Soyinka's writing is probing and energetic; he moves easily between European and Yoruba culture. Although set in such modern Nigerian cities as Lagos and Ibadan, the scenes and situations in his plays and novels seem familiar since they often are influenced by, are adapted from, or imitate well-known works of European literature. Shaped by myth and imagery, the narrative moves back and forth in time. The events are powerful; the language is filled with puns and witty word-play, references, and allusions. Soyinka has an excellent sense of dramatic rhythm and visual theater. Although he is a poet who creates rich layers of images and symbols, his plays resemble those of Ben Jonson and Bertolt Brecht in their energy, knock-about humor, satire, sharply outlined characters, sense of society, unexpected development, and use of popular culture. Besides Yoruba expressions, songs, and myth, he uses a Yorubaized English in his poetry, which, while creating a strange syntax and artificial diction, is in expression highly metaphoric, allusive, and economical.

Soyinka was originally part of a group associated with the University of Ibadan, the Mbari Club, and *Black Orpheus* magazine that included the novelist Chinua Achebe and the poet Christopher Okigbo. In the early 1960s these writers made Nigeria the successor to the Harlem renaissance and the francophonic negritude movement as the torchbearer of a renaissance of black culture. Blending traditional African arts with those of modern Europe, they shaped a contemporary African culture. Soyinka is the only one of the Mbari group who has continued to develop after the Nigerian civil war. Christopher Okigbo died for Biafra. Achebe, author of *Things Fall Apart* (1958) and *Arrow of God* (1964), has written little since the war; nor have the poets Gabriel Okara and J. P. Clark. Although imprisoned by the federal military government in conditions meant to lead to his death, Soyinka continued to write; denied writing paper, he managed to use scraps of cigarette and toilet paper to smuggle out *Poems from Prison* (1969). His powerful prison diary, *The Man Died* (1972), and other prison poems, *Shuttle in the Crypt* (1972), were published after his release from prison in 1969. The prison writings are quietly angry, broody, detailed in observation of his cell and guards, satirical and personal in their sense of confrontation with the head of the government and yet metaphysical as Soyinka tested his ideas by the reality he faced. A more introspective, imaginative Gulliver found himself imprisoned by the Lilliputians.

Soyinka's energy and his will to survive reflect a cosmology that he developed early and that is central to his writing, often providing an underlying mythical and psychological structure. He uses mythology from his Yoruba culture the way James Joyce and T. S. Eliot use classical and Christian material to bind together writing that otherwise seems fragmented or discontinuous. His novel about alienation of the young university-educated intellectuals from the older corrupt politicians, *The Interpreters* (1965), one of the best novels to come from English-speaking Africa, has no central narrator, narrative, or plot; Soyinka jumps without warning between various scenes and times and the consciousness of different individuals. It is organized by recurring images, symbols, and analogy to Yoruba mythology. The events occurring toward the conclusion of his powerful play *Kongi's Harvest* (1967), a satire on the tyrannies and ideologies of postcolonial Africa, are confusing; and perhaps they can be best explained by the harvest and Ogun myths they embody. Organization by analogy to myths and by recurring images has similarities to the dramatic structures Soyinka studied in Yoruba ritual in which, instead of narrative, the underlying story is represented by significant contrasts and parallels.

At the heart of the vision, used in Soyinka's epic poem *Idanre* (1967) and explained in his difficult *Myth, Literature, and the African World* (1976), is Ogun, god of iron, roads, creativity, and destruction. After the division of an original unity and the creation of the world, man was separated from the gods. Ogun then undertook an epic voyage through the void of unformed matter (like Satan's first journey from hell to earth in *Paradise Lost*) to reach man, thus bridging the gods and man, and the living and the dead. Because of this dangerous voyage Ogun became a leader of the Yoruba and settled among them, enjoying palm wine and women until one day, drunk in battle, he savagely destroyed both the enemy and his followers and in remorse withdrew to live by himself. Most of Soyinka's writings bear some analogy to part of this story. The significance of Ogun is personal and psychological as well as communal and religious. The writer, the prisoner, the actor, the hero must survive an equivalent to Ogun's dangerous journey through the void as part of the process of creation.

The Ogun myth (together with its complementary legend of Sango, the Yoruba king who became god of lightning) enables Soyinka to establish a coherent African cosmology to replace European mythology and Christianity. Such a decentering of an alien vision involves a necessary part of authentic modernization for a Third World writer. Soyinka does not reject foreign culture, as have some African nationalists; nor, as was common in the colonial period, does he judge the validity of African beliefs by their similarities to Western and Christian ideas. Instead he places his Yoruba world at the center, seeing European and Indian myths as analogous to African beliefs. The claim that Yoruba tragedy developed out of Ogun ritual and masquerade is similar to claims that Greek tragedy evolved from funeral rites and that medieval and Renaissance drama grew out of the Catholic mass. Hindu notions of reincarnation illustrate Soyinka's concept of history as recurring cycles from which it is difficult to escape. The African agrarian view of life as a seasonal harvest-rebirth cycle also provides the basis of his "Abiku" poem, which refers to the Yoruba belief that when a mother often loses her children it is the same child dying and being reborn again and again.

Even as a student Soyinka showed great talent. While at the University of Leeds, he wrote the witty, humorous verse drama *The Lion and the Jewel* (1957). Based on the false eunuch theme of Terence, *Volpone*, and *The Country Wife*, *The Lion and the Jewel* is one of the more charming works of early modern Nigerian literature. Its classical motif of deception in the game of sexual warfare and conquest is ingeniously transposed into a metaphor for the continuing relationship of old Africa to new Africa. The wily old chief who wins the vain maiden from the young, priggish, Western-educated suitor has the energy and cunning of those who succeed, but he is also like the "rust" of Soyinka's poem "Season," the rich autumnal maturity that must infuse the new in the cycle of birth, death, and renewal.

On his return to Nigeria, Soyinka's playfulness and sense of humor increasingly were overshadowed by pessimism. In the elaborately symbolic *Dance of the Forests*, performed to celebrate Nigeria's independence in 1960, he mocks negritude claims of an ideal Africa before the coming of the Europeans. He recalls that slavery existed before colonialism and warns that the rulers of the new nation will repeat the past in oppressing and exploiting the people. Soyinka already was integrating music and dance into his plays to make them more Nigerian, closer to Yoruba popular theater. He shifted the action backward and forward through time, creating a puzzling, highly theatrical dramatic form. Such plays embody unexpected revelations that deepen the significance of the events.

Soyinka often includes in his writings an African separatist preacher, since he is fascinated by the power they wield in his community, by their often comic corruption, and by their attempts like his own to syncretize African and Western thought. *The Road* (1965), perhaps one of the great plays of our age, portrays a preacher who searches for the meaning of existence, not realizing that it cannot be put into words, whether English or Yoruba. The truth is already experienced by a masquerader in the play who, having been hit by a truck while possessed during the Egungun ceremony, is permanently embodied in a moment of ritualistic immersion in Ogun's transitional voyage. The play is rich in language, humor, social observation, themes, visual symbols, and spectacle. The quest for life's metaphysical significance is dramatized within a context of political violence, police corruption, dangerous roads, and syncretic and chaotic cultural values revealed in varied kinds of English. The mythic structure and even the coherence of the plot are probably overlooked by many readers, but Soyinka's sense of theater holds audiences through the rhythm of events.

The Western Region crisis (1965) in Nigeria developed from an attempt by the ruling conservative northerners to split the Yoruba tribe and impose a minority government. As violence became widespread, Soyinka held up a radio station to call on the government to resign; he was imprisoned, tried, and then freed on a technicality. Within two years he was arrested once more, this time for attempting to create a third force that might prevent the start of a civil war between the federal government and Biafran secessionists. After twenty-seven months in prison, mostly in solitary confinement, he was freed; still opposing the military government, he went into exile for five years, 1970–75. After his release he published the bitter, grotesque play *Madmen and Specialists* (1971), in which war and the use of power are forms of cannibalism and *Season of Anomy* (1973), an allegorical novel about the Nigerian civil war, in which an Orpheus descends into the hell of northern Nigeria (where Soyinka was imprisoned) to bring back his Eurydice and start the process of renewal. Although indicating how an African democratic socialism might be born from the example of one Yoruba village, the novel seems facile and lacks the imaginative depth of Soyinka's best writing. He has long been interested in the *Bacchae* of Euripides. The version [*The Bacchae of Euripides: A Communion Rite*] (1973) that he wrote for the National Theatre in London combines a Marxist and a ritualistic interpretation of the theme and treats Dionysos as similar to Ogun. Since 1977 most of his plays have been political satires, aimed at corrupt politicians, tyrannical governments, and South African racism; they include *Opera Wonyosi* (1977), a Nigerian adaptation of Brecht's *Threepenny Opera*. A major work is *Aké* (1981), the story of his childhood, with its rich characterizations and observant portraits of the vigorous varied life of a Yoruba community, in which Christianity and animism are near neighbors, often in the same family.

Death and the King's Horseman (1976), which Soyinka directed in New York in 1987, is based on events in Yorubaland during the 1940s when an English district commissioner tried by imprisonment to prevent an Oba from performing a ritualistic suicide which had been demanded of the chief's horseman by tradition. Humiliated by his father's dishonor, the Oba's son commits suicide instead; the father then kills himself in the presence of the district officer. Although based on history, the circumstances have been altered by Soyinka; the events occur during the second world war, an English prince visits during the play's action, and the horseman's son is a Western-educated student of medicine. These and other changes create parallels and contrasts between European and Yoruba notions of personal honor, of self-sacrifice for communal purposes, and of the need to face death.

Soyinka affirms what may have been by the 1940s a dying tradition of ritualistic self-sacrifice because it exemplifies the central themes of his own vision, a vision which he claims is based on the African sense of communal well-being. In traditional Yoruba society the preservation of the community is the central concern. Gods are created by the community to be worshiped for the protection and welfare they give in return. There is continuity, based on reciprocality, between the living and their ancestors, the human and the divine, man and nature, sky and earth. If the horseman does not perform his duty as sacrificial messenger to the gods, the community is put at risk.

There is a double focus in the play, almost as if the world of British skepticism and power only superficially impinged on the real world of the Yoruba community. The play is constructed so that the focus moves from themes of cultural conflict to a revelation of the horseman's weakness when he is faced by death. The horseman, despite his imprisonment, can kill himself if he wants. He is reluctant to abandon the fruits of life, the pleasure represented by the young bride he acquires the night he is to die. If he does not die, if his son dies first, the cycle of life, of generations, of seasonal harvest, planting, rebirth, is ruptured. The richness of the play results from this poetic vision, expressed through image, symbol, and allusion, of an organic process threatened by an act of human weakness, which is contrasted to the blindness of the British district officer, who sees only a clash of cultures. The symbols are those of Yoruba mythology; the infusing of the old into the new is like lightning because it is the god Sango's lightning entering the receiving earth. While Soyinka's play resembles Yoruba ritual, in the way that *Murder in the Cathedral* is analogous to the Catholic mass that it reenacts, the king's horseman is less a victim than someone guilty of lack of will. The real action involves the psychological struggle of the main character with his beliefs, not the constraints imposed on him. Having suffered from a weakness of will, he sees himself forever shamed and he wonders if the gods have fated him to be the one whose dereliction will destroy his society. Death, as an act of will, affirms his identity and destiny.

Will is at the heart of Soyinka's vision. Tragedy results from will, the will of the hero to challenge the world, to cross the transition between life and death, to be sacrificial messenger, to enter the destructive abyss known by the masquerader and Ogun. Such determination marks Soyinka's own life—his risks in defying governments, his survival after two years in solitary confinement, his political involvement, and his continuing creativity. Soyinka's work and life celebrate the human spirit. In this affirmation he resembles writers from eastern Europe who have been awarded Nobel prizes. As a novelist, poet, dramatist, director, theorist, intellectual, and citizen, he shows that a unified personality may still be possible in our time.

To see Soyinka's assertion of a Yoruba cosmology as a later, more sophisticated response to colonialism than the negritude idealization of Africa does not limit the achievement to a specific historical moment. Such mythmaking should also be seen within the context of claims that a dissociation of sensibility occurred in western Europe during the late Renaissance. The rich layers of imagery, the grounding of myth in ritual and harvest cycles, the creative imitation of literary classics, the organizing of the discontinuous by analogy to myth, and the creation of a private cosmology are all familiar from Eliot and Joyce. Behind the assumption of a crisis in modern culture is a desire to return to a unity of personality in which art, religion, and society are not separate realms. Soyinka is one of the great mythmakers of our time; like Yeats, Eliot, Graves, Lawrence, and others, he has created a total vision. A problem with such mythologies is that they are anti-science and therefore essentially romantic and conservative. Soyinka, however, has made full use of African adaptability: Ogun becomes the god of roads, iron, and of telephone wires and carries the electricity of Sango. Instead of a backward-looking return to the middle ages or to prerational blood thought, Soyinka's mythology is part of an active, dynamic, liberating African cultural and political assertion.

The award of the Nobel Prize for Literature to Soyinka also shows that Africa and the Third World will increasingly have a place in international modern culture.

THE WORKS OF JONATHAN SWIFT

***

"The Irish Tracts"
by David Ward, in *Jonathan Swift: An Introductory Essay* (1973)

***

INTRODUCTION

Calling for a reexamination of Swift as an Irish writer, David Ward describes the way Swift captures the experience of British colonization and the way Swift's works arise "from a particular, local situation, and the concreteness of that situation." By showing how Swift's works respond to historical realities, Ward locates Swift as both an Irishman and a Protestant defending his homeland.

There is no comfort for any man in the history of Ireland; 'the Irish Problem' has always been there, not just for the English, but for the Irish too, ever since the two nations began to have contacts with each other. Other nations have been conquered, dispossessed, exploited, starved, dominated, divided, degraded, pacified and decimated; other nations have been given independence and yet remain hopelessly dependent economically; other nations have suffered from recurrent states of declared and undeclared civil war, and have seen

***

Ward, David. "The Irish Tracts." *Jonathan Swift: An Introductory Essay*. London: Methuen and Company Ltd., 1973. 100–120.

indiscriminate murder become a way of life; but there is no nation among whom embittered memories remain so powerful a force, entering into every aspect of life, impoverishing, distorting and, out of such contrary passions, breeding both deadly waste and, from time to time, such extraordinary creative fertility. I, an Englishman, one of Ireland's hereditary tormentors, can perhaps resolve to understand my responsibility to my neighbour nation a little better than my ancestors; I can even ask as much forgiveness for my country as it deserves, if it deserves any; I cannot (and this must limit any claims this chapter may have to deal with its, subject fully) feel the whole force of Ireland's tragic history bearing upon me, now, as it does, say, upon a resident of the Bogside, or a prisoner at Long Kesh, or a Belfast shipyard worker, or a doctor in a Derry hospital emergency ward, or a five-year-old boy playing war among the ruins.

Swift himself was not, in an unqualified way, an Irishman; and perhaps because of this, Swift's Irish tracts can be a better way for an alien to find his way into the terror of Ireland than his daily newspaper, with its brutalizing, repetitive tale of atrocities and opinionated stubbornness on every side. Or at least Swift will help us to see some of the depth of this hell, so that we can no longer dismiss it as a problem for whichever men have most power now. Sometimes Ireland seems like a cracked record stuck in the one groove, with the same voices singing the same songs over and over again, but ever more worn with time; perhaps Swift can help us in some way to feel how the needle scores and abuses the desperate, the violent, the unhappy; how deep are the roots of hatred and despair.

It was in the last quarter of the sixteenth century that England at last achieved military control over Ireland; Elizabeth, a great Queen of England in so very many ways, was a brutal mistress of the Irish; Lord Mountjoy, her general in Ireland, suppressed the rebellion of Hugh O'Neill, Earl of Tyrone, and proceeded to confiscate the lands of the defeated chieftains, dividing them between English adventurers, and thus creating a new Protestant aristocracy. The early Stuarts continued the process of colonization, importing large numbers of Scottish presbyterians into Ulster, dispossessing landlords and persecuting the Catholic priesthood. A Catholic rebellion in Ireland in 1641 helped to precipitate the English Civil Wars, and, as soon as Cromwell felt sufficiently confident to leave England, in 1649–50, he devastated Ireland and established a rule of terror. The

Act for the Settlement of Ireland which followed soon after in 1652 dispossessed almost every landowner in Ireland either wholly or partially; some sixty or seventy per cent of all the landed property in the island was seized and redistributed to reward those who had assisted in Ireland's rape. Dispossessed landlords—whether Catholic or Protestant—were dumped in the west, and their tenants and labourers exploited by new and alien masters.

During the next forty years the English government continued to reapportion land with regard only to English political exigencies, never to the needs of unhappy Ireland. Some land was returned to loyalists at the Restoration, though most of it remained in the hands of those who had been favoured by Cromwell, and hardly any of it went back to Catholic landlords. James II made his last stand in Ireland after 'the Glorious Revolution' of 1688; his 'patriot parliament' dispossessed some 2,000 supporters of William of Orange; when James was defeated at the Battle of the Boyne (1690) the land changed hands once again, and his supporters lost their lands to the Orangemen, many of whom were neither Irish, English, nor Scottish. Even the English protested against this, and once again, in 1700, land was repossessed by the Government and sold to the highest bidder.

The new masters of Ireland found no security in their dominance; they petitioned for union with England in 1707, hoping to gain the benefits, in terms of freedom of trade with England, and the colonies and representation in the English parliament, which the Scots had won by their Act of Union in the same year. But Union was not granted. There was, it is true, a separate Irish Parliament. But the Dublin Parliament was subject to a fifteenth-century law which allowed it to pass only those laws which had previously been agreed to by the Privy Council in London. It very rarely submitted itself to the electorate, and therefore was representative of little but itself, and in any case usually only met once every two years to vote supplies.

Nevertheless, with the connivance of the English Government, it managed to pass a series of laws designed to strip Catholics of any vestige of power they still had: Roman Catholics could not vote or stand for Parliament, become lawyers or members of the armed forces; they could not sit on a municipal council. When the owner of one of the few remaining Catholic estates died, the land had to be divided between all the surviving children, and since the families were often large, this meant that Catholic holdings tended to be smaller and smaller, and therefore less viable. If the eldest son turned Protestant, on the other hand, he took all.

But though all this ensured Protestant dominance, it could not ensure prosperity, even for the Protestant landlords. Ireland's economy was in the hands of the English, and the English were determined to avoid any competition they could possibly prevent in industry or trade. The infamous Wool Act of 1699, for instance, prevented Irish exports of wool or cloth to foreign countries or to British Colonies; all woollen products were to be sent to England, where heavy import duties were levied on them. Of course there was a good deal of smuggling from Irish ports to the Continent. But it was a sore blow to the Irish people, both landowner and peasant. The English Parliament took care to consolidate its power to do such things by the Declaratory Act of 1719, which asserted that Ireland 'hath been, is, and of right ought to be, subordinate unto and dependent upon the Imperial Crown of Great Britain, as being inseparably united and annexed thereto; and that the King's Majesty, by and with the advice and consent of the Lords Spiritual and Temporal and the Commons of Great Britain in Parliament assembled, had, hath, and of right ought to have, full power and authority to make laws and statutes of sufficient force and validity to bind the kingdom and people of Ireland'.

These are the bare bones of a terrible story. The detail has to be filled in with the suffering of peasants in loathsome hovels, their hand-kerchief of land rack-rented from an absentee landlord acting through a voracious agent; a diet of potatoes which would fail in a season of bad weather or blight, causing starvation; lank cattle bled for food; barefoot adults and children; the young men and women emigrating to England or the American Colonies; beggary, theft, murder, prosti-tution, vicious penal laws, epidemic disease, dirt and cruel bankrupting tax-laws. Ireland was degraded and demoralized; it was also deeply divided, and lacked the kind of dedicated, compassionate and articu-late leadership which was necessary if ever Protestant and Catholic, landowner and peasant, Irish and Anglo-Irish, tradesman and farmer were to make common cause about anything; if ever any movement of resistance or protest were to be mounted to ameliorate, in however small a degree, the terrible poverty and the terrible demoralization of the Irish people.

Swift may seem to have been an unlikely candidate for leadership of such a kind. An Anglo-Irishman who would dearly have loved to leave Ireland for good; a minister of the Established Church, hostile both to the Catholics and the Presbyterians; a Tory devoted to tradition and the monarchy he could, perhaps, have devoted his life to port and hunting, mumbling somebody else's sermons every Sunday and intriguing in cloister politics during the week.

Indeed, the first six years of his exile in Ireland passed peacefully enough, to all outward appearance. But his intimacy with Harley and Bolingbroke had given him a taste for action, and he was easily roused to anger by injustice and suffering, though like everyone else he was sometimes blind to some aspects of it. Much of Ireland's suffering could be traced to the Wool Act of 1699 and other related pieces of legislation; Swift recognized this and seized on the fact. However, characteristically he did not attack the Act directly, but proposed a scheme for improving the condition of Ireland without disobeying the law. Even more characteristically, deprived as he was of access to the executive centres of power, he appealed directly to the ultimate source of power, the people. In *A Proposal for the Universal Use of Irish Manufacture* (1720) he argues that, if the manufactures of Ireland may not freely be exported, then the Irish themselves should use them exclusively, and refuse to accept imports of woollen goods from England. One would have thought that, embarrassing as this may have been to the authorities, no one could have considered a proposal for the Irish to wear Irish cloth seditious, treasonable or in any other way actionable at law, but here is Swift's own account of what happened, in a letter to Pope dated a few months after the pamphlet was published:

This Treatise soon spread very fast, being agreeable to the sentiments of the whole nation, except those gentlemen who had Employments, or were Expectants. Upon which a person in great office here immediately took the alarm; he sent in haste for the Chief Justice, and inform'd him of a seditious, factious, and virulent Pamphlet, lately publish'd with a design of setting the two kingdoms at variance.... The Printer was seized, and forced to give great bail: After his tryal, the jury brought him in Not Guilty, although they had been culled with the utmost industry; The Chief Justice sent them back nine times, and kept them eleven hours, until being perfectly tired out, they were forced to leave the matter to the mercy of the Judge, by what they call a Special Verdict.

As is to be expected, there were accusations of Jacobitism laid against the printer and the author (who was, of course, anonymous) but, after a long and tedious delay, the Lord Lieutenant, the Duke of Grafton, granted a *noli prosequi*, and the case was dropped.

It is possible to read all the most famous of Swift's works, *Gulliver's Travels*, *A Tale of a Tub*, *The Battle of the Books*, *A Discourse Concerning the Mechanical Operation of the Spirit*, even *A Modest Proposal*, as satires of universal application; and this is, indeed, why they are still so famous, and so much read. But each one of these works arises from a particular, local situation, and the concreteness of that situation, the particularity of the problem, gives fulness and energy to the satire: 'the grandeur of generality' in Johnson's phrase, may be what makes art last, but only because it forces itself upon a great variety of readers, living in worlds so different that only the most essential things remain in common between them, as strikingly relevant to their own particular worlds. Universality is not arrived at by a process of reduction, by missing out all the particular detail which gives one age and one culture its unique, unrepeatable colour and flavour, its intricate texture and ambience; it is achieved by re-creating that culture, that time, by fighting the battles which are special to it, but in such a way that everything is related to certain great and abiding issues; so great art has a high degree of convertibility: like good currency, it is backed by ample resources held in the bank of issue.

So, *A Tale of a Tub* is incredibly rich in reference to the London of the last few years of the seventeenth century; its author can be identified as a typical representative of a particular community of a few hundred men and women, living in an acre or two of land in a shabby part of London making money by scribbling for hire. He is a Grub Street hack; but now, when Grub Street no longer exists, we can recognize the character of the hack, with all his habits and pretensions so characteristic of a place and time, as a point of reference for placing similar absurdities in our own, very different time.

Now, if there is one thing obvious about *A Proposal for the Universal Use of Irish Manufacture*, and most of Swift's other Irish Tracts, it is that it is written for a particular purpose at a particular time; it is a very practical document, appealing to the Irish people in the year 1720 to undertake a certain course of action:

> What if we should agree to make *burying in Woollen* a *Fashion*, as our neighbours have made it a *Law*? What if the Ladies

should be content with *Irish* Stuffs for the Furniture of their Houses, for Gowns and Petticoats to themselves and their Daughters? Upon the whole, and to crown all the rest, Let a firm Resolution be taken, by *Male* and *Female*, never to appear with one single *Shred* that comes from England; *'and let all the People say, AMEN.'*

The tract is as topical as an article in an 'underground' newspaper of today in the United States, Britain or the U.S.S.R. There are, however, several ways in which the pressures of Swift's indignation propels the pamphlet in the direction of a more universal satire; ways, one might say, in which it tends towards the greatest of all English prose satires, *Gulliver's Travels*—particular towards the third book of that masterpiece. The means by which this further reach to the argument is implied is the ironic idiom.

Consider how Swift turns from addressing Parliament to urging, first shopkeepers, then clergy, to do their share; then, with a curious, passing, dismissive irony, deflates all the pomp and circumstance of the army: 'I have not Courage enough to offer one *Syllable* on this subject to *their Honours* of the Army: Neither have I sufficiently considered the great Importance of *Scarlet* and *Gold Lace*.' We are already more than half way towards the tone and manner of Lilliputian satire: 'Whoever performs his Part with most Agility, and holds out the longest in *leaping* and *creeping*, is rewarded with the Blue-coloured Silk . . . ', sharing with this later manner the shrewd and light effect of distancing the reader from the subject. The army is made to seem contemptible, in passing, but not in a way that could possibly provoke the army to legal action, or even a brawling duel; so the reader is, partly at least, relieved of his fear of authority and power. Then Swift employs the method of fable for the next stage: notice how he appeals to Ovid, giving a point of reference as remote as may be from the actual sufferings of Ireland, but familiar to most of his readers from their school days. Swift tells the story with simplicity, as if to a schoolboy; he mentions his own reactions to it as a boy, thus suggesting, lightly enough, that no very great experience or wisdom are necessary for judging the case. The fables of Ovid show scant respect for the gods; Olympian power is not necessarily administered with integrity and justice in his tales; in fact the gods generally behave like overgrown babies. The ethos of Ovid is thus entirely suitable to

Swift's purpose, which is to adjust the reader's attitude towards power; to redraw the boundaries of power where that power, is administered without respect for justice or morality. Thus, though it would seem to elevate the dignity of England to compare her with Pallas Athene, the goddess of wisdom, in fact the comparison encourages contempt; while the comparison of Ireland with Arachne, the maiden turned into a spider, does not in the least belittle Ireland, but stresses her skill, innocence and injury:

> The Fable, in *Ovid*, of *Arachne* and *Pallas*, is to this Purpose. The Goddess had heard of one *Arachne* a young Virgin, very famous for *Spinning* and *Weaving*: They both met upon a Tryal of Skill; and *Pallas* finding herself almost equalled in her own Art, stung with Rage and Envy, knockt her *Rival* down, turned her into a Spyder, enjoining her to spin and *weave* for ever, *out of her own Bowels*, and *in a very narrow Compass.* I confess, that from a Boy, I always pitied poor *Arachne*, and could never heartily love the Goddess on Account of so *cruel and unjust a Sentence*; which, however is fully *executed* upon *Us* by *England*, with further Additions of *Rigor* and *Severity*. For the greatest Part of *our Bowels and Vitals* is extracted, without allowing us the Liberty of *spinning* and *weaving* them.

What follows is a sinuous little ambiguity which gains a great deal of its inner strength from Swift's obsessive concern with two related ideals, sanity and liberty, and his equally obsessive, indignant fear of their two opposites, madness and oppression or imprisonment (whether the imprisonment be physical or metaphorical). Madness recurs again and again as a leading metaphor in Swift's work, from *A Tale of a Tub* to *The Legion Club*, the horror growing and the laughter acquiring more bitter inflections on each occasion. The hatred of oppression grows greater, and becomes more and more linked with fear of madness, after Swift was obliged to return to Ireland, and after the hated Whigs took power in England. The capture of Gulliver in Lilliput, his impotence and vulnerability in Brobdingnag, the sufferings of Balnibarbi, the desperate uncertainties of Gulliver in Houyhnhnm Land, all these suggest remarkably strong feelings both of protest and fear in the face of power. As these complex feelings are expressed here, they are perhaps too compressed for complete understanding; the words of the Preacher (*Ecclesiastes* 7, 7) are a thought ambiguous, but Swift's development of them chases its own tail in a most disturbing way:

> The Scripture tells us that *Oppression makes a wise Man mad*; therefore, consequently speaking, the Reason why some Men are not *mad*, is because they are not *wise*: However, it were to be wished that *Oppression* would, in Time, teach a little *Wisdom* to *Fools*.

The complexity and disturbing nature of this depends on the ambiguity of the word 'mad'; so much is clear. Mad may mean insane, it may. mean very stupid, it may mean terribly angry; and any of these meanings would have been current at Swift's time. But the borderlines between them would have been much hazier for Swift and his audience. A man might have been committed to Bedlam for any of these three reasons: there were none of the fine drawn (though in some ways insensitive) distinctions between levels of intelligence which psychologists and educationalists now employ; no understanding of the physical diseases, like diabetes or epilepsy, which might affect rational behaviour; no distinction between neurotic and psychotic states of mind. 'Mad' was a word of fear: it meant anything which could disturb the proper disposition of things by loosening a man's command over his powers of reason. For a deeply conservative man like Swift it could almost mean not being able to accept life as it is; and yet the life all around him was so clearly not to be accepted that complacency was a more despicable kind of madness. So, oppression of this kind must force upon the sensitive observer, like Swift—himself so much in fear of madness—an odd, almost unbearable distinction: oppression of this degree partitions the kingdom of madness into the madness of the wise and the madness of the foolish, but sanity whole and entire is made impossible.

Some of this ambiguity in attitude towards madness can be recognized in *A Tale of a Tub* already, but there at least there is a Martin who, despite mad Peter's oppression, survives to be sane, and despite mad Jack's frenzy, overcomes his foolishness and preserves his coat entire. But in later life Swift was not so sure of things: *Gulliver's Travels* at several points displays a man sane amidst madness; at several points shows the same man mad amidst sanity. He is sane when, like Gulliver in Lilliput, he does not accept things as they are, and has power to act; sane when, like Gulliver in Laputa, he is an alien and can dissociate himself entirely from things as they are. He is mad, when like Gulliver in Brobdingnag, he is impotent to act; but accepts complacently the world as it is. Again, in Houyhnhnm Land, Gulliver is impotent to act. But on the other hand he is unable to accept the world as it is; man, himself, for what he is. And this terrible combination is something new: impotence without complacency. Does such a state necessarily lead to madness? If so, Swift implies, wisdom and madness are so close to each other that the first must contain in it a share of the second.

The vigorous sarcasm which follows, of 'how *grievously* POOR England *suffers by Impositions from* Ireland', is particularly effective in the way in which it moves from complaints which the English certainly did make—against the smuggling of Irish wool to France, for instance—through ever more unreasonable complaints to the most farcical: '*The Ballad upon* Cotter is *vehemently suspected to be* Irish *Manufacture; and yet is allowed to be sung in our open Streets, under the very* Nose, of *the Government.*' By comparison with the *Tale* or the *Discourse* it is crude satire; but it is intensely practical in purpose, designed to accomplish an immediate object by influencing as large a number of people as possible; not only the highly sophisticated reader at whom the earlier satires were aimed, but every shopkeeper, every merchant, anyone with a scruple of patriotic self-interest and a penny piece in his pocket.

For the meanwhile, then, the problem of wisdom and madness is solved by action; and yet Swift has not entirely solved the problem of communication which this kind of action presents. To be sure, his *Proposal* was read widely, most Irishmen agreed with its arguments, and drapers found it harder to shift their English woollens for a while. But Swift writes as if he is not quite sure which audience he is aiming at: at times, as in the reflection upon a text from *Ecclesiastes*, he seems almost to be talking to himself; at times to shopkeepers, at times to landowners; even: at times, he returned nostalgically to the old stamping grounds of his early satires, belittling the new English-sponsored aristocracy by associating them with Grub Street dullness, and so writing as if he had Pope or Arbuthnot in mind as an audience:

It is not many Years, since I remember a *Person* who, by his Style and Literature, seems to have been *Corrector* of a Hedge-Press[1] in some *Blind-Alley.* about *Little-Britain,* proceed *gradually* to be an *Author,* at least a *Translator* of a lower Rate, although somewhat of a larger Bulk, than any that now *flourishes* in *Grub-street*; and, upon the Strength of this Foundation, come over *here; erect* himself up into an *Orator* and *Politician,* and lead a *Kingdom* after him.

But action of the kind that might restore the self-respect of the Irish, and give them a means of living decently, needed more concentration of purpose; an Anglo-Irish *Dunciad* couldn't set matters straight, even if its satiric butts were more substantial than Colonel Bladon, or the 'booby lord', Viscount Grimston. When immediate self-interest, such as the saving of a few pence on an article of clothing or the buying of a smarter hat than one's neighbour's, comes into conflict with a longer-term self-interest, such as helping to restore the economic health of one's nation, then the longer-term consideration usually withdraws from combat early. A very sharp and narrow issue was necessary to focus the attention of the public; it had to be pursued with intense persistence; the manner of persuasion had to be clear enough to convince any man who could read, and many who could not, and above all the recommended course of action had to be one which would not put any man out of pocket or deprive a single pretty woman of a single scrap of lace. It had to be legally defensible as far as was possible in an age which allowed considerable political pressure on courts; it had not to be directly against the king or his principal minister, and yet it had to be an issue sufficiently big to show both England and Ireland the potential strength of the Irish people when they were aroused enough to work together as one.

The perfect issue came along at last; the matter of Wood's halfpence satisfied every one of these requirements. The rights and wrongs of the question hardly matter at all: perhaps Wood's halfpence might have been good honest coin as Sir Isaac Newton and his fellow assayers were prepared to assert after weighing, heating and hammering a random sample and comparing it with other coins of similar value. That was not important; what was important was that it provided a rallying point for a divided population.

I have remarked on the ways in which *A Proposal for the Universal Use of Irish Manufacture* tends towards the satire of *Gulliver's Travels*, widely different though the tones, methods and purposes of the two works are. The relationship between the *Travels* and *The Drapier's Letters* is even closer: as Harold Williams points out:

> their close relationship is due mainly to the fact that the travels of Gulliver were actually interrupted by the activities of the Drapier in Irish politics. Towards the end of January, 1724, Gulliver was approaching the end of his travels: 'I have left the Country of Horses, and am in the flying Island, where I shall not stay long, and my two last Journyes will be soon over'. But actually two years or more passed before the travels were over, and in that time Gulliver was to learn much from the experience of the Dublin draper, just as the latter was able to profit from the benefits that Gulliver had obtained by reason of his stay among the Brobdingnagians and Houyhnhnms.

However, when we begin to try and define the ways in which Gulliver and 'M.B. Drapier' resemble each other, there begin to be difficulties. They are, both of them, rather ordinary men, practical, patriotic, intelligent; the kind of men most of us would welcome as a neighbour. They are, also, Swiftian *personae*; means by which Swift creates an illusion, persuades us to look at certain events or situations from a special point of view. Swift has used such *personae* before, of course, but never, as in the case of M. B. Drapier, endorsing everything his creation says, using him as a mouthpiece. And, of course, Swift's relationship with Gulliver is far more complex than his relationship with the Drapier. We are made to feel that Gulliver is like us; sometimes we are flattered by the relationship, as when he entertains a nation by letting its army march between his legs: at other times we are humiliated by the similarity, as when the King of Brobdingnag says what odious vermin Gulliver's race must be. *Gulliver's Travels* constantly questions the wisdom of the human animal, and it is Gulliver's job to take us where the questions are. The power of the Drapier, on the other hand, is in our conviction that the ordinary, simple human, the man next door who chats about the weather as he sells a couple of yards of material (all good Irish stuffs and silks, of course) is as good as any man when it comes to political economy. Most men are happy, as they say, to 'listen to common sense', because common sense consists of what one believes is right, or can be persuaded is true, without going too deeply into the matter or seeking expert advice. Sometimes such judgements are right; just as often they are wrong, as anyone who has talked to men in draper's (or tobacconist's, or greengrocer's) shops must know. But, increasingly, such men were becoming the measure of Swift's society, and its core, a fact upon which the extraordinary career of Daniel Defoe was based. The Drapier, perhaps, is even closer to Robinson Crusoe than he is to Gulliver, closer than Gulliver and Crusoe were to each other, despite their common experience of shipwreck. Like Crusoe, he is devised especially to appeal to the man who has won a little comfort and a few possessions by trading in a very competitive world, and is scared of losing it all. Crusoe reassures him that he would make out all right, even if he did lose everything. The Drapier warns him that there is a plot afoot to steal everything he has worked for, and tells him how to fight back:

> What I intend now to say to you, is, next to your Duty, to God, and the Care of your Salvation, of the greatest Concern to your selves, and your Children; your *Bread* and *Cloathing*, and every common Necessary of Life entirely depend upon it. Therefore I do most earnestly exhort you as *Men*, as *Christians*, as *Parents*, and as *Lovers* of *your Country*, to read this Paper with the utmost Attention ...

Indeed, the soundness of a currency is important. The way in which this soundness used to be guaranteed was by minting coins whose value as metal when melted down was nearly equal to the face value of the coin. Thus, no one would profit by forging in gold or silver of equal quality, and baser alloys could be easily detected by a variety of tests. As the economy began to be based more and more upon trade, more and more coins were needed, and the demand outstripped the supply of gold and silver. Baser metals began to be used for smaller coins, and gradually it became clear that coins of very little value indeed were greatly useful to the economy as a whole, enabling a finer adjustment of prices, and therefore more competition and more rapid exchange of money and goods. But forgery was made easier, and, perhaps more important than this, it was made easy for governments to increase the money supply at will, and this in its turn could produce inflationary tendencies. Economists still argue about the matter, some stressing the need to stabilize the value of money, others stressing the need to encourage trade and industry by a ready supply of money and credit.

Economists of any school would agree that it was bad practice to license a private individual to issue coin for a whole nation. But there are places where Swift, perhaps, carries his ironies too far, exaggerating the probable effect of the new coinage. The sophisticated would enjoy the joke; the unsophisticated would be scared out of their wits by the prospect of a farmer having to pay his rent with three horse loads of halfpence, a lady having to go out shopping with a carriage full of copper following her, Squire Conally having to pay his rent with two hundred and fifty horse loads, and so on. The mad mathematics assume that there is no other currency, and this is a valid enough distortion for the purposes of satire, but satire depends upon an audience possessed of considerable analytical and critical ability. The *Letter to the Shopkeepers* is, avowedly, addressed to the illiterate as well as the literate, to the simple as well as the sophisticated, and while it does not lie to those who are aware of its satirical aspect, there are ways in which, in addressing its avowed audience, it uses improper methods.

The problem is that Swift is acting more than one role here. He is concerned to give solid, honest advice to the citizens of Ireland. He is concerned to fight irresponsibility and negligence in government. He is concerned to restore self-respect to the Irish nation. But he sees all these concerns in the context of a larger view of the world; in *A Tale of a Tub* he promises *A Description of the Kingdom of Absurdities*; in *Gulliver's Travels* he gives us, not one, but many such absurd kingdoms; but all the time, between writing the *Tale* and the *Travels* and before and after too, he is irresistibly drawn towards the absurd, and to the satirist's habit of giving the naturally absurd a half twist more, until it becomes grotesque caricature. Consider, for instance the progression from Squire Conally, with his two hundred and fifty horseloads of rent, to this, in the *Letter to Harding*:

> But if I were to buy an hundred Sheep, and the Grazier should bring me one single Weather, fat and well fleeced by way of *Pattern*, and expect the same Price round for the whole hundred, without suffering me to see them before he was paid, or giving me good Security to restore my Money for those

that were *Lean*, or *Shorn*, or *Scabby*; I would be none of his Customer. I have heard of a Man who had a Mind to sell his House, and therefore carried a Piece of *Brick* in his Pocket, which he showed as a Pattern to encourage Purchasers: And this is directly the Case in Point with Mr. *Wood's Assay*.

Consider, too, the further progress from this to the various mad projectors of Lagado, particularly those concerned with the 'Scheme for entirely abolishing all Words whatsoever':

> An Expedient was therefore offered, that since Words are only Names for *Things*, it would be more convenient for all Men to carry about them, such *Things* as were necessary to express the particular Business they are to discourse on.... many of the most Learned and Wise adhere to the new Scheme of expressing themselves by *Things*; which hath only this Inconvenience attending it; that if a Man's Business be very great, and of various Kinds, he must be obliged in Proportion to carry a greater Bundle of *Things* upon his Back, unless he can afford one or two strong Servants to attend him.

All three passages are concerned with the way in which we *represent* things or ideas. Today we are all quite used to the idea that coins and notes are not *in themselves* wealth: they *represent* wealth. If the government which issues a paper currency ceases to guarantee it, it becomes worthless, as did Confederate currency, or Czarist paper money. If the same thing happens to coins which are not made in valuable metals, the only value of the coins, over and above the small value of the metal, is a curiosity value for the collector. Swift's campaign against Wood was based on the idea that this was bad practice; that money should be intrinsically valuable, as the gold sovereign or the old silver dollar are now worth more than face value, even though they are not official coinage any more. So a coin, according to Swift, should be a valuable *thing*; it can be exchanged for other valuable *things*, and its only advantages over other *thing* as a medium for exchange are that it is small, easily carried, and that it is commonly accepted as of a known value, as a measure for the relative value of other *things*. If you take away these two advantages, and have currency consisting of kilos of lead, or gas-filled balloons, or currency of so little intrinsic value in

proportion to weight that you have to count it by the horse load; or
if a community disagrees about the acceptable value of a coinage, and
one man says a six-inch nail is worth a pigeon pie and two cream buns
whereas another says it is only worth the iron in a six-inch nail, then
the point of coinage is lost.

In the *Letter to Harding*, Swift explores another angle of this business of representation. We cannot, he says, represent any whole by any
one of its parts. Newton's assay only tested a sample of the coins, and
therefore need not be reliable as a measure of its worth. Swift empha-
sizes the point by homely language, easily understandable by either
townsman or farmer. What he does not mention here, though he does
so elsewhere, is that the assay sample was chosen at random, from
several packets of coins, over a period of one year. How else could one
test a coinage, if to test it involves destroying it, as Newton's methods
did? But ultimately the value of coinage depends upon trust in the
authority behind the currency. Swift was attempting to undermine
this trust, and was assisted by the ambiguity about who the issuing
authority was. Wood guaranteed the money, but was authorized to do
so by the English parliament. By distrusting Wood Swift was opening
up doubts in the Irish people's minds as to the trustworthiness of
the English government, and therefore opening up doubts about its
right to authority. In the process some of his arguments may be faulty,
even dishonest; but the grand strategy of the process was important
enough to justify the aim for Swift, and the grand strategy was this:
governments need assent to govern, and assent depends upon trust.
If government is bad, trust and assent may be withdrawn. Therefore
the process of government is dependent upon winning trust and
assent, and this can only be done by a mutual process; by government
representing its actions and motives honestly to the people, by the
people being allowed to represent its needs and complaints directly
to the government. Otherwise a government is a flying island; the
governors, wrapped in their own concerns, cannot communicate with
their subjects except by force; their subjects are forced to respond in a
similar way, and the contract of government is broken, by a failure in
communication, by a failure of truth in representation.

The passage from the third book of the *Travels* applies some of
these considerations in a different area. One well-established theory of
language works upon the principle that words *represent* things (or ideas,
or actions and so forth). The kind of representative function which

words have is not precisely like the function, say, of a paper currency. Currency acts as a standard of value and a medium for exchange, but, according to this ancient theory, each word represents one thing; or, one idea derived from a group of similar things. If this were true, we could, theoretically, do without language altogether; and Swift satirically plays with this idea, unfolding its absurdity: and, of course, one of the ways in which it is absurd is similar to the way in which Wood's halfpence are made to look absurd with the image of Squire Conally carrying his rents on two hundred and fifty packhorses. Words are even more compact a currency than gold: they occupy no space at all, so it is absurd to imagine doing away with them. Why should Swift go to the trouble of saying this? No contemporary thinker had begun to suggest that one could do away with words: the closest approach was the interest Leibniz showed in a plan to develop a universal language, as logical and rational as mathematics; based upon an ordered analysis of the universe of things. It is most unlikely that Swift had Leibniz in mind; he was thinking of a more widespread tendency in contemporary science: the obsession with the physical aspect of the universe, the growing tendency to disregard the role of the human mind in a moral, intellectual and spiritual universe. The *savants* engaging in conversation with *things* instead of words are not absurd simply because they act in an awkward and unnecessary way; they are absurd because they place crippling limits upon knowledge and communication—precisely the grouse Swift had against contemporary science. This, one aspect of the madness of materialism, is closely linked in Swift's mind to that other aspect, bad government caused by narrow material self-interest, which engages his attention in the *Drapier's Letters*.

Contemporary science and technology, Swift believed, had set out to engineer the universe in such a way as to destroy the accumulated wisdom of man; and one most important aspect of this is language. This same obsession with theory, this disregard of the inherited wealth of knowledge is what leads to the devastation of Balnibarbi: 'The People in the Streets walked fast, looked Wild, their Eyes fixed, and were generally in Rags ... except in some very few Places, I could not discover one Ear of Corn, or Blade of Grass.' Balnibarbi is a somewhat distant account of Ireland under the domination of an English Parliament in some ways, but in others it is pretty close, allowing for the stretching effect of the satirical rack. The closest match of all is the account of the Lindalinian rebellion:

> The People were unanimous, and had laid in Store of
> Provisions, and a great River runs through the middle of the
> Town. The King hovered over them several Days to deprive
> them of the Sun and the Rain ... not a Person offered to send
> up a Petition, but instead thereof, very bold Demands ... This
> Incident broke entirely the King's Measures and (to dwell
> no longer on other Circumstances) he was forced to give the
> Town their own Conditions.

This is not necessarily an account after the event of what happened
in the matter of Wood's halfpence: Swift was already 'in the Flying
Island' before he began to write as the Drapier. It is, as it were, a model
of the kind of action the Irish might take to redress their grievances.

Swift's campaign against Wood's halfpence culminated in the
finest of the four letters, *To the whole People of Ireland*, and in this
latter he makes clear something which has been implicit in all the
other three: that the quarrel about coinage implied an even deeper
question—the true relationship between the Crown and the people of
Ireland; the status and rights of Ireland as a nation. This was the letter
which forced Carteret, the new Lord Lieutenant, to issue a Proclama-
tion, offering three hundred pounds for information about the author,
and for publishing which Harding the printer was taken to court.

The reason for this reaction is not difficult to discover: it lies in
the assertion that there is 'no Law that makes *Ireland depend* upon
England; any more than *England* doth upon *Ireland*'. Nor was there
any such law; the Declaratory Act of 1719 had only made Ireland
'subordinate unto and dependent upon the Imperial Crown of Great
Britain': but everybody knew what that meant. There was no Declaratory Act to say that England or Scotland were 'subordinate unto and
dependent upon' the Crown. Instead there were such instruments as
the Act of Union with Scotland (1707) which declared that the two
kingdoms of England and Scotland shall for ever 'be united into one
kingdom by the name of Great Britain'. So the quarrel about Wood's
halfpence implies a deep and urgent constitutional question, as well as
innumerable social and human problems.

Almost by accident Swift's determined action led to the invention of techniques of civil disobedience (though they were not called
that) which have since played an increasing role in the world whenever state and people come into sharp conflict. There are many ways

in which the matter of Wood's halfpence prepared the way for the long subsequent history of Irish resistance to English power, and also taught the American colonists a thing or two which they were to remember half a century later. It was a significant incident in the pattern of changing relationship between governor and governed which led eventually, for instance, to the campaign of the Congress movement under Gandhi. But it is only with hindsight that we can see this; radical in effect though Swift's arguments were, they were loyalist, patriotic and conservative in theory: 'next under God, I depend only on the King my Sovereign, and the Laws of my own Country'. The core of his argument, apart from the dispute about the constitutional status of Ireland, was the proper limitations of royal power within the social contract, and this was a matter which had been discussed for some time, by Bacon, Hobbes and Locke, and given constitutional sanction at the accession of William of Orange, in The Bill of Rights (1680) which has the significant subtitle 'An act for declaring the rights and liberties of the subject and settling the succession of the crown'. Swift himself quotes Bacon to support his argument; but notice how the chosen quotation expresses an essentially conservative view of the nature of monarchy; that monarchy is modelled upon divine government:

> as God governs the World by the settled Laws of Nature, which he hath made, and never transcends those Laws, but upon high important Occasions: So among earthly Princes, those are the Wisest and the Best, who govern by the known Laws of the Country, and seldom make Use of their *Prerogative*.

Swift was no democrat; the model of human government which approaches closest to perfection in *Gulliver's Travels* is that of Brobdingnag, where the King is benevolent, intelligent and governs by consent, but where the King *is* a king. A Houyhnhnm democracy, based upon the total integrity, intelligence and freedom from malice of each member of society, is not put forward as a serious model for mankind, and yet neither is Lilliputian society, where the governors in whom the king trusts are distinguished by their malice, envy and narrowness of vision. This is the kind of perspective in which the *Drapier's Letters* are written; the boycott of Wood's halfpence was not a bid for popular power, the first stage in a rebellion—Swift would have been terribly shocked if it had turned out that way. It was an attempt to restore a proper relationship between monarch and subject, the kind of desperate act which should be as rare as the monarch's use of his prerogative, but was just as necessary to the health of the state. And its intended social effects were not what we should think of as social justice or civil rights: equality of opportunity, freedom of religion, or anything of the sort. Swift would want the Protestant squirearchy in control of the land again, and the Protestant tradesman prosperous in the towns. The following shows clearly enough for whom he spoke:

> One great Merit I am sure we have, which those of *English* Birth can have no Pretence to; that our Ancestors reduced this Kingdom to the Obedience of ENGLAND; for which we have been rewarded with a worse Climate, the Privilege of being governed by Laws to which we do not consent; a ruined Trade, a House of *Peers* without *Jurisdiction*; almost an incapacity for all Employments, and the Dread of *Wood's* Half-pence.

NOTE

1. A clandestine printing house, often engaged in libellous, pornographic or even treasonable work.

THE TEMPEST
(WILLIAM SHAKESPEARE)

"'Had I Plantation of this Isle, My Lord–':
Exploration and Colonization in
Shakespeare's *The Tempest*"
by Robert C. Evans,
Auburn University at Montgomery

Exploration and colonization are important themes in Shakespeare's *The Tempest*, and have been discussed extensively in recent criticism. Indeed, such discussion has been so extensive and detailed, and has involved so many diverse and divergent perspectives, that (as often happens when any topic is exhaustively studied) the basic issues now seem more perplexed and perplexing than ever. Some critics, for instance, have argued strongly that European exploration and colonialism in the New World in general (and British exploration and colonialism in Virginia in particular) are especially relevant contexts for any understanding of Shakespeare's play. Other critics have questioned this approach or have dismissed its relevance altogether. More recently, British colonialism in Ireland has been seen as the most significant parallel to the kinds of colonialism presented in Shakespeare's play, while others have argued for the importance of Mediterranean contexts, African parallels, and classical (especially Virgilian) backgrounds. Many recent commentators have seen Caliban, in particular, as a victim of Prospero's colonialist oppression. Critic David Lindley has helpfully complicated matters even further by suggesting that it is possible to "argue that Caliban is not an indigenous native, but rather a first-generation colonist himself. His enslavement by Prospero repeats his mother's earlier imprisonment of Ariel, who might be considered the island's 'real' indigenous inhabitant" (39). In responding to the play, in short, readers and audiences have many perspectives on exploration and colonialism to consider and (perhaps) to choose from.

When it is viewed with exploration and colonialism in mind, one of the most striking aspects of this drama is how few of the characters fit common stereotypes about explorers or colonizers. None of the characters—with the possible exception of Ariel—seem to have set out with any deliberate intention to discover this particular unnamed island, or to take up anything approaching permanent residence there. The "damned witch Sycorax" (Caliban's mother), who originally lived in Algiers, was banished to the island after having committed "mischiefs manifold and sorceries terrible" (1.2.264)—at least according to Prospero, with whose angry account Ariel readily concurs. On the island, Sycorax gave birth to Caliban and imprisoned Ariel within a tree. Ariel was only freed (after 12 years of painful torment) when Prospero and Miranda, having been set adrift in the ocean after Prospero's overthrow as Duke of Milan, happened to arrive "By providence divine" on the island (1.2.159). Prospero then liberated Ariel from the curse imposed by Sycorax, who had died in the meantime. Neither Sycorax nor Prospero, then, visited the island as an intentional explorer or purposeful colonizer; for them the place was, if anything, a penal colony—a kind of proto-Australia—rather than a place they deliberately sought out to explore or exploit. Prospero, meanwhile, hardly seems an explorer: he rarely ventures far from his "full poor cell" (1.2.20), a dwelling which may in fact be a mere cave and which, in any case, is not the sort of elaborate residence we might expect an aristocratic magician to construct if he had any intention of making the island his permanent home. A man with Prospero's wondrous powers could easily have transformed the island into a pleasant and splendid colony if he had wished; he could even have populated it with hundreds of compliant colonists. Instead, his main concern seems is to return to Milan and reestablish his ducal authority in Italy. Exploring the island, or establishing an elaborate colony there, is unimportant to him.

Meanwhile, the island once again functions as a kind of penal colony for its next set of unwilling visitors—Alonso, the king of Naples;

Antonio, Prospero's conniving brother and his usurping successor as duke of Milan; Sebastian, the similarly conniving brother of Alonso; and the various servants and courtiers (including the good-natured Gonzalo) who find themselves shipwrecked on the island, thanks to the tempest Prospero has engineered. The island becomes their prison and Prospero (unbeknownst to them) now functions as their warden, with Ariel as an ever-vigilant guard and enforcer. Like Sycorax and Prospero, none of these men deliberately intended to land on this island, let alone explore it or turn it into a colony. Most of them assume they will somehow quickly return to their native Italy, even though their ship (as far as they know) is now at the bottom of the ocean, and the island seems uninhabited and perhaps uninhabitable. Among the group of aristocrats and courtiers, only Gonzalo (and, to a much lesser extent, another courtier named Adrian) gives much serious thought to the prospect of long-term residence on the island. Adrian notes that the island seems "to be desert" (i.e., deserted) as well as "Uninhabitable and almost inaccessible," yet he also comments that "It must needs be of subtle, tender and delicate temperance" and that "The air breathes upon us here most sweetly" (2.1.37–49). Partly, of course, he is trying, in making these comments, to cheer up Alonso, the disconsolate Neapolitan king who assumes that his son and heir, Ferdinand, has died in the shipwreck. However, Adrian is also beginning to think in pragmatic terms about their prospects for survival on the island.

Even more pragmatic, in some ways, is Gonzalo, a character whose speeches and personality are difficult to interpret. In part he seems a garrulous and even simpleminded old man, and in both respects he has sometimes been compared to Polonius in *Hamlet*. On the other hand, Gonzalo seems genuinely compassionate in his efforts to cheer Alonso; he also seems to understand that any further success for the survivors (however such "success" is defined) depends on reviving the flagging spirits of their leader. Gonzalo's optimism can be seen, then, either as foolishly naïve, or as pragmatically wise; either as genuine, or as partly studied. In any case, his words and personality are not cynical (which is much more than can be said of either Antonio or Sebastian). Gonzalo seems to understand instinctively that if the shipwrecked group hopes to survive and prosper, they must not give in to the sort of despair that afflicts the Neapolitan king. Gonzalo considers their "preservation" a "miracle" (2.1.6–7)—phrasing that implies his humility, his gratitude, and his spiritual sensibilities. Meanwhile, he also urges Alonso to "wisely . . . weigh / Our sorrow with our comfort" (2.1.8–9)—phrasing that implies his own wisdom as well as his commitment to practical reason. These qualities help make Gonzalo an intelligent and well-motivated counselor. Gonzalo, in short, is precisely the sort of man who might in other circumstances make a good colonist, and who might help establish a successful colony. He is an embodiment of some of the best qualities of Western European civilization, and he who would make a good member of a common-wealth just about anywhere.

Unfortunately, also among the survivors are the cynical, treacherous Antonio and the self-serving Sebastian—exactly the sort of persons who corrupt societies wherever they happen to be. These are the kinds of people who undermine any hope of making a fresh start or of establishing a truly "New World"; they symbolize the sinful selfishness that Christians of Shakespeare's time would have seen as endemic in human nature. Antonio and Sebastian personify the perverse pride that both led to, and resulted from, the fall of Adam and Eve in the Garden of Eden. They embody the inevitable flaw in any colonial project—any effort to establish a utopian society anywhere. Just as the European colonists arrived in America with hopes of spreading the blessings of Christianity among supposedly unenlightened heathens, but inevi-tably brought with them their own perversities and innate corrup-tions, so Antonio and Sebastian symbolize the predictable futility of any effort to start over, to begin again, to create a brave new world different from or better than the world the explorers and colonists have left behind. Just as the European colonists in America introduced devastating physical infections unknown to the native inhabitants, so Antonio and Sebastian bring with them, to this seemingly uninhab-ited island, their own (but also quite common) moral corruptions and spiritual flaws. Yet these sorts of flaws and corruptions, of course, are already present on the island, partly in the personality of Prospero and partly in the character of Caliban. Pride, selfishness, and ethical and spiritual shortcomings (Shakespeare seems to suggest) are part of the inevitable human condition. We bring them with us wherever we go because they are so deeply engrained in our nature. They are inescap-able, and they inevitably doom any utopian colonial dreams.

This is part of the point of the sniping by Antonio and Sebastian against Gonzalo and Adrian in the first scene of the second act of *The*

Tempest. Antonio and Sebastian consider themselves very clever and witty in the ways they mock and abuse Gonzalo and Adrian, and at first Shakespeare seems to be encouraging his audience to identify with this joking and seemingly sophisticated pair (2.1.10–48). It soon becomes evident, however, that both men are sarcastic cynics, and it isn't long before their sneering witticisms begin to boomerang. Thus, when Adrian comments that "The air breathes upon us here most sweetly," Sebastian immediately retorts, "As if it had lungs, and rotten ones," and Antonio adds, "Or, as 'twere perfumed by a fen" (2.1.49–51). If, however, anything is "rotten" in this play, it is Sebastian himself, just as Antonio's reference to a "fen" (commonly associated with disease and rank odor) suggests his own putrid moral nature. Moreover, the cynicism of both men is implicitly pessimistic and defeatist. When Gonzalo remarks that "Here is everything advantageous to life," Antonio responds, "True, save means to live" and Sebastian concurs by saying, "Of that there's none, or little" (2.1.52–54). Gonzalo's comment may seem either unintentionally naïve or calculatedly optimistic, but at least it is not cynically hopeless. If a colony on the island had any hope at all for practical or moral success, such hope would depend on Gonzalo and Adrian, not on scoffing and pessimistic misanthropes Antonio and Sebastian.

Gonzalo's next comment—"How lush and lusty the grass looks! How green!" (2.1.55)—symbolically associates him with the very vitality he praises. In contrast, the predictable cynicism of the ripostes by Antonio ("The ground is indeed tawny") and by Sebastian ("With an eye of green in't") once more imply their own sarcastic and life-denying outlooks. Indeed, Sebastian's comment seems especially intriguing. Most editors, following the *Oxford English Dictionary*, gloss the word "eye" as meaning "slight shade, tinge" (see Lindley, Orgel, the Vaughans, and Hulme and Sherman), and that is obviously the main meaning. However, it is hard not to overhear, also, an echo of one of Shakespeare's own most famous phrases from two of his most significant plays, *The Merchant of Venice* and *Othello*. In the first of those works, Portia refers to "green-eyed jealousy" (3.2.110), while in the latter Iago cautions Othello to beware of "jealousy," the "green-eyed monster" (3.3.168). Jealousy and envy, in fact, seem to be among the main motives of Antonio and Sebastian, not only in the dealings with Gonzalo but also in their general outlooks on life. Those motives have already led Antonio to usurp the dukedom of Prospero, his own brother, and they will soon lead Antonio and Sebastian together to plot the murder both of Sebastian's brother Alonso and of the good-hearted Gonzalo, whom they apparently consider more dangerous than their studied contempt for him might suggest. Having been on the newly discovered island for only an hour or two, Antonio and Sebastian have already manifested a plethora of old-world corruptions and vices. If the island symbolizes, in some ways, an escape from death and the possibility of a fresh start, Antonio and Sebastian symbolize the inherent perversity that lies deep in human nature and that makes any hope of an earthly paradise realistically impossible.

The contrast between Gonzalo and Adrian and between Antonio and Sebastian is the main point of Act Two, Scene One. Gonzalo and Adrian represent the best and literally most hopeful aspects of human nature; they are the kinds of civilized beings who might indeed be able to establish and sustain an ethical, thriving colony. They are the sorts of Europeans who might be welcomed by the natives of a new and unknown land; they are the kinds of Christians who might win converts through their exemplary attitudes and behavior as much as by any overt proselytizing or preaching. They embody the best aspects of a humanity originally created (as Renaissance Christians believed) in the image of God. Thus, although Gonzalo is literally an old man, he seems more full of vitality and freshness than either of the younger cynics, Antonio or Sebastian. Indeed, Shakespeare goes out of his way to link Gonzalo with the words "fresh" and "freshness" in this scene (1.2.65, 70, 98, 103), and it is typical of Gonzalo to look on life with optimism and to see the best in his surroundings and in other people. (At the same time, he is not so naïve as to overlook the cynicism of such persons as Antonio and Sebastian.) In contrast, Antonio and Sebastian are essentially egotists whose union (here and later) is merely temporary and self-serving. They make common cause in their wit-combat against Gonzalo, just as they will later connive in the planned murder of Gonzolo and Alonso, but each man is too full of pride and self-regard to be a true friend (or even a true brother) to anyone. At the beginning of the scene they appear to be two witty humorists with whom the audience might identify; but by the time they reach their tedious and tiresome jokes about "Widow Dido" (2.1.78–102), they have revealed their true colors. Commentators and editors have often wondered why and how Shakespeare could write such vapid and wearisome dialogue, but perhaps he knew what he was doing, since this episode helps expose Antonio and Sebastian as superficial narcissists who love to hear themselves prattle.

The fundamental cruelty that lies beneath the surface wit of these men becomes especially evident when Sebastian bluntly blames his brother, Alonso, not only for the death of Ferdinand, Alonso's son, but also for the loss of Claribel, Alonso's daughter, through her recently arranged marriage to an African king (2.1.124–35). It was on the return voyage from this African wedding that the shipwreck occurred, and Sebastian not only reminds Alonso that Claribel and many courtiers opposed the marriage, but he even rubs salt into the wound by emphasizing that "Milan and Naples have / More widows in them of this business' [i.e., the wedding's] making / Than we bring men to comfort them" (2.1.133–35). He then brusquely concludes by saying "The fault's your own" (2.1.136). Rather than being admirably and honestly plainspoken, however, this remark seems almost sadistic, as Gonzalo immediately observes: "My lord Sebastian, / The truth you speak doth lack some gentleness, / And time to speak it in. You rub the sore / When you should bring the plaster" (2.1.137–40). Gonzalo, significantly, does not deny the validity of Sebastian's words, but he does dispute their appropriateness given the pain Alonso is already suffering. Gonzalo thereby exhibits, once more, his own commitment to both "truth" *and* "gentleness." Just as typically, however, Sebastian makes no effort to apologize, while Antonio (apparently) merely cracks another joke (2.1.141).

The first half of Act Two, Scene One, is highly relevant to the famous set piece that now ensues: Gonzalo's memorable speech outlining his utopian vision of a potential "plantation" (or colony) on the island. No other passage in the play is more germane to themes of exploration and colonization than this one, and the fact that the speech is indisputably indebted to Montaigne's noted essay "Of the Caniballes" (i.e., cannibals) makes it especially noteworthy. "Of the Caniballes" discusses European contact with so-called "savages" of the New World (whom Montaigne considers in some ways far less savage than the allegedly Christian colonizers), and at points Gonzalo's wording follows the Frenchman's almost verbatim. As Gonzalo outlines his vision of an earthly paradise, however, he is continually interrupted—as he has been throughout the entire scene—by the sarcastic Antonio and the equally cynical Sebastian. Their interruptions remind us that any hope of an earthly utopia is impossible, precisely because of the inevitable presence in it of such corrupted human beings as these men themselves. They mock Gonzalo's dreams (which may be deliberately fanciful to begin with), but in the final analysis their mockery reflects as much on their own flawed characters as on Gonzalo's possible naïveté. In any case, their mockery illustrates why any hope of a brave new colonial world is doomed from the start. It is impossible to build the kind of ideal society Gonzalo extols because any such society will necessarily include people such as Antonio and Sebastian. Indeed, most Renaissance Christians would have believed that it is impossible to build such a perfect society because any such society would include human beings in general, who are all fundamentally flawed by original sin.

Gonzalo no sooner begins explaining his ideal vision than he is immediately—and sarcastically—interrupted by Antonio and Sebastian:

> GONZALO
> 　　Had I plantation of this isle, my lord–
> ANTONIO
> 　　He'd sow't with nettle-seed.
> SEBASTIAN
> 　　Or docks, or mallows.
> GONZALO
> 　　And were king on't, what would I do?
> SEBASTIAN
> 　　'Scape being drunk, for want of wine. (2.1.144–47)

Paradoxically, however, it is people such as Antonio and Sebastian who are the figurative weeds in any potential earthly garden, and the figurative (and often literal) irrational drunks in any human society. The corruption of such persons would be especially likely to surface in any newly founded colony that lacked long-standing institutions and ancient traditions of law and justice. In any recently established society, particularly in one geographically distant from the home country, the influence of such corrupt persons (most Renaissance Christians would have believed) would be likely to be far greater than in a well-regulated culture with settled laws and potent churches. Only in heaven could the ideal society Gonzalo now outlines truly exist; on earth, the kind of commonwealth he envisions could only be "utopian" in both etymological senses of that word: a good place that is also literally no place.

Even so, the fact that Gonzalo is capable of imagining such an ideal speaks well of him and of his fundamentally noble character. His vision of a utopia free both from riches and from poverty, lacking in treason, felony, and violence, and emphasizing the purity of "innocent people" (2.1.148–69; see esp. 165) implies his own essential innocence and goodness. Yet even as he expounds upon the prospective virtues of his ideal "commonwealth" (2.1.148), his phrasing reminds us of the practical problems inherent in any such scheme. Thus, his praise of a society in which "all men" will be "idle" (i.e., free from the need to toil and labor, as in the Garden of Eden) cannot help but remind us of the idleness of the lazy and indolent Antonio and Sebastian, who employ themselves only in ostensibly witty sarcasm. Likewise, when Gonzalo praises a society in which "treason" will not exist, he reminds us of the treason Antonio has already committed, just as his words also unintentionally foreshadow the treason against Alonso that both Antonio and Sebastian will soon attempt. Likewise, Gonzalo's vision of a utopia in which there will be no need for swords or knives will seem ironic when Antonio and Sebastian plot the murder of Alonso and Gonzalo with precisely such weapons (2.1.291–97). Similarly, when Antonio mocks the "knaves" who will populate Gonzalo's commonwealth, we are reminded that perhaps the greatest of all the knaves presently residing on Prospero's island is none other than Antonio himself. The presence of people such as Antonio and Sebastian therefore subverts any realistic hope for a "commonwealth" that will "excel the Golden Age" (2.1.148, 169). The practicality of Gonzalo's dream is undercut even as he outlines its particulars. Even as Gonzalo imagines the establishment of an earthly paradise, Shakespeare reminds us of all the reasons why any such paradise is impossible.

The problems inherent in establishing any kind of ideal colony are obviously reflected in the documents of the Virginia Company, which attempted to establish a Christian British outpost in pagan North America. Various critics have argued that some of these documents had a direct influence on *The Tempest*. In any case, they reveal how quickly the lofty hopes that lie at the root of most colonial enterprises are soon complicated by mundane and unattractive realities. In this respect the documents reflect the general experience of European colonialism in the New World. Thus, the so-called "First

Charter of Virginia," issued by King James in 1606, proclaimed the King's support of

> soe noble a worke which may, by the providence *of* Almightie God, hereafter tende to the glorie of His Divine Majestie in propagating of Christian religion to suche people as yet live in darkenesse and miserable ignorance of the true knoweledge and worshippe of God and may in tyme bring the infidels and salvages living in those parts to humane civilitie and to a setled and quiet govermente. (Grizzard and Smith 250)

By the time a second charter was issued in 1609, however, conflict among Christians themselves was already reflected in that charter's revised language:

> because the principall effect which wee cann desier or expect of this action is the conversion and reduccion of the people in those partes unto the true worshipp of God and Christian religion, in which respect wee would be lothe that anie person should be permitted to passe that wee suspected to affect the superstitions of the Churche of Rome, wee doe hereby declare that it is oure will and pleasure that none be permitted to passe in anie voiadge from time to time to be made into the saide countrie but such as firste shall have taken the oath of supremacie. (302)

Colonists, in other words, could now journey to Virginia only if they had first sworn allegiance to Protestant King James. Finally, by the time of the third charter, issued in 1612, the situation had become even more complex. The third charter begins by reiterating that the main purpose of the colony is "the propagacion of Christian religion and reclayminge of people barbarous to civilitie and humanitie" (307), but by this point the main concern is with ostensibly Christian colonists who,

> by their insolent and contemptuous carriage in the presence of our said Counsaile, have shewed little respect and reverence, either to the place or authoritie in which we have placed and appointed them; and others, for the colouring of their lewdnes

and misdemeanors committed in Virginia, have endeavored them by most vile and slanndrous reports made and divulged, aswell of the cuntrie of Virginia as alsoe of the government and estate of the said plantacion and Colonie, as much as in them laie, to bring the said voyage and plantacion into disgrace and contempt; by meanes where of not only the adventures and planters alreadie ingaged in the said plantacion have bin exceedingly abused and hindred, and a greate nomber of other our loving and welldisposed subjects otherwise well affected and inclyning to joine and adventure in soe noble, Christian and worthie an action have bin discouraged from the same, but allsoe the utter overthrow and ruine of the said enterprise hath bin greatlie indanngered which cannott miscarrie without some dishonor to us and our kingdome ... (319).

In the space of a few short years, in other words, the colonists had begun to realize that the main challenges to the success of the colony lay less with the land or the natives they encountered there than with the corruption inherent in the colonists themselves. The "insolent and contemptuous carriage" of some of the colonists resembles, in various respects, some of the attitudes and behavior of Antonio and Sebastian. In Shakespeare's play, as in any New World (and even Old World) colonial enterprise, the explorers and colonists had inevitably brought with them the very sort of barbarity, incivility, and inhumanity they sought to eliminate in the so-called "savages." Gonzalo's dream of a renewed colonial "Golden Age" is appealing as an ideal, but it is unclear that even Gonzalo really takes the idea seriously. In any case, Shakespeare clearly does not, and *The Tempest* provides ample evidence of the disappointments and disillusionments inherent in any colonial enterprise.

WORKS CITED OR CONSULTED

Andrews, John F., ed. *The Tempest*, by William Shakespeare. *The Everyman Shakespeare*. London: Dent, 1994.

Grizzard, Frank E., Jr., and D. Boyd Smith, *The Jamestown Colony: A Political, Social, and Cultural History*. Santa Barbara, CA: ABC-CLIO, 2007.

Hulme, Peter and William H. Sherman, eds. *The Tempest*, by William Shakespeare. Norton Critical Edition. New York: Norton, 2004.

Lindley, David, ed. *The Tempest*, by William Shakespeare. *The New Cambridge Shakespeare*. Cambridge: Cambridge University Press, 2002.

Orgel, Stephen, ed. *The Tempest*, by William Shakespeare. *The Oxford Shakespeare*. Oxford: Clarendon Press, 1987.

Phelan, James D. and Gerald Graff, eds. *The Tempest*, by William Shakespeare. New York: Macmillan, 2000.

Vaughan, Virginia Mason and Alden T. Vaughan, eds. *The Tempest* by William Shakespeare. London: Arden Shakespeare, 2000.

THINGS FALL APART
(CHINUA ACHEBE)

"Exploration and Colonization in
Chinua Achebe's *Things Fall Apart*"
by Eric Sterling,
Auburn University at Montgomery

In his first novel, *Things Fall Apart* (1958), Nigerian author Chinua Achebe portrays a peaceful, innocent, and traditional Igbo society that is irrecoverably transformed and corrupted by British Christian missionaries and British government officials. Achebe begins his novel with a vivid depiction of Umuofia, an Igbo village in southeastern Nigeria. This description shows readers how Igbo culture used to be— and what has been lost because of the invasion by Christian missionaries and government workers. Rather than write his novel in his Igbo language, Achebe chooses to write in English, in order to show a large audience, particularly British readers, how colonization has negatively altered the society in which he was raised. Before the arrival of the missionaries and government officials, the inhabitants of Umuofia (and the other villages in the community) are content with their lives and obey cultural customs that ensure stability, order, and tradition. Achebe presents Nigerian society in a matter-of-fact and objective fashion, portraying the beauty of the Igbo society and its traditions, yet also depicting the problems that are inherent in the culture, such as killing a member of the community (in this case, Ikemefuna) because of an order from an oracle; or killing *osu* (twins) because of a superstition. Achebe chooses not to glorify his Igbo culture, but nonetheless

191

indicates that a rich and beautiful society has been changed by English colonists who explore and transform village life with their own customs and faith. Achebe portrays most of the colonists as imperialistic, prejudiced, and condescending. For the most part, the colonists do not have good intentions toward the native villagers.

The first Englishman appears in the village of Abame; he is a lost missionary seeking directions to Mbaino. He is clearly an outsider, and he frightens the natives, who have never seen anyone like him (they consider him an albino) and do not understand his intentions. In fact, even after the novel is over, readers might have trouble discerning the true intentions of the missionaries. The first missionary, whose role is to help and guide lost sheep (people who have lost their way spiritually) and direct them toward the correct path, is himself lost. Do they come to Nigeria to convert the natives to Christianity, or are they exploring the region in search of areas to colonize? Not knowing his intentions, the villagers murder him. Obierika, the best friend of Okonkwo, the protagonist, mentions that the people were afraid and thus unwilling to explore new relationships with different people. Instead, they consulted their Oracle, which declared that they should slay him:

> The elders consulted their Oracle and it told them that the strange man would break their clan and spread destruction among them.... And so they killed the white man and tied his iron horse to their sacred tree because it looked as if it would run away to call the man's friends.... It said that other white men were on their way. They were locusts, it said, and that first man was their harbinger sent to explore the terrain. And so they killed him. (120)

Although the murder seems heinous, one should bear in mind the villagers respond out of fear. In defending their culture, they seek self-preservation, tying up an "iron horse" (bicycle) to a sacred tree to prevent it from riding away and telling on them. The Oracle, which expresses the thinking of the ruling class, fears outsiders who wish to explore and exploit the Igbo culture. To the spiritual leaders of the villages, exploration correlates with colonization. When the white outsiders arrive and wish to meet and interact with the natives, the religious leaders sagaciously decide that the explorers are setting up a new home that will ultimately lead to the destruction of their culture. The English explore to learn more about the villages and the people, but then ultimately wish for—and ultimately coerce—the natives to learn and adapt to their Western way of life, which includes Christianity and modernization. Thus, the missionary's murder indicates the villagers' fear of foreign exploration of their land and the concomitant resistance to British colonization.

This murder leads to the arrival of soldiers, who shoot and kill practically all of the inhabitants of Abame, destroying the village. All the soldiers know is that the missionary's bicycle is tied to a tree. Without investigating what has happened to the missionary, the soldiers murder many innocent people. The life of the Christian missionary has been sacrificed for the good of the colonizer: the missionary's death provides the British government with the motivation and cause they need to invade and destroy the village, thereby intimidating the inhabitants of the other eight villages. This show of force scares the villagers into allowing the British to enter and colonize this region. There is a question as to the motives of the missionaries. Do they arrive to explore the region and the culture so that they can determine how they can best teach the natives about Jesus Christ, or have they been sent by the British government to begin the process of colonization, with soldiers following them shortly thereafter? In other words, it is quite conceivable that the imperialistic English government, when determining how best to add to its empire, sends the missionaries first, so that the exploration of the Igbo villages seems innocuous. After the missionaries arrive, seemingly harmless and benevolent, the government sends soldiers, ostensibly to protect the unarmed missionaries but surreptitiously to colonize and usurp power from the unsuspecting Nigerian natives. Ode Ogede claims that several

> factors joined forces to make European powers unable to resist the idea of taking actual political control of the African continent. Not the least significant of these elements were calculations related to how European powers could monopolize and maximize profits from this external trade with Africa, as well as ideas regarding the burden of bringing [spiritual] enlightenment to the dark corners of the world. Thus, 1892–1904 saw the forcible imposition of colonialism by Britain on virtually all the areas now known as Nigeria. (2)

The emergence of the missionaries in the village of Okonkwo's motherland, Mbanta, shows how the missionaries view their mission as an effort to explore and civilize, while the native inhabitants see an annihilation of their culture. Although the missionaries express their desire to know the village and its people, these same missionaries bring with them Western culture and a mandate to save the "heathens." The missionaries want the Nigerians to learn all they can about Western tradition, particularly Christianity. The goal is to convince the Africans to understand the ways of Jesus Christ, and ultimately to convert the Africans to Christianity. The missionaries believe that their ways of life and their faith are vastly superior to those of the Nigerians, so perhaps they wish to help the Africans to live a better life and, upon their deaths, go to Heaven. Yet readers should also consider the prospect that the missionaries know that if they successfully convert the natives, it will be easier for the British soldiers to colonize them.

Mr. Brown, the missionary who speaks in Mbanta, begins by telling the natives that the gods in their polytheistic society are worthless, dead pieces of wood that cannot help them. Mr. Brown begins in this manner because he realizes that he must incite the natives to distrust their gods before they will begin to explore the ways of Christians. He then informs the natives about the Holy Trinity, but this concept confuses them because they think of gods in human terms. As the villagers contemplate the meaning of Christ, Okonkwo asks Mr. Brown about God's wife. Exploring the Holy Trinity in human and cultural terms, Okonwko ponders how Christ could be the son of God when God is not married (127). Unable to comprehend how an unmarried God can have a child, Okonkwo becomes convinced that the missionary is insane, and wishes to beat the man until he flees. His desire to drive out Mr. Brown suggests that Okonkwo instinctively realizes that Brown's appearance presents danger to the clan and can lead to British colonization of the village. Perhaps he remembers Obierika's remark, cited above, that the Oracle prophesies that strange men—outsiders to the clan—will destroy their culture.

Because of Mr. Brown's patience and persistence, some of the natives, such as Nwoye, Okonkwo's son, decide to explore Christianity. Nwoye is entranced by the harmonious Christian music, and wishes to flee his hard-hearted father. Others are also moved to explore this new religion, primarily because their polytheistic gods have failed to protect or help them; the same holds true for their *chi*, or personal god.

The natives who decide to leave their gods and explore a new faith are the societal outcasts, the *efulefu*, who have nothing left to lose and much to gain. Thus, the missionaries attract followers by seeking out the malcontents and the disenfranchised, those who are easy to entice to leave their faith for Christianity. Obierika notices that Nwoye has visited a missionary to discover more about the new faith, but the missionaries refuse to allow Obierika near the convert because new initiates are vulnerable and easily lost back to their original religion. The narrator says that it is only "after many difficulties the missionaries had allowed him to speak to the boy" (124). This indicates how proprietary the missionaries are of their converts. After attracting a new initiate to Christianity, the Christians refuse to allow the converts to spend time with their unconverted family members for fear of losing that person. These converts are important to the missionaries because the new Christians now belong to God and to the colonists; as the missionary Mr. Kiaga says to Nwoye when the latter leaves Okonkwo's *obi* (hut) for good, "Blessed is he who forsakes his father and his mother for my sake.... Those that hear my words are my [new] father and my [new] mother" (132). These converts create a tension between the native Igbos who convert and those who do not. This civil strife makes it much easier for colonists to conquer the land and take over the government. The natives who remain true to their polytheistic faith would be reluctant to attack the British government officials and soldiers because the white strangers now have Nigerian converts in their groups. Furthermore, the traditional Africans are so upset and distracted by their neighbors' conversion to Christianity that they are blind to the genuine threat: the imperialistic British government officials who seek to usurp power. Joseph McLaren notes that the clan leader Akunna uses analogies to manifest "combined elements of missionary efforts and colonial administration. Akunna's allusion to the District Commissioner as an agent of the British nation is a sign of this connection between church and state" (111). The colonists employ the missionaries, to some extent, as a distraction to their true purpose—imperialism.

After the missionaries arrive, they set up their church in the natives' Evil Forest, a segment of land where the Nigerians leave diseased people to die and where they place twins whom they kill. Twins are considered an abomination in part because the natives believe that a natural birth involves only one baby. Historically, part of the reason why missionaries came to southeastern Nigeria was because they had heard about the supersitious practice of slaughtering twins. Thus, the missionaries come not only to bring the natives Christianity and ultimately to bring British rule, but also to save the lives of twin babies. The problem is exacerbated because the native females give birth to many sets of twins. For example, Nneka is disowned by her husband and in-laws, who permit her to join the Christians, because she has given birth to four sets of twins and thus lost eight children (131). Some scientists believe that the unusually high rate of twins in the culture derives from an excessive eating of yams, the staple "male" crop of the region. Nneka, like other disenfranchised natives, joins the missionaries out of desperation, not out of faith. Because of this desperation, they unwittingly place themselves wholly in the power of the Christian visitors and are used as a weapon against their own people. Another part of the clan is also used by the colonists: the intelligent and intellectually curious natives who want to explore Western culture and receive an education. These people, the brightest and most ambitious in the clan, are targeted by the colonists and separated from the rest of the native inhabitants, enticed with the reward of social advancement through education. However, Kalu Ogbaa notes that in books written by the colonists, Igbo words were misspelled, and the natives were forced to learn the new spellings of words in their own language (104). Ogbaa adds that "as an educated African, indeed, an educated Igbo, Achebe realized early enough that the colonial educational system deliberately did not teach African students things African" (106). The European educational system was designed to entice the natives away from their traditions. Clayton G. MacKenzie says that for these natives, exploring Western tradition and education "promises advancement within the prevailing socio-economic system; for Mr. Brown it accords the opportunity to convert to Christianity those who have entrusted their education to his care.... The knowledge and understanding that Mr. Brown's school seeks to promulgate is openly abrasive to the organization and culture of the clan" (100).

After the natives of Mbanta grant the Evil Forest to the Christians, both sides rejoice and explore. The Christians thank God for the land and eagerly explore it, deciding where to build their church. They clean the area and make it habitable for the first time. Meanwhile, the natives rejoice because they believe that they rid themselves of the Christians. They firmly believe that within a few days, all of the missionaries will be dead because the visitors tread on and explore the land containing the Evil Forest. The narrator comments that when the missionaries continue to explore the Evil Forest and build their church, the natives rationalize

> that their gods and ancestors were sometimes long-suffering and would deliberately allow a man to go on defying them. But even in such cases they set their limit at seven market weeks or twenty-eight days. . . . And so excitement mounted in the village as the seventh week approached since the impudent missionaries built their church in the Evil Forest. The villagers were so certain about the doom that awaited these men that one or two converts thought it wise to suspend their allegiance to the new faith. At last the day came by which all the missionaries should have died. But they were still alive. . . . That week they won a handful more converts. (131)

When the Christians fail to perish as expected, the natives feel compelled to re-evaluate their views on faith. The Nigerians question their faith and wonder why the missionaries succeed and thrive despite the efforts of their gods. They also wonder why the Christian god is more powerful than their gods and successfully protects His adherents. The failure of the natives' gods and the success of the Christian god result in the desire of some Africans to explore the tenets of Christianity and to convert to the new faith, ultimately helping in the British movement to colonize the region.

Achebe demonstrates the effect of these successful conversions in relation to colonization when he describes the behavior of one convert—Enoch. Enoch wishes to manifest his newfound allegiance to the European visitors, so he willfully defies sacred laws of the natives. For instance, he kills and eats the sacred python. Furthermore, he unmasks an *egwugwu*—a current member of the tribe who dresses as, and is supposed to be seen by all people as, the living embodiment of an ancestral hero and spiritual guide. No one is allowed to see the face beneath the mask of an *egwugwu*. By ripping the mask off the head of an *egwugwu*, Enoch destroys the ideology of the natives' religion, suggesting to the Nigerians that their beliefs in the Igbo gods are based on illusion and deception, not faith. Witnessing the unmasking of their faith, the natives must explore other aspects of their religion, an exploration that results in the destruction of Umuo-fia's autonomy and their successful colonization by the British settlers. Some of the natives inevitably will be disillusioned by the unmasking of the illusion surrounding their faith; yet others, such as Okonkwo, exact revenge by burning down the Christian church. The natives who resist European imperialism are kidnapped and humiliated by government officials, fined for burning down the church, and embarrassed when released from prison. The British government's refusal to allow the natives to congregate clearly demonstrates the tyrannical power and imperialistic dominance of the European colonists. Okonkwo commits suicide after slaying a government official who attempted to break up a meeting between the natives. According to Richard Begam, Okonkwo's suicide shows, from Okonkwo's perspective, how "Igbo culture has willingly succumbed to its own annihilation, committing what is a form of collective suicide by submitting to the British" (10–11).

After Okonkwo commits suicide, the District Commissioner wishes to explore more about the natives—not because he cares about them but rather because he is writing a book in which he will write condescendingly about their lives:

> In the many years in which he had toiled to bring civilization to different parts of Africa he had learned a number of things. One of them was that a District Commissioner must never attend to such undignified details as cutting a hanged man from a tree. Such attention would give the natives a poor opinion of him. In the book which he planned to write he would stress that point. . . . The story of this man who had killed a messenger and hanged himself would make interesting reading. One could almost write a whole chapter on him. Perhaps not a whole chapter but a reasonable paragraph, at any rate. (179)

He wants to learn about the culture not because he cares about the people but because he wishes to profit from his book. Begam claims that Igbo culture is no longer seen from the natives' perspective but rather "from the outside as an object of anthropological curiosity, and its collapse is understood not as an African tragedy but as a European triumph . . . [The District Commissioner becomes] a 'student of primitive customs'" (11). The title of his intended book is *The Pacification of the Primitive Tribes of the Lower Niger.* The title indicates unequivocally that the colonist considers the natives to be primitive savages, unequal intellectually and socially to the people of his own culture. That the District Commissioner reduces the life of Okonkwo, which has merited an entire novel by Chinua Achebe, to a mere paragraph, indicates that the Europeans who colonize the African lands feel precious little respect for the native inhabitants.

WORKS CITED AND CONSULTED

Achebe, Chinua. *Things Fall Apart.* New York: Knopf, 1992.

Aguwa, Jude C. "Christianity and Nigerian Indigenous Culture." In *Religion, History, and Politics in Nigeria.* Eds. Chima J. Korieh and G. Ugo Nwokeji. Lanham: University Press of America, 2005. 13–28.

Begham, Richard. "Achebe's Sense of an Ending: History and Tragedy in *Things Fall Apart.*" *Bloom's Modern Critical Interpretations: Chinua Achebe's* Things Fall Apart. Ed. Harold Bloom. Philadelphia: Chelsea House, 2002. 5–18.

Cobham, Rhonda. "Problems of Gender and History in the Teaching of *Things Fall Apart.*" *Bloom's Modern Critical Interpretations: Chinua Achebe's* Things Fall Apart. Ed. Harold Bloom. Philadelphia: Chelsea House, 2002. 19–30.

Falola, Toyin. *Culture and Customs of Nigeria.* Westport: Greenwood, 2001.

Isichei, Elizabeth. "Ibo and Christian Beliefs: Some Aspects of a Theological Encounter." *African Affairs* 68, no. 271 (1969): 121-134.

Jenkins, Philip. *The Next Christendom: The Coming of Global Christianity.* Oxford: University Press, 2002.

MacKenzie, Clayton G. "The Metamorphosis of Piety in Chinua Achebe's *Things Fall Apart.*" *Bloom's Modern Critical Interpretations: Chinua Achebe's* Things Fall Apart. Ed. Harold Bloom. Philadelphia: Chelsea House, 2002. 89–101.

McLaren, Joseph. "Missionaries and Converts: Religion and Colonial Intrusion in *Things Fall Apart.*" *Bloom's Modern Critical Interpretations: Chinua Achebe's* Things Fall Apart. Ed. Harold Bloom. Philadelphia: Chelsea House, 2002.103–112.

Ogbaa, Kalu. *Understanding* Things Fall Apart: *A Student Casebook to Issues, Sources, and Historical Documents.* Westport, CT: Greenwood Press, 1999.

Ogede, Ode. *Achebe's* Things Fall Apart: *A Reader's Guide.* London: Continuum, 2007.

Paas, Steven. *The Faith Moves South: A History of the Church in Africa.* Zombia:
     Kachere, 2006.
Pratten, David. "Conversion, Conquest, and the Qua Iboe Mission."
     Christianity and Social Change in Africa: Essays in Honor of J.D.Y. Peel. Ed.
     Toyin Falola. Durham, NC: Carolina Academic Press, 2005. 413–439.
Sterling, Eric. "Teaching Chinua Achebe's Novel *Things Fall Apart* in Survey
     of English Literature II." *Teaching the Novel Across the Curriculum: A
     Handbook for Educators.* Ed. Colin C. Irvine. Westport, CT: Greenwood
     Press, 2008. 64–72.
Walls, Andrew F. *The Cross-Cultural Process in Christian History: Studies in the
     Transmission and Appropriation of Faith.* Maryknoll, NY: Orbis, 2002.
Wren, Robert M. *Achebe's World: The Historical and Cultural Context of the Novels
     of Chinua Achebe.* Washington, DC: Three Continents Press, 1980.

"UNITED FRUIT CO."
(PABLO NERUDA)

"'United Fruit Co.,' *Canto General*, and Neruda's Critique of Capitalism"
by Jeffrey Gray, Seton Hall University

The Chilean poet and Nobel laureate Pablo Neruda is one of the most famous Latin American poets in history. For a period in the 1950s and 1960s, he was arguably the most famous poet in the world. In his long career, Neruda was variously a love poet, a Symbolist, a surrealist, an elegist, a nature poet, a historical poet, and a political poet. *Canto General*, the collection in which Neruda first published "United Fruit Co.," partakes of all these elements, most especially the historical and political: the subjects of Neruda's poems in *Canto General* span the entire history of the New World, often lamenting the effects of global capitalism on the indigenous people of Latin America. *Canto General* was published in 1950 in Mexico City, with drawings by the great Mexican muralists Diego Rivera and David Alfaro Siqueiros. Indeed, the mural is an appropriate analogy here, not only in the sense that *Canto General* shared Rivera's anti-imperialist ethos, but that the book imitates the mural's epic sweep: beginning with pre-Columbian America, passing through the conquest, tracing the movements toward independence, and extending its reach to the mid-twentieth century, Neruda's collection details oppression. The sections of the book that deal with relatively recent times are among the most famous, especially that section in which "United Fruit Co." appears, depicting a dictators' betrayal of revolutionary aspirations, and emphasizing the hope that lay, for Neruda, in socialism. The poem itself, rich with image and metaphor, is a relatively direct indictment. Its themes, images, and historical references run through many other poems of *Canto General*.

By the time Neruda published *Canto General*, he had already achieved fame as both a surrealist and a love poet—to this day, his most read book is *Twenty Love Poems and a Song of Despair* (*Veinte Poemas de Amor y una Canción Desesperada*), which he wrote at the age of 20. Neruda experienced a major upheaval in his view of the world and the purpose of art during his consularships in Barcelona and Madrid (it was common in twentieth-century Latin America for writers to be appointed to diplomatic posts). This turn began with the Spanish Civil War and, particularly, with the senseless assassination in 1936 of the great Spanish poet and Neruda's friend, Frederico García Lorca. Neruda compromised his position as a diplomat in Spain by taking the Republican side and by writing his first politically engaged book of poems, *Spain in My Heart* (*España en el Corazón*, 1937). It was this artistic and political conversion that eventually led to the writing of *Canto General*.

Having joined the Chilean communist party in 1945, Neruda was given a commission to write an epic on Chile. His early concept of the book, accordingly, was called *Canto General de Chile* (published under that title in 1946). However, motivated by the victory of the fascist forces in Spain and by events in his own country, he soon realized he had to write something larger, "a lyric attempt to confront our whole universe," as he said (qtd. in Belitt 140). The result is *Canto General*— roughly translated "General Song" or "Song for Everyone"—a book engaging not only Chile but all the Americas, embracing its prehistory, geology, and its diverse flora and fauna. Neruda also fills his poems with references to pre-Columbian cultures, the successive eras of the conquistadors, the liberators, and finally the Cold War with its corporate and anti-communist interventions from North to South.

The circumstances under which Neruda wrote *Canto General* inform its content as well as the poet's evolving view of the world. In 1949 Neruda was forced to flee Chile and go into exile after President González Videla, under U.S. pressure, began to shut down unions and persecute communists. Two-thirds of *Canto General* was written in 1948–49 in France, Mexico, Guatemala, and other parts of Europe. All of this—but particularly Neruda's time in Guatemala, where the United Fruit Company had its headquarters—is important for a reading of the poem "United Fruit Co."

The United Fruit Company (UFC) is perhaps the most charged symbol of U.S. political and economic exploitation of Latin America in the twentieth century. From 1899 to 1970, the UFC was a holding company that included 20 different businesses operating in Central and South America and the Caribbean, importing bananas, cocoa, and sugar, among other crops, to markets in the U.S. and Europe. The company, with headquarters in the town of Bananera, Guatemala, was known in Central America as *la frutera* ("the fruit company") or *Mamita Yunay* ("Mommy United"). Exempt from taxes, the company controlled production and exportation as well as railway service, telecommunications, and shipping in Guatemala and in most other countries where it had operations. Its properties included autonomous enclaves with greater power than the national governments. The UFC even used local armies to depose governments it considered hostile to its interests (as happened, with the aid of the CIA, in Guatemala in 1954). The company eventually ran into financial difficulties, changed its name to United Brands, and finally was bought by Del Monte, which runs the operations today, no longer with significant intervention in the affairs of host nations.

The poem "United Fruit Co." forms part of a section titled "The Sand Betrayed," which spans both the nineteenth and twentieth centuries, and includes poems on the theme of betrayal at the hands of conquistadors, politicians, governments, and corporations: "Standard Oil Co." and "Anaconda Copper Mining Co.," for example, precede "United Fruit Co." Related poems include "The Dollar's Lawyers" and "Exploiters." "United Fruit Co." is part of this suite of poems treating a whole procession of landowners, political tyrants, and corporations.

The poem begins wryly with a creation scene in which God himself favors, if not represents, the corporations:

> When the trumpet blared everything
> on earth was prepared
> and Jehovah distributed the world
> to Coca-Cola Inc., Anaconda,
> Ford Motors and other entities:
> United Fruit Inc.
> reserved for itself the juiciest,
> the central seaboard of my land,
> America's sweet waist ... (179)

If the Americas are a human female body, then Central America is that body's "sweet waist," a simile Neruda repeats in two other poems—both called "Central America"—in different sections of *Canto General*. In both cases the anatomical figure suggests the cultural and political vulnerability of the region: *"Bleak year—do you see our geography's / waist beyond the dense shadow / of the forests?"* and "O weeping waist-line" read the lines in one (*CG* 194–5, italics in original); "O, central waistline, O paradise / of implacable wounds" (207) in the other.

The creation scene is followed by a scene of consumption, in which the "juicy" organic riches of the Americas attract greedy dictators the way that "blood and jam" draw flies:

> Trujillo flies, Tacho flies,
> Carías flies, Martínez flies,
> Ubico flies, flies soaked
> in humble blood and jam,
> drunken flies that drone
> over the common graves . . . (179)

The image is tropical: the sticky, sweet substances attracting insects that may carry sickness or death. This scene of infection, parasitism, atrocity, and decadence particularly indicts the deeds of the named historical figures, the dictators who are the topic of still other poems in *Canto General*. For anyone not steeped in the history of the region, they need explanation: Jorge Ubico was president of Guatemala from 1931 to 1944. Neruda gives him his own short poem in "The Sand Betrayed," as he does also Maximiliano Martínez, president of El Salvador, installed by a coup in 1931. Martínez's 1932 anti-communist purge left 40,000 dead and effectively destroyed El Salvador's Indian culture. Three of the other dictators appear in the first lines of "The Satrapies," also from "The Sand Betrayed." Neruda heaps epithets upon them: "voracious hyenas, rodents . . . pandering merchants / of American bread and air . . . / Little vultures received / by Mr. Truman . . ." and much more (*CG* 160–1). These three are, first, Rafael Trujillo, president of the Dominican Republic from 1930, who, through nurturing the sugar companies, became not merely the president but the owner of his country. The second is Nicaragua's Anastasio Somoza (nicknamed "Tacho") and, following his assassination, his sons, Luis and Anastasio ("Tachito"). The "Tachos," through manipulating elections with the support of the U.S., ruled from 1931 to 1979. Finally, Tiburcio Carías is the strong man who, by winning the support of the UFC and imprisoning all opposition, ruled Honduras from 1932 to 1954.

The theme of betrayal in "United Fruit Co.," which connects it to the other poems in "The Sand Betrayed," emerges in the contrast between these new exploitative regimes and what they replaced. They "rebaptized" the Central American lands as "Banana Republics" and established their reign (a "comic opera") upon

> the slumbering corpses,
> upon the restless heroes
> who conquered renown,
> freedom and flags ... (179)

With the collusion of the dictators—the homegrown "bloodthirsty flies"—the UFC is able to ravage the coffee and fruits of entire nations, spiriting away their "submerged land's treasures ..." (179). Note that it is the lands that are submerged (*tierras sumergidas*), not the treasures.

The scene of the closing stanza of the poem is of the seaports'"sugary abysses." Neruda may be thinking here of Puerto Barrios on Guatemala's Caribbean coast, to which the United Fruit Company built a direct railway line from Bananera, and from which produce was shipped to various ports on the south coast of the U.S. The labor force of the United Fruit Company in Bananera was largely Indian. In the last lines of Neruda's poem, the Indians collapse and fall, "buried / in the morning mist":

> a body rolls down, a nameless
> thing, a fallen number,
> a bunch of lifeless fruit
> dumped in the rubbish heap. (179)

The poem ends not only in an indictment of an exploitative and heartless system, but also in the pathos of individual deaths: Indians collapsing from exhaustion while their culture collapses from foreign and internal destabilization. The burden of the poem is not merely a critique of colonialism, and of corrupt puppet regimes, but particularly of capitalism and of its alienation of the worker. The body that has fallen is described in a series of appositives: first as a "nameless thing," then as a "fallen number," and finally as "a bunch of lifeless fruit." The language of "nameless thing" suggests Marxism's central critique of industry: when individuals become things used to calculate profit, the process of alienation, not merely from the means of production but ultimately from the self, is complete. In the last of the three descriptions, the "bunch" (*racimo*) in Spanish does not mean "many," as it might in English, but rather a vegetative clump, as in bananas that grow in bunches. Thus the victim of the violence is both the individual and the group to which he belongs. This is particularly important when the question is one of indigenous people, an issue for many Latin American writers and a problem for Neruda.

Indeed, *Canto General* can be seen as structured around two major conflicts: that between Latin and Anglo America—obvious in a poem such as "United Fruit Co."—and that between Latin Americans and indigenous Indians, a subtler opposition that nevertheless permeates the book.

Neruda once remarked, by way of indicating his sympathies, "For my part I'm not just an Indianist but an Indian" (qtd. in Rovira 33, translation mine). Neruda was not in fact ethnically Indian. He once founded a literary journal called *Araucaria* (with reference to the Araucano Indians native to Chile, today called the Mapuches). The title did not agree with the president, who sent him a message saying, "Change the title or suspend publication. We are not a country of Indians" (qtd. in Covira 133). In spite of this example of Neruda's identification with indigenous people, however, they do not figure in Neruda's first several books. One has to wait until *Canto General*, where they appear immediately, in the italicized introductory poem "*Amor América* 1400," as part of pre-Columbian and almost pre-human Nature, without real contours:

> *Man was dust, earthen vase, an eyelid*
> *Of tremulous loam....* (*CG* 13)

By the end of the poem, the Indian begins to take metaphorical shape:

I searched for you, my father,
Young warrior of darkness and copper

. . . .

Mother cayman, metallic dove.
I, Incan of the loam. . . . (14)

After several pages of sweeping geographical survey, Neruda introduces, in a section called "Man," particular indigenous groups: the
Tarahumaras, Aztecs, Mayas, Tarascos, and Guaraníes, and finally
the Mapuches of Chile. Neruda apparently wished to assume
the role Walt Whitman, his most immediate poetic influence,
had assumed: that of a medium or channel for the spirits of the
oppressed and the forgotten. In *Song of Myself*, Whitman claims,
"Through me many long dumb voices, / Voices of the interminable
generation of prisoners and slaves." In a congruent reversal, Neruda
writes of the Indians, "I come to speak through your dead mouths"
(41). But the phrase "dead mouths" introduces a problem, as do his
lines on the Mapuches, of whom he sees only ghosts and traces, even
though, during his childhood in Temuco, he saw Mapuches every
day. Nevertheless, he speaks of "the warriors' absence," and, repeated
five times, intermittently, "There's no one" (27). Indeed, all Indian
peoples in *Canto General* are presented elegiacally, as vanished,
even while the countries of which he writes have enormous Indian
populations (more than fifty percent in the case of Guatemala).
For Neruda, the Indians were lost to the conquistadors; they are an
absent presence in the Americas.

The second problem with regard to Indians is Neruda's conflation
of Indians with the oppressed proletariat of the world. Numerous
other poems in *Canto General* address Indian peoples: consider "The
Indians" (also part of "The Sand Betrayed"), which traces the Indians'
path from a natural, "immortal dwelling," to the "arid dung heap
of misery . . ." (184). The forces of imperialism and capitalism are
described as invisible cancers that enter Indian civilization almost
undetected until the Indian is forced to pass through

        the only door open to him,
    the door of the other poor, that
of the entire earth's downtrodden. (184)

In such passages, the specificity of the Indians seems often to be veiled by their state of oppression. When Neruda describes the lost Machu Picchu he does so elegiacally. But he does not do so nostalgically, since, for the poet, Machu Picchu was a site of oppression: his focus is on the enslaved victims of the caste system of the Incas. The Indians of Central or South America, however, do not constitute an urban proletariat as Marx and Lenin envisioned; they are a rural agricultural people who have sometimes been drafted into servitude by multinational corporations. (I am speaking here of Neruda's perspective, since apologists for the UFC would certainly point out that laborers for this company were paid better than their peers working elsewhere in Guatemala.) As Kuhnheim remarks: "the indigenous people function as a metaphor for workers and the dispossessed" (65). Neruda never altered these two views of the Indians in his work: as vanished victims and as exploited workers.

"The world has changed and my poetry has changed," Neruda wrote (March 1939, epigraph to "Las furias y las penas," *Tercera Residencia* II [*OC* 230]). Neruda's experiences in the first months of the Spanish Civil War ended his poetic self-absorption forever, purging his poetry of its Symbolist and Romantic elements. His poem "Let Me Explain a Few Things" ("Explico unas cosas"), implicitly renounces the introspective self in favor of a commitment to realism and the material life of the people. The "I" of that poem, as of later poems, became subsumed in the physical abundance of a public world, the marketplace, foods, sensations, voices, agglomerations, the beating of hands and feet. This evocation of a public life is not in itself, however, necessarily a "political" move. His *Elemental Odes* (*Odas Elementales*), for example, are not political in the way that, say, "United Fruit Co." or "Standard Oil Co." are political.

In a 1971 Canadian interview only recently translated from the French, Neruda rejects the category of "political poet": "I am only the echo in a certain part of my poetry of the anxieties of the contemporary world, of the anxieties of the Latin American world. But I refuse to be classified as a political poet" (Bockstael). He goes on to say that "reactionary poets and writers"—those "who have never made contact with the feelings of their people ... or [who have] preached a poetry far removed from a certain pressing reality" are the real political poets (Bockstael). Moreover, he remarks that "the part of my work that one can call political or social, it doesn't make up a fourth or a fifth part" (Bockstael).

As regards those poets who are *not* in "contact with the feelings of their people," Neruda took, in *Canto General*, the Soviet view. He heaps invective on what he calls "Celestial Poets," calling them "false existentialist / sorcerers, surrealist / butterflies," "cadavers of fashion," "pale worms of capitalist cheese," and so on. He asks rhetorically what such writers did when the people needed them, and answers, "You did nothing but flee . . ." (*CG* 166–167).

Looking over the long arc of Neruda's work, it can be argued that the historical-political preoccupation, essential though it was in the poet's development, does indeed occupy a relatively minor space. Nevertheless, given the monumentality of the single volume *Canto General*—that is, the book's size as well as its historical significance— the theme cannot be ignored. It contains some of Neruda's greatest poetry as well as some of his greatest errors. For, in spite of his vast experience and world travel, and in spite of his informed critique of international capitalism, Neruda was sometimes naïve. He remained a staunch supporter of Stalin (see "On the Death of Stalin," *CG*), even after the truth of the Gulags had emerged. He also unquestioningly embraced Castro: "Fidel, Fidel, the people are grateful / for word in action and deeds that sing," he wrote. One of the last poems of *Canto General* warns North America: "But if you arm your hordes" to attack us, "we'll rise from the stones . . . we'll rise to burn you in hell" (266). He says the same regarding any U.S. incursion in France, Spain, Greece, Venezuela, Argentina, Peru, Nicaragua, Puerto Rico, Cuba, Mexico, China, and Russia. Indeed, the poem is a catalogue of threats directed at the United States, ending with the nuclear threat, among Neruda's most embarrassing moments:

> And from the laboratory covered with vines
> the unleashed atom will also set forth
> toward your proud cities. (269)

When a leftist movement swept Chile in the 1960s, Neruda was able to return and participate in the government once more. Indeed, he was nominated for president but stood down in favor of Salvador Allende, who, in 1970, became the world's first democratically elected Marxist president. Not long after, because of the prospect of national- ization, the CIA intervened and with the help of the Chilean military, deposed Allende (who disappeared, his death undetermined), and in

1973 installed August Pinochet, one of the most brutal dictators Latin
America has known. Neruda died of cancer, certainly aggravated by deep
disappointment, shortly after the coup. He had seen all this before—the
toppling of a democratically elected leftist president—in Guatemala.

Neruda's love poems, wide travel, political persecution, and many
love affairs all contributed to his fame. Two decades after Neruda's
death, Michael Radford's film *Il Postino,* based on a novella about
Neruda (*Ardiente Paciencia*), by his compatriot Antonio Skármeta,
renewed his appeal and introduced him to millions who had not
known his work. The film, however, depoliticizes the novel, which was
originally set not in Italy in the 1950s, but in Chile at the time of the
death of Allende.

Neruda's readership in the English-speaking world has always been
large, as regards both the political and the love poetry. But the U.S.
is not a country that has produced, as a rule, politically explicit poets.
One can single out poets such as Adrienne Rich, Allen Ginsberg,
Muriel Rukeyser and others, but poems with titles such as "Anaconda
Copper Mining Inc." or "United Fruit Co."—explicit critiques of
specific events or institutions—are seldom found in the North. In
Latin America they are less rare. One thinks of Ernesto Cardenal in
Nicaragua with his poems on the Somozas, or the Guatemalan poet
Otto Rene Castillo. Neruda's love poetry will continue to be read by
millions. It would be unfortunate if some of the best "political" poetry
in *Canto General* were not also remembered.

Neruda's mission was to reassert the vision of an organic society
in which artists and poets addressed the concerns of common people.
In Neruda's view, the role of the romantic poet—of Keats, Goethe,
or Hugo—had been lost with the emergence of the industrial bour-
geoisie. In this connection, the title *Canto General* suggests Neruda's
critique of the mutual isolation of the nations of Latin America, where
it is possible to know everything about the United States and nothing
about your neighboring countries. Neruda saw the struggles of Latin
American people as a single cause. *Canto General* poignantly demonstrates and passionately argues for this view.

WORKS CITED

Belitt, Ben. "Pablo Neruda: A Revaluation." *Modern Critical Views: Pablo
    Neruda.* Ed. Harold Bloom. New York: Chelsea, 1989. 139–166.

Bockstael, Eric. "An Interview with Pablo Neruda." *Memorious* 4 (2009). www.memorious.org.

Brotherston, Gordon. "Neruda's *Canto General* and the Great Song of America." *Modern Critical Views: Pablo Neruda.* Ed. Harold Bloom. New York: Chelsea, 1989. 117–130.

Cortázar, Julio. "Neruda Among Us." *Modern Critical Views: Pablo Neruda.* Ed. Harold Bloom. New York: Chelsea, 1989. 83–92.

Kuhnheim, Jill. "Quests for Alternative Cultural Antecedents: The Indigenism of Pablo Neruda, Ernesto Cardenal, and Gary Snyder." *Pablo Neruda and the U.S. Culture Industry.* Ed. Teresa Longo. New York: Routledge, 2002. 61–81.

McCard, Victoria L. "El Banquete Nerudiano." *Literatura y Lingüística* 10 (1997). Santiago, Chile. No p.#.

Neruda, Pablo. *Canto General.* Trans. Jack Schmitt. Berkeley: U California P, 1991.

———. *Obras Completas.* Ed. Hernán Loyola. 5 volumes. Barcelona: Galaxia Gutemberg-Círculo de Lectores, 1999–2002.

Rovira, José Carlos. *Neruda: Testigo de un Siglo.* Madrid: Centro de Lingüística Aplicada Atenea, 2007.

Santí, Enrico. *Pablo Neruda: The Poetics of Prophecy.* Ithaca: Cornell UP, 1982.

WAITING FOR THE BARBARIANS
(J.M. COETZEE)

"*Waiting For the Barbarians:*
Narrative, History, and the Other"
by Lorena Russell, University of
North Carolina at Asheville

Written by South African novelist J. M. Coetzee during South Africa's period of apartheid, *Waiting for the Barbarians* is not set in South Africa, but rather broadly conveys events taking place during the sunset years of an (unnamed and unspecified) "Empire." The scene of this decline is alternately marked by extremes of violence and torpidity as the Empire battles to keep the "Barbarians" at bay. The narrative unfolds within the context of this struggle between Empire and Barbarians, exposing a number of ideological and psychological dynamics central to colonialism. The storyline itself is simple enough: a civil servant learns to question authority in the twilight of a repressive regime. But in the telling of the story, the text employs narrative devices that draw the reader into complex considerations of power and knowledge central to exploration, imperialism, and colonization; postcolonial issues largely centered on the distance between Self and Other.

Set in an outpost settlement on the borders of an ill-defined Empire, the story is narrated from the perspective of an unnamed Magistrate, a judicial official whose goal at the opening of the story is to live out his days quietly and simply until his pending retirement. At the opening of the story, the Magistrate knows enough to doubt any official story that is sent down from the government, but is nevertheless content to carry out his role as judge. When officials spread stories of increasing raids, rape, and ravishment, he wisely weighs the rumors against his own experience, noting, "Of this unrest I myself saw nothing" (8). He quietly develops his own understanding of the "Barbarians" through private excavations of their ancient dwellings, and even though he fails to decipher the scripted slips of wood he covets, he comes to understand that they are a quiet people—fishermen, nomads, and tent dwellers—far from the bloodthirsty Barbarians the official stories and associated rumors describe.

The Magistrate can live with this basic incongruity until a turn of events forces him to engage with the bodily suffering the Empire can inflict on its erstwhile enemies. When the sadistic official Colonel Joll comes to town and instigates torture and interrogation against some helpless captives, the Magistrate's position vis-à-vis the Empire shifts. Although he has lived quietly as a servant of the law up until this point, it is when he recognizes the physical sufferings of the Barbarians that his faith in the system is undermined. This shift in the Magistrate's position creates a crisis of conscience. It confirms his increasing awareness of how the Empire maintains itself through its projected fears of Barbarians, implying that these identity categories may in some sense be purely relational, existing in the realm of language, outside of history. At the same time, he is confronted with the bodily evidence of death and torture: the material suffering of colonialism.

As Coetzee puts it, *Waiting for the Barbarians* is centrally about a basically decent, but nonheroic man, "about the impact of the torture chamber on the life of a man of conscience" ("Into the Dark Chamber: The Writer and the South African State" 363). Once the Magistrate has knowledge of Colonel Joll's methods, it leads him towards a broader understanding of the injustice of the Empire he serves, and he is shifted, in effect, towards a different subject position: "I know somewhat too much; and from this knowledge, once one has been infected, there seems to be no recovering. I ought never to have taken my lantern to see what was going on in the hut by the granary" (*Waiting for the Barbarians* 21). As Samuel Durrant describes it, "[t]he Magistrate's crisis of consciousness/conscience is ultimately a crisis of knowledge: although his mind is now radically opened up to the existence of otherness, this existence still remains inaccessible to him . . ." (44). Thus, his knowledge of the torture precipitates his growing understanding of otherness and difference, but he is nevertheless left outside the experience and full knowledge of the Other.

Much of the story engages the Magistrate's varied and basically unsuccessful attempt to close this gap and to "know" the other. He enters into a relationship with one of Joll's victims, a young woman who is left behind after the rest of her people leave. This woman, known only as "the Barbarian girl," becomes a key figure in the text. Her body bears the traces of the violence it endured: she is blinded and terribly crippled from having her feet smashed with a hammer and eyes scarred with a hot poker. As though to make amends for her suffering, the Magistrate takes her into his apartment. There he begins ritual bathings, massages her feet and legs, shares her bed, but (to his own surprise) falls short of having sexual intercourse with her:

> First comes the ritual of the washing, for which she is now naked. I wash her feet, as before, her legs, her buttocks. My soapy hand travels between her thighs, incuriously, I find. She raises her arms while I wash her armpits. I wash her belly, her breasts. I push her hair aside and wash her neck, her throat. She is patient. I rinse and dry her. (30)

These ritual cleansings and massages inevitably devolve into a deep sleep, where he experiences a number of disquieting dreams broadly representative of his search to know the Other who appears as a hooded girl. The expected activity of sexual play is displaced instead by his ministrations, surface probing and a sequential flaccid torpor and oblivion.

While the Magistrate was in the habit of enjoying affairs with a number of the servant women in the compound, this relationship is different. According to David Attwell, the Magistrate's lack of sex signals a change in his power relationships: "In disallowing penetration, therefore, Coetzee both acknowledges and refuses to perpetuate these generalized implications of dominance" ("Politics" 79). Despite the woman's attempted seduction, the Magistrate's obsessive ministrations are stripped of any erotic desire. It is not until they have left the world of the compound that they have sex, and this event is passed over without much comment. For the most part in his relationship with the girl, he is driven instead by his need to understand the girl's pain and her personal history (here one should consider the pun on the sexual nuances of the verb "to know"). He struggles in vain to remember what she looked like before the torture, but cannot summon an image. His dreams are haunted by her hooded figure. He fingers her misshapen ankles, and attempts to read the scarring at the corner of her eyes. He yearns for knowledge, yet remains unsatisfied: "until the marks on this girl's body are deciphered and understood I cannot let go of her" (31).

These scenes invite readers to consider power dynamics between victim and oppressor on several levels, yet offer no certain answers. Instead, the relationship is marked by a deep ambivalence and frustration. In spite of his seeming good intentions, the Magistrate's actions nevertheless reenact the oppressiveness of the Empire, a dynamic of which he is aware: "with this woman it is as if there is no interior, only a surface across which I hunt back and forth seeking entry. Is this how her torturers felt hunting their secret, whatever they thought it was?" (43). While the rituals enacted on the girl's body fall short of sexual domination, there is still a strange, erotic energy underlying their engagement, and the obvious difference of his status as an imperial official, and the girl's status as a displaced Barbarian. Despite the supplication that seems to be implied through the Magistrate's compulsive foot washing, he remains, as Barbara Eckstein notes, separate from the woman and from any language that could connect: "he is not the humbled and perfect Christ. He cannot read her, and she cannot put her pain into words he understands" (Eckstein 188). The distance between the two remains.

Eckstein's useful reading of the frustration at the center of the Magistrate's efforts to "know" the Other depends largely on the observations of Elaine Scarry, whose book, *The Body in Pain: The Making and Unmaking of the World*, explores the intersection of bodily pain and language. For Scarry, pain is characterized by its very private and incommunicative quality: "it is to the individual experiencing it overwhelmingly present, more emphatically real than any other human experience, and yet is almost invisible to anyone else, unfelt, and unknown" (55). It is pain's very quality of inexpressibility combined with the intensity with which it is experienced that marks the limits of intersubjective exchange, what Scarry describes as "this absolute split between one's sense of one's own reality and the reality of other persons" (4). In the novel, the Magistrate comes to realize this "absolute split" between himself and the girl: "These bodies of hers and mine are diffuse, gaseous, centreless, at one moment spinning about a vortex here, at another curdling, thickening elsewhere; but often also flat, blank, I know what to do with her no more than one cloud in the sky knows what to do with another" (34). What should be real, absolute and ultimately knowable is instead unknowable and itself unstable, ultimately unrepresentable.

Upon his realization that he will never successfully decipher the Barbarian woman, the Magistrate decides to return her to her people. He gathers a small party and they set out into the harsh environment of the frontier. There they fight storms and lose horses to exhaustion, and finally, they meet up with a group of Barbarians who accept the girl. Before this point, the Magistrate and the girl (at her instigation) have sex, yet this moment is still marked with the same ambivalence that plagues the Magistrate in all his dealings with the Barbarians:

> ... it has not escaped me that in bed in the dark the marks her torturers have left upon her, the twisted feet, the half-blind eyes, are easily forgotten. Is it then the case that it is the whole woman I want, that my pleasure in her is spoiled until these marks on her are erased and she is restored to herself; or is it the case ... that it is the marks on her which draw me to her but which, to my disappointment, I find, do not go deep enough.... is it she I want or the traces of a history her body bears? (64).

Upon returning to the town, he finds that the war against the Barbarians has been reinstituted, and now the Magistrate, in part by virtue of his expedition and contact with the Barbarians, is himself arrested as a suspected spy. When he tries to intervene against the public beating of prisoners, he is himself subjected to beatings, but not before he defends himself and the Barbarians as "miracle[s] of creation" (107). Beyond claiming a shared humanity, he extends his sense of grace to all living creatures: "It occurs to me that we crush insects beneath our feet, miracles of creation too, beetles, worms, cockroaches, ants, in their various ways" (107). This broadening sensibility of an animal ethic points towards another persistent theme that runs through many of Coetzee's writings, including *Disgrace*, *The Lives of Animals*, and *Elizabeth Costello*.

There is little reward for the Magistrate's broadening ethical sensibility. The next section of the novel follows the Magistrate's term of imprisonment, deprivations, and regime of torture. He is cruelly beaten and sickened, allowed to fester in his filth until his previous position in the town is forgotten, and the people regard him as subhuman. In one penultimate act of torture and humiliation, he is made to wear a woman's smock and then hung and beaten. He cries out in a voice quite beyond language: "From my throat comes the first mournful dry bellow ... I bellow again and again, there is nothing I can do to stop it" (121). The townspeople watch, delighted with the spectacle of the suspended Magistrate: "That is barbarian language you hear," they mock (121).

This moment implies the impossibility of one entering into the experience or the pain of another, either imaginatively, cognitively, linguistically, or on the level of the body, thus reiterating Elaine Scarry's central point. Even though the Magistrate experiences the pain of torture and the injustice of the Empire, he does not ultimately have access to the Other because they do not share a common language. As Michael Moses summarizes,

> The 'language' that connects the civilized magistrate with the barbarian victims of the [Empire] proves indistinguishable from the subhuman roar of a tortured animal body. The unmediated and prehistorical language of men and beasts naturally contains no discrete or articulate words; in such a tongue the name of justice cannot be spoken. (127)

Paradoxically, the language that would connect him with the other is really no language at all, even as it bonds him with all animals through an ethics of mutuality and recognition.

In the conclusion of the novel, the Empire slowly abandons its claims on the town, and the troops depart while a tattered remnant of citizens remains. In a precarious situation with dwindling rations, the Magistrate resumes a marginalized version of his previous official position. He helps the people prepare for the challenges of the future, but in the final moments of the story he is lost in a passive reverie, staring at a snowman. Throughout the narrative, the Magistrate had slipped into any number of seemingly prophetic dreams of a hooded figure in the snow, yet the meanings remain elusive and enigmatic. In the conclusion, he admits his failure as a reader, "feeling stupid" as he stares upon the nonreflective face of the snowman, "like a man who has lost his way long ago but presses on along a road that may lead nowhere" (156).

This lack of a satisfying conclusion is typical enough in post-modern fiction, but for David Attwell the open-ended nature of Coetzee's conclusion further implies that "[w]hat is renounced is the large agenda, the need for final conclusions" (86). Barbara Eckstein, in a cautiously optimistic reading, notes how the conclusion reiterates the theme of humility, and links that potentially redemptive quality with the Magistrate's growing understanding of his own limitations: "'feeling stupid' is neither despair nor humiliation. It is the absence of controlling language and disembodied certainty. It is humility, the humility he tried to achieve by the gesture of washing the girl's crip-pled feet" (198). The Magistrate does come to realize his complicity with the dynamics of power even as he tried to relate to the girl: "I was not, as I liked to think, the indulgent pleasure-loving opposite of the cold rigid Colonel. I was the lie that Empire tells itself when times are easy, he the truth that Empire tells when harsh winds blow" (135). In times of peace, states can maintain themselves through ethics and compassion; in times of war, states depend on war and torture. Either way, the state goes on.

Coetzee is consistently concerned in his writings—at least in his earlier works—with the role and expectations surrounding the writer in South Africa. He defends the division between history and fiction, noting that too often novels have been treated as appendages to historical record, with a premium put on realism as a preferred mode of fictional discourse ("The Novel Today" 2–3). If judged against standards of realism, *Waiting for the Barbarians* would be a failure. It teaches very little about the specifics of lived experi-ence within South Africa. Paul Rich, for example critiques the text because it fails to engage the specifics of racial difference, calling the novel "a moral dead end" (389). Most critics, however, praise the novel's postmodern and allegorical approach to the complexities of the postcolonial predicament.

For Bill Ashcroft, the ambivalence in the novel productively links to irony. He follows the works of Linda Hutcheon to explore how "[w]hat we detect in Coetzee's novels is that the subject, which is in most respects *subjected* to the dominant discourse, can act in resistance by making use of the fractures which open up within it" (102). Ashcroft describes the Magistrate's position as "profoundly ambiguous. His face turned in two directions, he is both judge and judged, law and transgressor, protector and enemy, imperial official and imperial outcast. He is, in fact, an embodiment of the profound and disabling ambivalence of imperial rule, of imperial discourse itself" (Ashcroft 104). It is only within this ironical relationship that resistance is possible, and this resistance, as is the case in *Waiting for the Barbarians*, ultimately remains ambivalent and incomplete.

Susan Gallagher links the allegorical ambivalence in the novel to its general comment on its careful approach to torture: "Coetzee's unusual combination of allegory, often thought to be a precise technique, and a text full of gaps, absences and uncertainties represents in part his solution to the moral issue of how a novelist should treat torture in fiction" (Gallagher 278). Samuel Durrant also links the novel's postmodern style to what it contributes to our understanding of discourse and torture: " ... *Waiting for the Barbarians* ... is the novel that most explicitly dramatizes the question of how to address oneself to a history that remains inaccessible even in the very moment of its occurrence. ... The novel forces us to consider our own relation to the history of torture, as part of a history that takes place 'out of sight'" (451).

For Coetzee, the darkened space of the torture chamber is akin to the imaginative world of the author, thereby linking the work of the author and that of the State in problematic ways: "The dark, forbidden chamber is the origin of novelistic fantasy per se; in creating an obscenity, in enveloping it in mystery, the state unwittingly creates the preconditions for the novel to set about its work of representation" ("Into the Dark Chamber" 365). Approaching torture directly within the detailed and mimetic mode of realism could trap the author into replicating the dynamic of horror and intimidation upon which interrogation depends. The ambivalence and allegory in *Waiting for the Barbarians* effectively short-circuit any easy sense of knowledge, and communicate the complexities of the relationship between the state and its subjects.

Furthermore, the thematic pairing of Colonel Joll and the Magistrate point to the ways in which the ideologies of the state are replicated in the darkened spaces of the boudoir. As Angela Carter argues in her essay on pornography and power, people like to think that consensual sexual acts are driven purely by our private desires, but in fact, these acts are largely informed by a broader ideological context. Carter writes:

> Flesh is not an irreducible human universal. Although the erotic relationship may seem to exist freely, on its own terms, among the distorted social relationships of a bourgeois society, it is, in fact, the most self-conscious of all human relationships, a direct confrontation of two beings whose actions in the bed are wholly determined by their acts when they are out of it. (Carter 9)

Thus, while the Magistrate sought a space outside of history, a pastoral retreat in the darkened spaces of his chamber, he nevertheless had to confront how his private relationship with the blind woman was in fact determined by the broader historical relationship between the Empire and the Barbarians, a position he deplores but cannot escape:

> [W]hat has made it impossible for us to live in time like fish in water, like birds in air, like children? It is the fault of the Empire! Empire has created the time of history. Empire has located its existence not in the smooth recurrent spinning time of the cycle of the season but in the jagged time of rise and fall, of beginning and end, of catastrophe. Empire dooms itself to live in history and plot against history. (133)

The Magistrate is a product of this history, and although he comes close to a realization of an underlying suffering that unites all sentient beings, he is nevertheless unable to sustain this vision, or to imagine a different future from his stance within the Empire.

The specter of history and the materiality of bodily suffering are thus intimately connected with the novel's persistent concerns with language, ideologies and meanings, and remind us of the gap between lived experience and representations. Coetzee does not deny historical reality; he merely resists the simple and straightforward narrative forms in which history tends to be written. As Laura Wright observes, "Coetzee's novels never exclude this historical reality from which they are drawn: instead, Coetzee's rhetorical choices simply deny that there

is merely one way to tell *any* story, including the stories of colonization, apartheid, and democracy in South Africa" (2). *Waiting for the
Barbarians* thus leads readers towards a critique of those narrative
forms that replicate the vagaries and imperatives of Empire.

Dereck Attridge warns against strict allegorical readings of the
novel whereby the meanings of the text are neatly mapped onto events
in South African politics. His reader-centered approach focuses on
the formal elements of the narrative structure, and generates some fine
interpretations of the text. A large part of *Waiting for the Barbarians'*
allegorical value is that it can be applied broadly to a range of situations. Apartheid-era South Africa is not the only place where citizens
find themselves living in a regime engaged in human rights violations.
As Patrick Lenta points out, the themes of the novel hold special
implications for United States' citizens during the Bush era, when
state-sanctified torture techniques were implemented as part of the
"War on Terror." The broadly allegorical and ambivalent nature of the
story—with its ill-defined characters, incoherent meanings, and frus-
trated struggle towards empathy—points to the complexity of truly
knowing the Other, offering readers a range of potential approaches
to understanding the complex relationship between the colonizer and
the colonized in the postcolonial world.

Works Cited

Ashcroft, Bill. "Irony, Allegory and Empire: *Waiting for the Barbarians* and *In
the Heart of the Country.*" *Critical Essays on J. M. Coetzee.* Ed. Kossew, Sue.
Critical Essays on World Literature. New York: G. K. Hall & Co., 1998.
100–16.

Attridge, Derek. "Against Allegory: *Waiting for the Barbarians* and *Life & Times
of Michael K.*" *J.M. Coetzee & the Ethics of Reading: Literature in the Event.*
Chicago: University of Chicago Press, 2004. 32–64.

Attwell, David. *J. M. Coetzee: South African and the Politics of Writing.* Berkeley:
U California P, 1993.

Carter, Angela. *The Sadeian Woman and the Ideology of Pornography.* 1st
American ed. New York: Pantheon Books, 1978.

Coetzee, J. M. "Into the Dark Chamber: The Writer and the South African
State." *Doubling the Point: Essays and Interviews.* Ed. Attwell, David.
Cambridge, MA: Harvard UP, 1992. 361–68.

———. "The Novel Today." *Upstream* 6 1 (1988): 2–5.

————. *Waiting for the Barbarians*. New York: Penguin Books, 1982.

Durrant, Sam. *Postcolonial Narrative and the Work of Mourning: J. M. Coetzee, Wilson Harris, and Toni Morrison*. Suny Series: Explorations in Postcolonial Studies. Albany, NY: State U of New York P, 2003.

Durrant, Samuel. "Bearing Witness to Apartheid: J. M. Coetzee's Inconsolable Works of Mourning." *Contemporary Literature* 40.3 (1999): 430–63.

Eckstein, Barbara. "The Body, the Word, and the State: J. M. Coetzee's *Waiting for the Barbarians*." *NOVEL: A Forum on Fiction* 22.2 (1989): 175–98.

Gallagher, Susan Van Zanten. "Torture and the Novel: J. M. Coetzee's *Waiting for the Barbarians*." *Contemporary Literature* 29.2 (1988): 277–85.

Lenta, Patrick. "*Waiting for the Barbarians* after September 11." *Journal of Postcolonial Writing* 42 (May 2006): 71–83.

Moses, Michael Valdez. "The Mark of Empire: Writing, History and Torture in J. M. Coetzee's *Waiting for the Barbarians*." *Kenyon Review* 15.1 (1993): 115–27.

Rich, Paul. "Apartheid and the Decline of the Civilization Idea: An Essay on Nadine Gordimer's *July's People* and J. M. Coetzee's *Waiting for the Barbarians*." *Research in African Literatures* 15.3 (1984): 365–93.

Scarry, Elaine. *The Body in Pain: The Making and Unmaking of the World*. Oxford and New York: Oxford UP, 1985.

Wright, Laura. *Writing 'Out of All the Camps': J. M. Coetzee's Narratives of Displacement*. Studies in Major Literary Authors. Ed. Cain, William E. New York & London: Routledge, 2006.

WIDE SARGASSO SEA (JEAN RHYS)

"Exploration and Colonization in *Wide Sargasso Sea*"
by Merritt Moseley, University of North Carolina at Asheville

Jean Rhys's 1966 novel *Wide Sargasso Sea* offers, at first reading, an exemplary fictional treatment of colonization, imperialism, and exploitation. Set in the 1830s, it depicts the decline of a Creole family living in Jamaica, whose lives become increasingly difficult and uncomfortable after the abolition of the slavery on which their wealth depended. The daughter, Antoinette Cosway, is the focal figure of Rhys's novel. Made a near-orphan by the death of her father and the madness of her mother, and near-homeless by the burning of her childhood home, she becomes an object of exploitation through marriage. She is, in effect, sold to an Englishman whose affection rapidly changes from love to hate. He deliberately torments her, and even renames her: Bertha Mason. In the last section of the novel he takes her from the only environment she has known back to England, where he imprisons her. Her last act, rendered impressionistically as a vivid dream, is to burn down the house in which she has been held. Her unnamed husband has colonized her, helped himself to her money, robbed her of her place in the world, and driven her to death. It is tempting to see the husband and Antoinette as metonymic figures for the "mother country" and the colony, the metropolis and the subaltern.

That is a perfectly valid reading of *Wide Sargasso Sea*, though a more nuanced understanding of the novel must take into account its relation to another book, Charlotte Brontë's (1847) *Jane Eyre*, for Rhys's novel is a response to and a rebuttal of Brontë's.

Jane Eyre is a bildungsroman, focusing on the growth toward maturity of a young orphan who is mistreated by the relatives with whom she lives; survives and to some extent flourishes in a brutal boarding school; then takes a position as governess in a gentleman's manor house. She gradually falls in love with its owner, Edward Rochester, though his love for a woman who is not only his paid employee but (as they both agree) "disconnected, poor, and plain" (Brontë 157), is improbable. On their wedding day, Jane learns that Rochester has a living wife, insane to the point of bestiality, immured in an upstairs room. This discovery explains various gothic details of Jane's time at Thornfield: an unearthly laughter, an arson attack on Mr. Rochester and the knifing of a house guest, and the appearance in Jane's bedroom of a purple-faced specter who rips up her wedding veil, all of which had been rather implausibly blamed on one of the servants. Despite Rochester's appeals to Jane to live with him as his wife, in defiance of the law, and despite Jane's strong temptation to do so, she leaves him and makes a new life for herself in another part of Britain. There she is courted by her cousin, a neurotic clergyman, but she escapes his attentions when she hears a supernatural appeal from Rochester. When Jane returns to Thornfield, she finds his home burned down. Though he has been maimed in the fire (blinded and with one arm disabled) and is depressed and abashed, his living wife perished in the blaze, so he is now eligible to marry her. As Jane says, in one of the most famous lines in Victorian fiction, "Reader, I married him" (448).

Jane is the narrator of her story, and of course the main character, and readers have tended to identify strongly with her in her longing for love. As a little girl she insists to her unfeeling aunt, "You think I have no feelings, and that I can do without one bit of love or kindness; but I cannot live so" (31). She finds the love of a man like Rochester compensation for the unhappiness she has endured, and in this emotional economy, the presence of Mrs. Rochester figures as a narrative obstacle. Jane has a moment of sympathy for her, when she scolds Mr. Rochester, then in the full flow of explaining his wife's degeneration, "you are inexorable for that unfortunate lady; you speak of her with hate—with vindictive antipathy. It is cruel—she cannot help being mad" (298–99), but generally the account Rochester gives of his marriage seems designed to exculpate him and to demonize his wife.

"Her relatives encouraged me," he insists to Jane; "competitors piqued me; she allured me: a marriage was achieved almost before I knew where I was . . . I never loved, I never esteemed, I did not even know her" (303). And this explanation of his marriage is followed by his account of how he discovered that his wife was insane, or morally mad, and possessed of alcoholic and erotic "giant propensities" that she, and increasingly he, could not control (304). It is a harrowing account.

For various reasons, one of which was certainly her identification with Bertha Mason rather than with Jane Eyre, Rhys objected to Brontë's depiction of the first Mrs. Rochester. Rhys grew up in the island of Dominica, in the British West Indies; she was the child of a Welsh doctor and a (white) Creole mother. And in letters and interviews she credits her reaction to Bertha Mason as the seed of *Wide Sargasso Sea*: "I've never believed in Charlotte's lunatic; that's why I wrote this book" (*Letters* 296); "the Creole in Charlotte Brontë's novel is a lay figure—repulsive which does not matter, and not once alive which does . . ." (*Letters* 156). In her fullest statement, she told an interviewer in 1979:

> When I read *Jane Eyre* as a child, I thought, why should she think Creole women are lunatics and all that? What a shame to make Rochester's first wife, Bertha, the awful madwoman, and I immediately thought I'd write the story as it might really have been. She seemed such a poor ghost. I thought I'd try to write her a life. (Vreeland 235)

In telling Bertha's story, Rhys makes a few adjustments. One is to set the novel just at the point where the freeing of slaves has radically changed the position of West Indies' families like the Masons. Another symbolically powerful change is to stipulate that Bertha Mason's real name is Antoinette Cosway. Her mother's second husband, Mr. Mason, supplies the new last name, but Antoinette "becomes" Bertha through an imperious and even imperialist act of aggression by her husband. Antoinette reports, "He never calls me Antoinette now. He has found out it was my mother's name" (113) and later the husband reports this dialogue:

"Don't laugh like that, Bertha."
"My name is not Bertha; why do you call me Bertha?"
"Because it is a name I'm particularly fond of. I think of
you as Bertha." (135)

It is hard to know what tone this name would have carried to a
contemporary of Brontë's. But twentieth-century readers would likely
regard the transition from Antoinette to Bertha as an act of malice on
the part of the namer.

Is Antoinette Cosway a lunatic because she is a Creole? Though
Charlotte Brontë was not innocent of xenophobia, Jane Eyre does not
place the blame for Bertha's insanity on her place of origin. The novel
does seem, however, to invite readers to accept Rochester's account
of his wife's madness. That is, she is the daughter of a woman who is
insane, and the evidence that it is hereditary comes from the mental
fragility of one brother and the fact that the other is a "complete
dumb idiot" (insanity and retardation apparently are regarded as the
same). Heredity, however poorly it may function as an explanation of
madness (and Rhys differs very sharply from Brontë on the etiology of
Bertha's mental disorders), is not geographic determination. But there
may be some of that nevertheless, as Sue Thomas explains:

> The discourse of white Creole moral degeneracy could offer
> Brontë a type, which might be construed as perverse, in
> accordance with James Cowles Prichard's theory of moral
> madness (Grudin 147). "There is a phase of insanity," Charlotte
> Brontë explains to W. S. Williams on 4 January 1848, "which
> may be called moral madness, in which all that is good or even
> human seems to disappear from the mind, and a field-nature
> replaces it. The sole aim and desire of the being thus possessed is
> to exasperate, to molest, to destroy, and preternatural ingenuity
> and energy are often exercised to that dreadful end. . . ." (3–4).

Thomas goes on to support the theory that Brontë associated this
moral madness (which contemporary theory assigned mostly to
women) with Creoles and life in the West Indies.

In *Wide Sargasso Sea* Rhys "writes back" against an act of colonial
expropriation. In the story, the Englishman is the colonial oppressor,
who comes to Jamaica only to exploit. His standard of judgment is that

of English life: "Everything is too much, I felt as I rode wearily after her. Too much blue, too much purple, too much green. The flowers too red, the mountains too high, the hills too near. And the woman is a stranger" (70). At their idyllic honeymoon retreat, he judges, "It was a beautiful place—wild, untouched, above all untouched, with an alien, disturbing, secret loveliness" (87). He sets about to make his surroundings more nearly correspond to what he considers normal and controllable: hence his strictures on the way the servants are treated, hence his ideas about the proper use of scent—and hence Antoinette must become Bertha.

Rhys's placement of Jamaica at the center of her narrative is one modernizing change, as she reenvisions the story of Jane Eyre. Another is her radically different explanation of the heroine's madness. In *Jane Eyre*, Rochester supplied an account of his wife's madness that nothing in the text contests: she inherited her insanity from her mother and the "idiocy" of one brother and the "feeble mind" of the other are further evidence that the madness is hereditary and inexorable. That Rochester saw no warnings of it is explained by his not knowing his future bride well before they were married; but afterwards she became "violent and unreasonable," "at once intemperate and unchaste" (304). It could not be otherwise, the explanation suggests, as the madness was in her blood.

In part because she rejected this explanation as equating "the Creole" with "the lunatic," and in part because of a century's increased understanding of mental illness, Rhys—while retaining the detail that Antoniette's mother is disturbed and her brother mentally afflicted—advances an alternate theory of the case. Both the mother and Antoinette are driven to madness by the conditions of their lives. Mrs. Mason endures the loss of status, home, and security. Christophine, the wise servant, tells the Rochester figure, "They drive her to it. When she lose her son she lose herself for a while and they shut her away. They tell her she is mad, they act like she is mad. Question, question. But no kind word, no friends, and her husban' he go off, he leave her" (157). Antoniette (whose life is better known to us, while that of her mother, after the fire that consumes their house, is shown in glimpses only) marries a man who takes her money and treats her with contempt. He renames her; he ostentatiously betrays her with a servant, making sure she hears them; he accuses her of infidelity with her cousin Sandi and of involvement with obeah (a kind of sorcery).

In both these accusations he is supported by ambiguous evidence that the text leaves indeterminate. Far from accidentally marrying a woman only to discover that she had "giant propensities," he initiates her into sexual desire:

> I watched her die many times. In my way, not in hers. In sunlight, in shadow, by moonlight, by candlelight. In the long afternoons when the house was empty. Only the sun was there to keep us company. We shut him out. And why not? Very soon she was as eager for what's called loving as I was—more lost and drowned afterwards. (92)

Christophine tells Antoinette's husband, "you make love to her till she drunk with it, no rum could maker drunk like that, till she can't do with out it. It's she can't seen the sun any more. Only you she see. But you want is to break her up" (153). The reference to the sun reminds the reader of Jane herself, who, while fraudulently engaged to Rochester, reflects, "He stood between me and every thought of religion, as an eclipse intervenes between man and the broad sun" (271).

Though his aroused jealousy of his wife, his growing hatred of her, his resentment of the climate and the servants and the house, and a feeling of victimization by marriage, all combine to change him, it is probably Christophine's suggestion that he set her free to marry someone else while keeping her money (rightfully his under English law of the time) that determines him to drag his wife back to England:

> She'll not laugh in the sun again. She'll not dress up and smile at herself in that damnable looking-glass. So pleased, so satisfied.
> Vain, silly creature. Made for loving? Yes, but she'll have no lover, for I don't want her and she'll see no other. (165)

Rhys's novel represents a postcolonial revision of the classic nineteenth-century bildungsroman, because it originates with a native of the islands, writing back against the automatic assumptions and unexamined Anglocentricity of the metropolis. It also approaches colonial appropriation—which is its subject, in the form of the colonizer's appropriation of the Creole woman's person, her fortune, her sense of self and finally her life—from the point of view of the colonized.

Writing in 1997, Laura E. Ciolkowski comments: "The story of imperial motherhood, of which the holy union of Jane and the reformed Rochester [in *Jane Eyre*] is one familiar variation, is explicitly recast in *Wide Sargasso Sea* as a tale of the battle over imperial control" (344). And H. Adlai Murdoch, in an essay specifically about Creole culture, writes:

> In Rhys's intertextual *Wide Sargasso Sea* (1966), she inscribes what purports to be the untold story of the Jamaican creole Bertha Mason's life prior to her marginal appearance in Jane Eyre. By deliberately underlining and interrogating the apparently oppositional tropes of metropolitan and creole identity, both by metonymically relating Rochester to the patters of colonialism and slavery at work in the Jamaica where he accrued his wealth, and particularly through her complex portrait of the "madwoman in the attic," this "prequel" to Brontë's test deliberately destabilizes received, supposedly singular notions of "colonizer," "colonized," and "creole" as they were used in 19th century British prose. (256)

But destabilization of one set of received opinions may produce another unstable picture, and recent scholarship has also sharply questioned the way in which Rhys, while reinscribing the Creole at the center of her story, has marginalized the black Caribbean population. If Rhys had "mixed feelings" about her own Creole heritage (Ochshorn 26), her attitudes toward black islanders was frequently unsympathetic, as her publisher Diana Athill reported. "She often used to talk querulously, or indignantly, about black people, like any other old exiled member of the Caribbean plantocracy: why had they hated 'us' so much? Hadn't they been better off in her youth, when 'we' were running things?" (quoted in O'Connor 406).

Whatever Rhys's private feelings, some critics have astutely observed the voicelessness of the black Caribbean characters. Carine M. Mardorossian interprets this as an approach by means of which Rhys critiques racism:

> Critics have impressively read against the grain of the husband's narrative in the novel's middle section in order to interpret the white Creole's life and identity; taking into account the representation of the black character compels us to read against the grain of Antoinette's narrative as well. Rhys distances herself from her protagonist through formal patterns, ellipses, and repetitions which expose Antoinette's colonialist assumptions. Thus *Wide Sargasso Sea*'s double narrative structure—which only gives us access to the black Creole voices and actions through the consciousnesses of the two major narrators—attests not to Rhys's imperialism but to her insight into the workings of the ideological system and its categories of representation. (1072)

Gayatri Chakravorty Spivak seems more inclined to see the novelist and novel—and possibly the reader—as implicated in Antoinette's colonialist assumptions. Regarding Christophine, the most important and powerful of the black characters and, for some readers, a moral norm and voice of reason, she declares, "Christophine is tangential to this narrative. She cannot be contained by a novel which rewrites a canonical English text within the European novelistic tradition in the interest of the white Creole rather than the native." (253) And Veronica Marie Gregg states vividly: "The racialist usurpation of the voices, acts, and identities of 'black people,' so central to Rhys's writing as a whole, is the psychological cement in the architecture of this novel ...." (114).

Yet the subtle complications of Rhys's novel cannot be exhausted by agreeing with either Mardorossian or Spivak. Both its divided narration and its impressionistic use of detail make it irreducible. And, after all, while Christophine is certainly more "native" than the husband, Antoinette is born on Jamaica; Christophine's history would be traced to Africa. This is not to conflate voluntary emigration for imperialist purposes with forcible enslavement: but who is "native"? Both women are indigenous to the Caribbean islands; both are the heirs of emigration; one is an agent of, while the other is the tool of, imperialism. Both are its victims. The Creole is the one in the middle: neither acceptably "at home" in Jamaica as Christophine is, nor plausibly English, despite her race. She is, in Rhys's telling, first the target of colonialism, the richness the colonizer has come to exploit, and then one of its many fatalities.

WORKS CITED

Brontë, Charlotte. *Jane Eyre*. 1847. New York: Harcourt, Brace & World, 1962.

Ciolkowski, Laura E. "Navigating the *Wide Sargasso Sea*: Colonial History, English Fiction, and British Empire." *Twentieth Century Literature* 42 (Autumn 1997): 339–59.

Gregg, Veronica Marie. *Jean Rhys's Historical Imagination: Reading & Writing the Creole*. Chapel Hill: University of North Carolina Press, 1995.

Mackie, Erin, "Jamaican Ladies and Tropical Charms." *ARIEL: A Review of International English Literature* 37 (2006): 189–220.

Mardorossian, Carine M. "Shutting up the Subaltern: Silences, Stereotypes, and Double-Entendre in Jean Rhys's *Wide Sargasso Sea*." *Callaloo* 22 (Autumn 1999): 1071–90.

Murdoch, H. Adlai. "Rhys's Pieces: Unhomeliness as Arbiter of Caribbean Creolization." *Callaloo* 26 (Winter, 2003): 252–72.

Ochshorn, Kathleen, "Of Woodlice and White Cockroaches: The West Indian Girlhood of Jean Rhys," *Frontiers: A Journal of Women Studies* 12 (1991): 25–35.

O'Connor, Teresa F. "Jean Rhys, Paul Theroux, and the Imperial Road." *Twentieth Century Literature* 38 (Winter 1992): 404–14.

Rhys, Jean. *The Letters of Jean Rhys*. Selected and Edited by Francis Wyndham and Diana Melly. New York: Viking Penguin, 1984.

———. *Wide Sargasso Sea*. London: Andre Deutsch, 1966.

Spivak, Gayatri Chakravorty. "Three Women's Texts and a Critique of Imperialism." *Critical Inquiry* 12 (Autumn, 1985): 243–61.

Thomas, Sue. "The Tropical Extravagance of Bertha Mason." *Victorian Literature and Culture* 27 (1999): 1–17.

Vreeland, Elizabeth. "Jean Rhys: The Art of Fiction LXIV." *The Paris Review* 76 (Autumn 1979): 219–37.

THE WOMAN WARRIOR: MEMOIRS OF A GIRLHOOD AMONG GHOSTS (MAXINE HONG KINGSTON)

"Maxine Hong Kingston's *Woman Warrior*: Filiality and Woman's Autobiographical Storytelling" by Sidonie Smith, in *A Poetics of Women's Autobiography* (1987)

INTRODUCTION

In her essay on the exploration of identity and gender in Maxine Hong Kingston's autobiographical *The Woman Warrior*, Sidonie Smith focuses on the way Kingston's work and her story of Ts'ai Yen fuse the voice of those dispossessed, colonized by a hierarchical society and culture: both Kingston and her mother. Thus, Smith concludes, "With her text she gives historical 'birth' to Brave Orchid, creating for her a textual space in the genealogical record, and she gives 'birth' to herself as the daughter who has passed through the body and the word of the mother."

It is hard to write about my own mother. Whatever I do write, it is my story I am telling, my version of the past. If she were

Smith, Sidonie. "Maxine Hong Kingston's *Woman Warrior*: Filiality and Woman's Autobiographical Storytelling." *A Poetics of Women's Autobiography: Marginality and the Fictions of Self-Representation.* Bloomington: Indiana UP, 1987. 150–173.

to tell her own story other landscapes would be revealed. But in
my landscape or hers, there would be old, smoldering patches
of deep-burning anger.

—Adrienne Rich, *Of Woman Born*

Since Harriet Martineau wrote her autobiography in 1856, many
hundreds of women have contributed the story of their lives to the
cultural heritage. Writers, artists, political figures, intellectuals, business-
women, actors, athletes—all these and more have marked history in
their own way, both as they lived their lives and as they wrote about
them. A tradition so rich and various presents a challenge to the critic of
twentieth-century autobiography. There is much to be written about the
works; indeed, studies of twentieth-century autobiography are beginning to emerge. Articles now abound. I do not want to conclude this
study of women's autobiographies without attention to a contemporary
work; but I also realize that there are many choices that would have
served my critical purposes. Nonetheless, for me at least, no single work
captures so powerfully the relationship of gender to genre in twentieth-
century autobiography as Maxine Hong Kingston's *Woman Warrior*.

And so it is fitting to conclude this discussion of women's autobiography with *The Woman Warrior: Memoirs of a Girlhood among
Ghosts*, which is, quite complexly, an autobiography about women's
autobiographical storytelling. A postmodern work, it exemplifies the
potential for works from the marginalized to challenge the ideology
of individualism and with it the ideology of gender. Recognizing
the inextricable relationship between an individual's sense of "self"
and the community's stories of selfhood, Kingston self-consciously
reads herself into existence through the stories her culture tells about
women. Using autobiography to create identity, she breaks down the
hegemony of formal "autobiography" and breaks out of the silence
that has bound her culturally to discover a resonant voice of her own.
Furthermore, as a work coming from an ethnic subculture, *The Woman
Warrior* offers the occasion to consider the complex imbroglios of
cultural fictions that surround the autobiographer who is engaging
two sets of stories: those of the dominant culture and those of an
ethnic subculture with its own traditions, its own unique stories. As
a Chinese American from the working class, Kingston brings to her
autobiographical project complicating perspectives on the relationship
of woman to language and to narrative.

Considered by some a "novel" and by others an "autobiography," the five narratives conjoined under the title *The Woman Warrior* are decidedly five confrontations with the fictions of self-representation and with the autobiographical possibilities embedded in cultural fictions, specifically as they interpenetrate one another in the autobiography a woman would write.[1] For Kingston, then, as for the woman autobiographer generally, the hermeneutics of self-representation can never be divorced from cultural representations of woman that delimit the nature of her access to the word and the articulation of her own desire. Nor can interpretation be divorced from her orientation toward the mother, who, as her point of origin, commands the tenuous negotiation of identity and difference in a drama of filiality that reaches through the daughter's subjectivity to her textual self-authoring.

Preserving the traditions that authorize the old way of life and enable her to reconstitute the circle of the immigrant community amidst an alien environment, Kingston's mother dominates the life, the landscape, and the language of the text as she dominates the subjectivity of the daughter who writes that text. It is Brave Orchid's voice, commanding, as Kingston notes, "great power" that continually reiterates the discourses of the community in maxims, talk-story, legends, family histories. As the instrument naming filial identities and commanding filial obligations, that voice enforces the authority and legitimacy of the old culture to name and thus control the place of woman within the patrilineage and thereby to establish the erasure of female desire and the denial of female self-representation as the basis on which the perpetuation of patrilineal descent rests. Yet that same voice gives shape to other possibilities, tales of female power and authority that seem to create a space of cultural significance for the daughter; and the very strength and authority of the material voice fascinates the daughter because it "speaks" of the power of woman to enunciate her own representations. Hence storytelling becomes the means through which Brave Orchid passes on to her daughter all the complexities of and the ambivalences about both mother's and daughter's identity as woman in patriarchal culture.[2]

Storytelling also becomes the means through which Kingston confronts those complexities and ambivalences. In dialogic engagement with her mother's word, she struggles to constitute the voice of her own subjectivity, to emerge from a past dominated by stories told to her, ones that inscribe the fictional possibilities of female selfhood, into a present articulated by her own storytelling. Her text reveals the intensity of that struggle throughout childhood and adolescence and the persistence of those conflicts inherent in self-authoring well into adulthood; for, not only is that effort the subject in the text; it is also dramatized by the text. In the first two narratives she re-creates the stories about women and their autobiographical possibilities passed on to her by her mother: first the biographical story of no-name aunt, an apparent victim and thus a negative model of female life scripts, and then the legendary chant of the warrior woman Fa Mu Lan, an apparent heroine and positive model. But as she explores their fates, Kingston questions the very basis on which such distinctions are predicated. Uncovering layer by layer the dynamics and the consequences of her mother's interpretations as they resonate with the memories of her past, the daughter, as she too passes them on to posterity, circles around them, critiquing them, making them her own. Next she reconstructs out of the autobiographical fragments of Brave Orchid's own Chinese experience a biography of her mother, discovering by the way the efficacies of powerful storytelling for the woman who has fallen in status with her translation to another culture. In the fourth piece, an elaborate fabrication played on actual events, she becomes even more keenly attentive to all autobiographical and biographical representations, including her own. Looking back to the beginnings of her own struggle to take a voice, she traces in the final narrative the origins of her own hermeneutics. The apparent line of progress, which as it ends returns us to the beginning, becomes effectively a circle of sorts, a textual alternative to the constricting patriarchal circle Kingston has had to transgress.

[. . .]

Whereas the first two narratives explore the consequences of Kingston's appropriation of her mother's stories, the third goes through the stories to the storyteller herself. Three scrolls from China serve as the originating locus of this biography of her mother pieced together with "autobiographical" fragments. Texts that legitimate her mother's professional identity as doctor, the scrolls stimulate biography because they announce public achievements, a life text readable by culture. They also announce to the daughter another mother, a mythic figure resident in China who resisted the erasure of her own desire and who pursued her own signifying selfhood. In her daughter's text, Brave Orchid becomes a kind of "woman warrior," whose story resonates with the Fa Mu Lan legend: both women leave the circle of the family to be educated for their mission and both return to serve their community, freeing it through many adventures from those forces that would destroy it. Both are fearless, successful, admired.

Kingston's biography accretes all varieties of evidence testifying to her mother's bravery and extraordinariness. Portrayed as one of the "new women, scientists who changed the rituals" (88), Brave Orchid bears the "horizontal name of one generation" that truly names her rather than the patronym signifying woman's identity as cipher silently bonding the patrilineage. Thus Kingston's awe-filled narration of her mother's confrontation with the Sitting Ghost takes on such synecdochic proportions in the text: "My mother may have been afraid, but she would be a dragoness ('my totem, your totem'). She could make herself not weak. During danger she fanned out her dragon claws and riffled her red sequin scales and unfolded her coiling green stripes. Danger was a good time for showing off. Like the dragons living in temple eaves, my mother looked down on plain people who were lonely and afraid" (79). The ensuing battle between woman and ghost unfolds as a primal struggle with the dynamics and the rhythms of an attempted rape. A physically powerless victim of the palpably masculine presence who "rolled over her and landed bodily on her chest" (81), Brave Orchid is initially unable to challenge his strength. But she ultimately prevails against the Boulder, defeating him with the boldness of her word and the power of the images she voices to taunt him into submission and cowardice. Such fearlessness and verbal cunning characterize subsequent adventures the daughter invokes: the coexistence with ghosts and strange monsters populating the countryside through which she travels on her way to administer to the sick; the bargain she drives with the slave dealer; her response to the birth of monster babies; and her bold orientation toward food.[3]

[. . .]

Kingston's narrative, as it interpenetrates her autobiography with her mother's biography, reveals how problematic such stories can become for the next generation. From one point of view, they can be exhilarating, creating in children the admiration that is so apparent in Kingston's text. But from another, they generate confusions and ambiguities, since as a child Kingston inflected the narratives with her own subjectivity, attending to another story within the text of female heroism. For Brave Orchid's tales of bravery and exoticism are

underwritten by an alternative text of female vulnerability and victimization. The story elaborating the purchase of the slave girl reaffirms the
servile status of women and actually gives legitimacy to Kingston's fears
that her parents will sell her when they return to China. The stories of
babies identify femaleness with deformity and suggest to the daughter
the haunting possibility that her mother might actually have practiced
female infanticide. The story of the crazy lady, scurrying directionless
on bound feet, encased in the mirror-studded headdress, caught in her
own self-destructive capitulations, dramatizes communal fear of the
anomalous woman who embodies the threat of uncontrolled female
sexuality and subversive alliances between women—always strangers
within the community—and the enemy outside.

All these tales from her mother's past, by reinforcing the representation of women as expendable, resonate with Kingston's sense
of displacement in her family and in the immigrant community in
America, her confusion about her sexuality, and her fears of her own
"deformities" and "madnesses." They leave her with food that suffocates
her, a voice that squeaks on her, and nightmares that haunt the long
nights of childhood. They also complicate Kingston's sense of identification with her mother by betraying the basis on which her tales of
extraordinariness are founded, that is, the powerlessness of ordinary
women and children and their cruel and insensitive victimization, even
at the hands of Brave Orchid herself. In fact, in her self-representation Kingston identifies herself with the "lonely and afraid," a victim
of her mother's stories, and thus no true heroine after her mother's
model. Paradoxically, her mother, the shaman with the power of word
and food, has, instead of inspiring her daughter to health and heroism,
made the daughter sick, hungry, vulnerable, fearful.

In the closing passage of this third narrative, Kingston re-creates
her most recent encounter with her mother and, through it, her
continuing resistance to her mother's victimizing presence. Ironically,
the scene recapitulates the earlier scene of her mother's biography. The
dark bedroom, the late hour recall the haunted room at the medical
school. Here Brave Orchid is herself the ghost who would continue to
haunt her daughter: "My mother would sometimes be a large animal,
barely real in the dark; then she would become a mother again" (118).
Like Brave Orchid before her, Kingston grasps the only weapon effective in overcoming that ghost—the words with which she resists her.
In the syncopated rhythm of statement and rebuttal, she answers her

mother's vision of things with her own, challenging unremittingly the power of her mother to control interpretations. She also offers an alternative representation of her in this closing scene, portraying her as an old woman, tired, prosaic, lonely, a woman whose illusions of returning to China have vanished, whose stories have become peevish, repetitious. In creating a portrait of her mother as neither fearless nor exotic, the daughter demystifies Brave Orchid's presence and diffuses the power of her word.

For all the apparent rejection of her mother as ghost, the final passage points to a locus of identification between mother and daughter and a momentary rapprochement between the two. In saying goodnight, Kingston's mother calls her Little Dog, a name of endearment unuttered for many years, and, in that gesture of affection, releases her daughter to be who she will. As a result, Kingston experiences the freedom to identify with her; for, as the daughter makes evident in her biography, her mother before her had strayed from filial obligations, leaving her parents behind in pursuit of her own desire: "I am really a Dragon, as she is a Dragon, both of us born in dragon years. I am practically a first daughter of a first daughter" (127). At this moment of closure, Kingston affectionately traces her genealogy as woman and writer to and through her mother in a sincere gesture of filiality, acknowledging as she does so that her autobiography cannot be inscribed outside the biography of her mother, just as the biography of her mother cannot be inscribed outside her own interpretations. Mother and daughter are allied in the interpenetration of stories and storytelling, an alliance captured in the ambiguous reference of the final sentence: "She sends me on my way, working always and now old, dreaming the dreams about shrinking babies and the sky covered with airplanes and a Chinatown bigger than the ones here" (127). As the motifs of the final pages suggest, both mother and daughter are working always and now old.

In the fourth narrative Kingston does not take the word of her mother as her point of narrative origin. She will reveal at the inception of the next piece that the only information she received about the events narrated in the fourth piece came from her brother through her sister in the form of an abrupt, spare bone of a story: "What my brother actually said was, 'I drove Mom and Second Aunt to Los Angeles to see Aunt's husband who's got the other wife'" (189). Out of a single factual sentence, Kingston creates a complex story of the two sisters, Brave Orchid and Moon Orchid. She admits that "his version of the story may be better than mine because of its bareness, not twisted into designs" (189); but the "designs" to which she alludes have become integral to her autobiographical interpretations.

In Kingston's designs Moon Orchid, like Brave Orchid in "Shaman," embodies her name: She is a flower of the moon, a decorative satellite that revolves around and takes its definition from another body, the absent husband. Mute to her own desire, attendant always on the word of her husband, she represents the traditional Chinese wife; a woman without autobiographical possibilities. "For thirty years," comments her niece, "she had been receiving money from him from America. But she had never told him that she wanted to come to the United States. She waited for him to suggest it, but he never did" (144). Unlike Brave Orchid, she is neither clever nor shrewd, skilled nor quick, sturdy nor lasting. Demure, self-effacing, decorative, tidy, refined—she is as gracefully useless and as elegantly civilized as bound feet, as decoratively insubstantial as the paper cutouts she brings her nieces and nephews from the old country. Having little subjectivity of her own, she can only appropriate as her own the subjectivity of others, spending her days following nieces and nephews through the house, describing what they do, repeating what they say, asking what their words mean. While there is something delightfully childlike, curious, and naive about that narration of other people's lives, there is a more profound sadness that a woman in her sixties, unformed and infantile, has no autobiography of her own.

When her husband rejects her, giving his allegiance to his Chinese-American wife, who can speak English and aid him in his work, he denies the very ontological basis on which Moon Orchid's selfhood is predicated and effectually erases her from the lines of descent. He also undermines with his negation of her role what autobiographical representations she has managed to create for herself. "You became people in a book I read a long time ago" (179), he tells the two sisters, dramatically betraying the elusiveness of the "fictions" on which Moon Orchid has sustained her identity as first wife. Once having been turned into a fairy-tale figure from a time long past, this woman loses the core of her subjectivity and literally begins to vanish: She appears "small in the corner of the seat" (174); she stops speaking because the grounds for her authority to speak have been undermined—"All she did was open and shut her mouth without any words coming out" (176); later she stops eating, returning to Brave Orchid's home "shrunken to the bone." Ultimately, she vanishes into a world of madness where she creates repetitive fictions, variations on a story about vanishing without a trace. Thus she fantasizes that Mexican "ghosts" are plotting to snatch her life from her, that "'they' would take us in airplanes and fly us to Washington, D.C., where they'd turn us into ashes. . . . drop the ashes in the wind, leaving no evidence" (184). The tenuousness, evanescence, and elusiveness of identity press on her so that everywhere she sees signs (sees, that is, evidence of the legitimacy of her own interpretations) that alien males threaten to erase her from the world, leaving no trace of her body as her husband has left no trace of her patrilineal existence. To protect herself she withdraws into the "house" of her sister, that edifice that has supported her construction of an identity as first wife. There she literally makes of the house what it has always been metaphorically—a living coffin—windows shut and darkened, "no air, no light," and she makes of storytelling itself a living coffin. As Brave Orchid tells her children, "The difference between mad people and sane people . . . is that sane people have variety when they talk-story. Mad people have only one story that they talk over and over" (184). Only after Brave Orchid commits her to a mental institution does she find a new fiction to replace the old one, a renewed identity as "mother" to the other women ("daughters") who can never vanish. In the end the story of vanishing without leaving a trace becomes the only trace that is left of her, an impoverished autobiographical absence.

Her mother Kingston now represents, not as the "new woman" of "Shaman," but as a traditional woman intent on preserving her family from harm by maintaining the old traditions against the erosions of American culture. Through the conventions of speaking (Chinese), eating, greeting, chanting, storytelling, she keeps China drawn around her family in a linguistic and gustatory circle. More particularly, she seeks to preserve the old family constellation and, with it, the identity of woman. Thus, from Brave Orchid's "Chinese" perspective, her sister is a first wife, entitled to certain privileges and rights, even in America. Yet, in her allegiance to the old traditions of filial and affinal obligations, Brave Orchid becomes shortsighted, insensitive, and destructive. She succeeds only in making other women (her niece, who remains trapped in a loveless marriage; her sister, who dies in a mental institution) unhappy, sick, even mad; and she does so because, failing to anticipate just how misplaced the traditions and myths have become in the new world, she trusts her word too well. The stories she tells create illusions that fail of reference to any reality.

The story of the Empress of the Western Palace is a case in point. "A long time ago," Brave Orchid tells her sister on the drive to Los Angeles,

> "the emperors had four wives, one at each point of the compass, and they lived in four palaces. The Empress of the West would connive for power, but the Empress of the East was good and kind and full of light. You are the Empress of the East, and the Empress of the West has imprisoned the Earth's Emperor in the Western Palace. And you, the good Empress of the East, come out of the dawn to invade her land and free the Emperor. You must break the strong spell she has cast on him that has lost him the East." (166)

The myth, however, is an inappropriate text through which to interpret Moon Orchid's experience. The Empress of the West is not conniving; the Emperor does not want freeing; and the Empress of the East cannot break the spell. Moreover, for all Brave Orchid's forceful narratives of the projected meeting among Moon Orchid, the husband, and the second wife, the actual scene is pitifully humorous, squeezed as it is in the backseat of the car. "What scenes I could make" (146), she tells her sister; but the only scenes she makes are in her fantasies of them (and her daughter the storyteller is the one who actually makes the scene). Though she is not entirely speechless when they confront Moon Orchid's husband, she is obviously awed by the wealthy, successful, and much younger man, and by the pressure of his young, efficient wife. Kingston creates a Brave Orchid bested in the game of fictionalizations. The husband has turned the two sisters into characters from a book read long ago, a devastating recapitulation of their efforts to turn him into the fictional Emperor. While the power of her myths to help define and situate identities has been eroded by another cultural tradition, Brave Orchid herself has not been destroyed because, unlike Moon Orchid, she is willful, hardworking, clever, intelligent, shrewd, stubborn, "brave"—all those qualities that have enabled her to cope with and to survive in her translation to another cultural landscape. Moreover, she can always fabricate another story, as she does when she urges her children to sabotage any plans her husband, now in his seventies, might have to marry a second wife. Nonetheless, other women are victimized by her words, their autobiographical possibilities cut off.

Through the "designs" in "At the Western Palace," Kingston confronts explicitly the problematics of autobiographical "fictions." Both Moon Orchid and Brave Orchid serve as powerful negative models for the perils of autobiography. Moon Orchid, bereft of the husband who defines her place and who sets the limits of her subjectivity within the structures of the patrilineage, succumbs to an imagination anchored in no-place, an imaginative rootlessness threatening Kingston herself. Overwhelmed by repetitive fantasies, her aunt vanishes into a world where alien males continually plot to erase her from existence, a preoccupation that resonates with Kingston's childhood fears of leaving no culturally significant autobiographical trace. A woman of no autobiography, Moon Orchid cannot find a voice of her own, or, rather, the only subjectivity that she finally voices is the subjectivity of madness. Brave Orchid, too, serves as a powerful negative model. She would write a certain biography of her sister, patterned after traditional interpretations of the identity of a first wife. In preserving her interpretations, however, she victimizes other women by failing to make a space in her story for female subjectivity in unfamiliar landscapes, by remaining insensitive to her sister's fears and desires, as she remains insensitive to her daughter's desires. Giving her unquestioning allegiance to language, she fails to recognize the danger in words, the perils inherent in the fictions that bind.

In the end Kingston, too, has created only a fiction, an elaborate story out of the one sentence passed by her brother through her sister; and she, too, must beware the danger in words as she constructs her stories of those other women, more particularly her mother. To a certain extent she seems to do so in this fourth narrative. For all the negative, even horrifying, aspects of Brave Orchid's fierce preservation and Moon Orchid's repetitive fantasies, both women come across in this section as fully human. Her mother, especially, does so; and that is because, releasing her mother to be her own character, under her own name "Brave Orchid," rather than as "my mother," the daughter penetrates her mother's subjectivity with tender ironies and gentle mercies. In doing so, she effaces her own presence in the text as character, her presence implied only in the reference to Brave

Orchid's "children." Unlike her mother, then, who does not imagine the contours of her sister's subjectivity, Kingston here tries to think like her mother and her aunt. Yet even as she creates the fullness of her mother out of her word, she recognizes the very fictionality of her tale—its "designs" that serve her own hermeneutical purposes. She, too, like her mother within her story, negotiates the world by means of the fictions that sustain interpretations and preserve identities. In the persistent reciprocities that characterize Kingston's storytelling, her mother becomes the product of her fictions, as she has been the product of her mother's.

Kingston represents in the final piece, "A Song for a Barbarian Reed Pipe," her adolescent struggle to discover her own speaking voice and autobiographical authority. This drama originates in the memory of her mother's literally cutting the voice out of her: "She pushed my tongue up and sliced the frenum. Or maybe she snipped it with a pair of nail scissors. I don't remember her doing it, only her telling me about it, but all during childhood I felt sorry for the baby whose mother waited with scissors or knife in hand for it to cry—and then, when its mouth was wide open like a baby bird's, cut" (190). Notably, Kingston remembers, not the actual event, but the reconstruction of the event in language, a phenomenon testifying to the power of the mother's word to constitute the daughter's history, in this case her continuing sense of confusion, horror, deprivation, and violation. Her mother passes on a tale of female castration, a rite of passage analogous to a clitoridectomy, that wounding of the female body in service to the community, performed and thereby perpetuated by the mother.[4] It is a ritual that results in the denial to woman of the pleasure of giving voice to her body and body to her voice, the pleasure of autobiographical legitimacy and authority.

In her re-creation of the confrontation with the Chinese-American girl in the bathroom of the Chinese school, Kingston evokes her childhood confusion about speechlessness: "Most of us," she comments, "eventually found some voice, however faltering. We invented an American-feminine speaking personality, except for that one girl who could not speak up even in Chinese school" (200). A kind of surrogate home, the Chinese school functions as the repository of old traditions and conventional identities within the immigrant community; and the bathroom is that most private of female spaces—only for girls, only for certain activities, which, as it locates the elimination of matter from the body, ultimately becomes associated with female pollution and shame. In that space, Kingston responds cruelly, even violently, to the female image before her, abhorring the girl's useless fragility: her neat, pastel clothes; her China-doll haircut; her tiny, white teeth; her baby-soft, fleshy skin—"like squid out of which the glassy blades of bones had been pulled," "like tracing paper, onion paper" (206). Most of all, she abhors her "dumbness," for this girl, who cannot even speak her name aloud, is ultimately without body or text. "You're such a nothing," Kingston remembers yelling at her. "You are a plant. Do you know that? That's all you are if you don't talk: If you don't talk, you can't have a personality. You'll have no personality and no hair. You've got to let people know you have a personality and a brain. You think somebody is going to take care of you all your stupid life?" (210).

Yet, while the girl stands mute before the screaming Kingston, they both weep profusely, wiping their snot on their sleeves as the seemingly frozen scene wraps them both in its embrace. Kingston remembers feeling some comfort in establishing her difference from the girl, taking pride in her dirty fingernails, calloused hands, yellow teeth, her desire to wear black. But the fierceness with which she articulates her desire for difference only accentuates her actual identity with the nameless girl: Both are the last ones chosen by teams; both are silent and "dumb" in the American school. An exaggerated representation of the perfect Chinese girl, this girl becomes a mirror image of Kingston herself, reflecting her own fears of insubstantiality and dumbness (symbolized for her in the zero intelligence quotient that marks her first-grade record). In the pulling of the hair, the poking of the flesh, Kingston captures the violence of her childhood insecurity and self-hatred. Striking the Chinese-American girl, she strikes violently at her own failure to take a voice and at all her mother's prior narratives of female voicelessness. Tellingly, her aggressive attack on that mirror image eventuates, not in the girl's utterance of her name, but in Kingston's eighteen-month illness, which ensures that she indeed does become like the other girl. Confined to bed, isolated inside the house, she is literally silenced in the public space, a fragile and useless girl. Attended always by her family, she too becomes a plant, a nothing. Ironically, she says of that time: "It was the best year and a half of my life. Nothing happened" (212). The admission betrays the tremendous relief of not having to prove to people she has "a personality and a brain," the powerful enticement of succumbing to the implications of her mother's narratives and her culture's maxims, the confusing attractiveness of not having to find a public voice, of not struggling with shame.

For, as her narrative recollection reveals, taking a voice becomes complicated by her sense of guilt. She is ashamed to speak in public with a voice like those of the immigrant women—loud, inelegant, unsubtle. She is ashamed to speak the words her mother demands she say to the druggist ghost because she considers her mother's words, as they exact compliance with traditional beliefs, to be outdated. She is ashamed to keep the same kind of silences and secrets her mother would keep because such secrets command her duplicity before the teachers she respects. For all these reasons she would not speak like her mother (and Chinese women) in her American environment; but her own efforts to take the appropriate American-feminine voice fail, and that failure too gives her cause for shame. In public her voice becomes "a crippled animal running on broken legs" (196), a duck voice; her throat "cut[s]" off the word; her mouth appears "permanently crooked with effort, turned down on the left side and straight on the right" (199). Her face and vocal chords continue to show the signs of her prior castration, the physical mutilation and discomfort that mark her relationship to language and to any public enunciation of subjectivity.

The landscape of her childhood, as she reconstructs it, reveals the underlying logic in Kingston's failure to overcome her symbolic disability. Seeing around her the humiliating representations of woman, hearing words such as "maggots" become synonyms for "girls," suspecting that her mother seeks to contract her out as the wife and slave of some young man, perhaps even the retarded boy who follows her around with his box full of pornographic pictures, she negotiates a nightmare of female victimization by adopting the postures of an unattractive girl, the better to foil her mother's efforts and to forestall her weary capitulation. Cultivating that autobiographical signature, she represents herself publicly as the obverse of her mother's image of the charming, attractive, practical young girl by becoming clumsy, vulgar, bad-tempered, lazy, impractical, irreverent, and stupid "from reading too much" (226). She becomes, that is, a kind of fiction; and the psychic price she pays for orchestrating such a public posture is high. Publicly appearing as the "dumb" and awkward girl, she does not earn the affection and respect of her family and community. Moreover, she must convince herself of the reality of her mind by constantly attending to the grades she earns in the American school, those signs, unrecognized in her Chinese culture, that signal her access to other discourses. She remains "dumb" in another sense, for she recognizes even in childhood that "talking and not talking made the difference between sanity and insanity," in that "insane people were the ones who couldn't explain themselves" (216). Since she cannot give voice to her subjectivity except by indirection and dissimulation, externalizing in an awkward masquerade the text of publicly unexpressed desires, she finds commonality with the anomalous women such as Pee-A-Nah and Crazy Mary, who retreat into imaginary worlds, there to haunt the outskirts of the immigrant community and the imaginations of its children.

The culmination of this struggle with voice comes when Kingston finally attempts to "explain" her silenced guilts, the text of which lengthens daily, and to represent her repressed desires to her mother, believing that by doing so she will establish some grounds for identification and overcome her profound isolation and dumbness: "If only I could let my mother know the list, she—and the world—would become more like me, and I would never be alone again" (230). Recapitulating the earlier castration, her mother cuts her tongue by refusing to acknowledge the daughter's stories as legitimate: "'I can't stand this whispering,' she said looking right at me, stopping her squeezing. 'Senseless gabbings every night. I wish you would stop. Go away and work. Whispering, whispering, making no sense. Madness. I don't feel like hearing your craziness'" (233). In response, Kingston swallows her words, but only temporarily. The tautness of her vocal cords increasing to a breaking point, she later bursts the silence, uttering in a cathartic moment the text of her inner life before her mother. Finally, this girl takes voice, albeit in great confusion, and thereby authors a vision, textualizes her subjectivity, and legitimizes her own desires. She embarks, that is, on the autobiographical enterprise, articulating her interpretations against her mother's.

In this battle of words, mother and daughter, products of different cultural experiences, systems of signs, and modes of interpretation, speak two different "languages" and inscribe two different stories—graphically imaged in the sets of quotation marks that delimit their separate visions and betray the gap in the matrilineage as the circle of identity, of place and desire, is disrupted. Unable to understand the mother, unwilling to identify with her, the daughter would, in ironic reciprocity, cut off her mother's word: "I don't want to listen to any more of your stories; they have no logic. They scramble me up. You lie with stories. You won't tell me a story and then say, 'This is a true story' or 'This is just a story'" (235). But her mother's reluctant admission—"We like to say the opposite" (237)—forces Kingston to question, at the moment of their origin, her own interpretations and thus the "truth" or "fictiveness" of the autobiography she would inscribe through her memories of the past. As a result, the young Kingston comes to recognize the relativity of truth, the very elusiveness of self-representation that drives the autobiographical enterprise. "Ho Chi Kuai" her mother calls her; and, even to the moment in her adult life when she writes her autobiography, she cannot specify, can only guess, the meaning of the name her mother gave her from that culture she would leave behind. In the end she can only try to decipher the meaning of her past, her subjectivity, her desire, her own name: "I continue to sort out what's just my childhood, just my imagination, just my family, just the village, just movies, just living" (239).

Kingston closes *The Woman Warrior* with a coda, returning it to silence after telling two brief stories, one her mother's, one hers. She starts with the former: "Here is a story my mother told me, not when I was young, but recently, when I told her I also talk-story. The beginning is hers, the ending, mine" (240). Notably, her mother's story is now a gift. Passed from one storyteller to another, it signals the mother's genuine identification with the daughter. Yet the two-part story also functions as a testament to difference, the simple juxtaposition of two words rather than the privileging of one before the other. Here, at last, Kingston lets her mother's word stand without resisting it.

Her mother's story, set in the China of the previous generation, presents Kingston's grandmother as a willful and powerful woman who, convinced "that our family was immune to harm as long as they went to plays" (241), loves to attend theater performances. Unfolding in the ironies of the unexpected, the contingencies of opposites, the absence of linear logic, the story is emblematic of Brave Orchid's individual narrative style and vision, of the kinds of stories she tells. It speaks both of the horrifying vulnerability of women and of their fierce and commanding power; and it tells of the power of art to sustain the continuity of life and the power of interpretations to turn adversity and victimization to triumph. Through her "gift," mother places daughter in the line of powerful "Chinese" women whose source of inspiration and whose very survival in the midst of vulnerability lie in the word of the creative imagination.

Kingston follows her mother's words with what she imagines might be the story on the stage at one of those performances. Turning toward rather than resisting her Chinese roots, she takes as her protagonist a Chinese poet who lived in the second century.[5] Forced to live among barbarians for twelve years, during which time she bears two children who cannot speak Chinese, Ts'ai Yen remains isolated beyond the boundaries that sustain her sense of place and identity. Nonetheless, she eventually discovers that even barbarians make music of life and longing, reflecting civilized, rather than merely primitive, sensibilities. In the midst of cultural difference, the poet finds a commonality of experience and subjectivity through the language of art, which enables her to give voice to her own desire for self-representation and, in doing so, to join the circle of humanity. Eventually, Ts'ai Yen is ransomed, returning to her home "so that her father would have Han descendants" (243); but the more momentous "birth" she contributes to posterity is the song of sadness, anger, and wandering created out of her experience in the alien land. Speaking of human yearning, it "translates well" through the generations and across communal boundaries. Ultimately, the story of Ts'ai Yen, the woman of words, is the tale of Brave Orchid, who finds herself hostage in the barbarian land of America where even her children, born like Ts'ai Yen's among the aliens, cannot "speak" her native language, cannot understand her. Yet the tale is simultaneously that of Kingston herself, whose sense of alienation is doubly complicated, since, as a product of two cultures, she remains outside the circle of both. Mother and daughter sing the songs of sadness, loneliness, and displacement, finding their common sustenance in the word. Thus through her storytelling Kingston can create the total identification of mother and daughter as they both become Ts'ai Yen, woman poet.

In that final juxtaposition of two stories, Kingston asserts the grounds of identification with her mother, affirming continuities rather than disjunctions in the line.[6] She is her mother's daughter, however much she may distance herself geographically and psychologically, learning from her the power and authority that enable her to originate her own storytelling. Carrying on the matrilineal trace, she becomes like her mother a mistress of the word in a culture that would privilege only the lines, textual and genealogical, of patrilineal descent.[7] With her text she gives historical "birth" to Brave Orchid, creating for her a textual space in the genealogical record, and she gives "birth" to herself as the daughter who has passed through the body and the word of the mother.

NOTES

1. Albert E. Stone comments that Kingston's autobiography joins others in "this terrain of contemporary autobiography which abuts the continent of fiction" (Albert E. Stone, *Autobiographical Occasions and Original Acts* [Philadelphia: Univ. of Pennsylvania Press, 1982], p. 25).

2. For a review article on recent literature on mothers and daughters, see Marianne Hirsch, "Mothers and Daughters," *Signs: Journal of Women in Culture and Society* 7 (Summer 1981): 200–222. See also Adrienne Rich, *Of Woman Born* (New York: Norton, 1976), esp. ch. 9.

3. As the daughter knows, "all heroes are bold toward food" (104). They demonstrate by their gustatory feats their power over the natural world, their high degree of aristocratic cultivation, and their association with the sacred. See Claude Lévi-Strauss, *The Raw and the Cooked*, trans. John and Doreen Weightman (New York: Harper & Row, 1969).

4. See Mary Daly, *Gyn/Ecology: The Metaethics of Radical Feminism* (Boston: Beacon Press, 1978), pp. 153–77.

5. For a brief biography of Ts'ai Yen, see Wu-chi Liu and Irving Yucheng Lo, eds., *Sunflower Splendor: Three Thousand Years of Chinese Poetry* (Garden City: Anchor, 1975), pp. 537–58.

6. For a discussion of the narrative rhythms of identification and differentiation in *The Woman Warrior* and *China Men*, see Suzanne Juhasz, "Maxine Hong Kingston: Narrative Technique and Female Identity," in *Contemporary American Women Writers*, ed. Catherine Rainwater and William J. Scheik (Lexington: Univ. Press of Kentucky, 1985), pp. 173–89.

7. See Aiken, pp. 175–84.

Acknowledgments

Denard, Hugh. "Seamus Heaney, Colonialism, and the Cure: Sophoclean Re-Visions." *PAJ: A Journal of Performance and Art* 22. 3 (September 2000): 1–18. © The MIT Press. Reprinted by permission.

Hawkins, Hunt. "Forster's Critique of Imperialism in *A Passage to India.*" *South Atlantic Review* 48.1 (Jan. 1983): 54–65. © The South Atlantic Modern Language Association. Reprinted by permission.

Helps, Sir Arthur. "Preface." *The Life of Las Casas: The Apostle of the Indies.* London: Bell and Daldy, 1868. v-xv.

King, Bruce. "Wole Soyinka and the Nobel Prize for Literature." *Sewanee Review* 96.2 (Spring 1988): 339–45. © The University of the South. Reprinted by permission.

Marx, Karl. "The Fetishism of Commodities and the Secret Thereof." *Capital: A Critique of Political Economy.* 1867. Ed. Frederick Engels. Trans. Samuel Moore and Edward Aveling. New York: The Modern Library, 1906. 88–90.

Moorman, Charles. "The Iliad." *Kings and Captains: Variations on a Heroic Theme.* Lexington, KY: UP of Kentucky, 1971. 1–29. © The University Press of Kentucky. Reprinted by permission.

Ortiz, Simon J. "Towards a National Indian Literature: Cultural Authenticity in Nationalism." *MELUS* 8.2 (Summer 1981) 7–12. Reprinted by permission.

Pereira, Malin Walther. "Periodizing Toni Morrison's work from *The Bluest Eye* to *Jazz*: the importance of *Tar Baby.*" *MELUS* 22.3 (Autumn 1997): 71–83. Reprinted by permission.

Smith, Sidonie. "Maxine Hong Kingston's *Woman Warrior*: Filiality and Woman's Autobiographical Storytelling." *A Poetics of Women's Autobiography: Marginality and the Fictions of Self-Representation.* Bloomington: Indiana UP, 1987. 150–173. © Sidonie Smith. Reprinted by permission

Ward, David. "The Irish Tracts."*Jonathan Swift: An Introductory Essay*. London: Methuen and Company Ltd., 1973. 100–120. © David Ward.

Zamora, Margarita. "Reading Columbus." *Reading Columbus*. Berkeley, CA: University of California Press, 1993. 9–20. © The Regents of the University of California. Reprinted by permission.

Index

A

absurd, 63, 67, 71–74, 82
Achaeans, 85–88
Achebe, Chinua, 152–153, 191–199
Achilles (*Iliad*), 87, 88–91, 94–96
Aegean colonization, 93
Africa
    colonization of, 76, 79, 81–82
    exploration of, 72–73
    modern, 151–152
African American beauty, 103–105
African American culture, 100
African Americans, cultural
  colonization of, 101–111
African culture, 152–153, 192–193
Agamemnon (*Iliad*), 86–89, 90,
  94–96
Aias (*Iliad*), 90
Aké (Soyinka), 156
Algeria, 57–59, 62–64
Allende, Salvador, 209–210
ancient Greece, 93–94
ancient history, 84–86
animalism, 39–40, 42, 46, 49
animals
    exploitation of, 40–41
    hunting imagery and, 42–44
Arab-European relationships,
  59–62
Ashcroft, Bill, 219–220
Attridge, Dereck, 222

Attwell, David, 215, 219
authenticity, 10, 11, 13–14
autobiography, 236–237

B

beauty
    decolonized perspective on,
      106–109
    notions of American, 103–104
    racial, 101–105
    white female, 103–106, 108–109
Begam, Richard, 198
Beloved (Morrison), 105
Beowulf, 84
bestiality, 48
betrayal, 205
bigotry, 134–135
Bill of Rights (1680), 177
Black Arts Movement, 101, 102
black female beauty, 103–105
Bloom, Harold, xi–xvi
blues, 107–108
Bluest Eye, The (Morrison), 101–102,
  103, 106–107
Brée, Germaine, 59
British colonialism, 81
    in Africa, 191–199
    in India, 133–145
    in Ireland, 159–162, 168, 176–178,
      179

in New World, 187–189
resistance to, 193
Brontë, Charlotte, 226–227, 228, 229

C

Camus, Albert, 57–64
Canto General (Neruda), 201–210
    writing of, 202
capitalism, 147–150, 201, 206,
    207–208
Carías, Tiburcio, 205
Carpentier, Alejo, 124
Carter, Angela, 220–221
Castro, Fidel, 209
Catholics, in Ireland, 33–34, 36, 41,
    161–162
Central America, 203–204
Ceremony (Silko), 12–14
Chile, 209–210
Christianity, 192, 194–198
Ciolkowski, Laura E., 231
civil disobedience, 176–177
Clinton, Bill, 32
Coetzee, J. M., 213–222
Collazos, Oscar, 125
colonial appropriation, 230–231
colonial discourse
    animalism in, 39–40
    construction of Other in, 40
    in *Cure at Troy*, 33–34, 37–39
    hunting theme in, 42–44
colonial education system, 196
colonialism
    British, 81, 133–145, 159–162,
        168, 176–179, 191–199, 193
    brutality of, 44–45, 47–49
    French, 57–58, 62–64, 73
    in India, 133–145
    process of, 34
    rebellion against, 58–59
    resistance to, 10–14

suffering caused by, 214
    in "The Guest," 57–64
colonists
    brutality of, 44–45
    identity of, 49
    stereotypes of, 180
colonization
    Aegean, 93
    in Africa, 76, 79, 81–82
    beauty and, 104–105
    Christianity and, 192–198
    cultural, 101–111
    economics of, 147–150
    experience of, 10–11
    impact of, 192–193
    of India, 133–145
    motivations for, 25–27
    in "My Kinsman, Major
        Molineux," 115–122
    of Northern Ireland, 36
    rejection of, 102
    resistance to, 193
    by Spanish, 8–11
    in *The Tempest*, 179–189
    as theme in works of Morrison,
        100–111
    in *Things Fall Apart*, 191–199
colonized
    identity of, 49
    as subhuman, 39–40
Columbus, Christopher
    petitions to Crown by, 24
    writings of, 15–30
Columbus, Ferdinand, 27n1
community, 157
Conrad, Joseph, 67–82, 140
conspiracies, 128
counter-colonialist ideology, 45–46
Creole culture, 231
Cromwell, Oliver, 160
cultural colonization
    of African Americans, 101–111

Cure at Troy, The (Heaney), 31–55
  Chorus in, 48
  colonial discourse in, 33–34, 37–53
  counter-colonialist ideology in,
    45–47
  fall of Troy in, 50–51
  hunting theme, 42–44, 46
  language in, 35–36, 51
  political discourse and, 32–34
  postcolonialism and, 49–50, 51,
    52–53
  readings of, 50–52
  as revision of *Philoctetes*, 34–39
currency, 171–172, 172–174, 174–175

D

Dance of the Forests (Soyinka), 155
Dante, xv
Death and the King's Horseman
  (Soyinka), 156–158
Declaratory Act (1719), 162, 176
decolonization, 100, 101, 105
Defoe, Daniel, 147–150, 171
dehumanization
  of colonialism, 44–45
Descartes, René, 58
Diario (Columbus), 16–20
Diomedes *(Iliad)*, 90, 96
dispossession, 36
Dorians, 85
Drapier Letters, The (Swift), 170–171,
  175–176
dual identity, 57–58
Durrant, Samuel, 214–215, 220

E

East India Company, 140
Eckstein, Barbara, 219
Eliot, T. S., 153
Elizabeth I (queen), 160

Ellison, Ralph, 107
estrangement, 63
Euro-American culture, 100, 101,
  102
European culture, 8–9
exploitation, 40–41, 204–205
exploration
  in "My Kinsman, Major
    Molineux," 115–122
  in *The Tempest*, 179–189
  theme of, xv–xvi
  in *Things Fall Apart*, 191–199

F

female beauty, 103–106, 108–109
female self-representation, 236–237,
  240
female victimization, 244–245,
  248–249
Ferdinand (king), 24–25
Forster, E.M., 133–145
French colonialism, 57–58, 62–64, 73
friendship, 133–134

G

Gallagher, Susan, 220
Gandhi, Mahatma, 138, 139, 140
global capitalism, 201
Gonzalo (*Tempest*), 181–187
government, trust in, 174
Greek tragedy, 34, 154
Grobe, Edwin P., 61
Guatemala, 203, 210
"Guest, The" (Camus), 57–64
  ethical dilemma in, 58–59, 63–64
  landscape in, 62–63
  relationship between central
    characters in, 60–62
Gulliver's Travels (Swift), 167–168,
  170–171, 174–175, 177

H

Hall, Bob, 13

Hawthorne, Nathaniel, 115–122

Heaney, Seamus, 31–55

Heart of Darkness (Conrad), 67–82, 140
  absurdity in, 68, 71–74, 82
  darkness in, 68, 75–76, 79–80, 81
  frame narrative of, 67–69
  irrational behavior in, 69–70
  Kurtz in, 70–71, 74–75, 78–81
  Marlow in, 67–82
  the Russian in, 76–79

Hector (*Iliad*), 90–91, 96

Hercules (*Cure at Troy*), 48–49

heroic age, 86

heroic myth, 84, 89

heroic values, 96–97

Hesiod, 86

Hinduism, 142

history
  ancient, 84–86
  Latin American, 124–131

Hittites, 85

Holy Land, 25–27

Holy Trinity, 194

Homer, xv
  The Iliad, 83–98

House Made of Dawn (Momaday),
  11–12

human-animal relationship, 40–44

humanity, shared, 217

human nature, 182

hunting theme, 42–44, 46

hybrid consciousness, 47, 49

I

Idanre (Soyinka), 154

Iliad, The (Homer), 83–98
  Achaeans in, 86–87
  Achilles in, 87, 88–91, 94–96
  Agamemnon in, 86–89, 90, 94–96

Hector in, 90–91

heroic values in, 96–97

historical basis for, 84–86, 87–88

Nestor in, 91

Odysseus in, 91–92

portrayal of war in, 96

purpose of, 92–94

imperialism. *See also* colonialism
  corrupting power of, 136–138
  critique of, 133–145, 207–208
  economics of, 139–140
  personal relationships and, 133–
    134, 138

India, colonialism in, 133–145

Indian independence movement, 138,
  139

Indian literature. *See* Native
  American literature

indigenous people
  bigotry toward, 134–135
  colonial education system and, 196
  effect of colonialism on, 57–64
  global capitalism and, 201
  in Latin America, 206–208

Inferno (Dante), xv

Interpreters, The (Soyinka), 153

Ionian colonies, 93

IRA, 32

Ireland, 32–34. *See also* Northern
  Ireland
  British rule of, 159–162, 168,
    176–178, 179
  Swift's writings on, 162–166,
    170–172, 176–178

Isabella (queen), 24–25, 26

J

James II (king), 161

Jane Eyre (Brontë), 226–227, 228,
  229

Jazz (Morrison), 103, 106–109

Jerusalem, 26–27
Joyce, James, 153, xvi

K

Kalkarni, Mangesh, 58
Kingston, Maxine Hong, 235–252
Kongi's Harvest (Soyinka), 153

L

labour division, 148–149
language
  lack of common, 218
  representative function of, 174–176
Las Casas, Bartolomé de, 1–6, 18
Latin America
  global capitalism and, 201
  indigenous people of, 206–208
  United Fruit Company and, 203
Latin American history, 123–131
Lazere, Donald, 62
leadership, 94
Lee, Don L., 102
Lenta, Patrick, 222
"Let Me Explain a Few Things"
  (Neruda), 208
Letter to Harding (Swift), 172–174
Lindley, David, 179–180
linear time, 128–129
Lion and the Jewel, The (Soyinka),
  154–155
literary influence, xii–xiii
literary themes, xi–xiii
Lorca, Frederico Garcí, 202
Lowell, Robert, 116–117

M

Machu Picchu, 208
Mackenzie Clayton G., 196
Madmen and Specialists (Soyinka), 156

madness, 166–168, 228, 243
magic realism, 123, 124
Man Died, The (Soyinka), 153
Mardorossian, Carine M., 231–232
marginalization, 36
Márquez, Gabriel García, 123–131
Martineau, Harriet, 236
Marx, Karl, 147–150
Mbari group, 152–153
MClaren, Joseph, 195
McNickle, D'Arcy, 11
Milton, John, xv–xvi
missionaries, 192–198
Momaday, N. Scott, 11–12
monarchy, 177–178
money supply, 171–175
Morrison, Toni, 99–111
  beauty theme and, 103–105, 106,
    108–110
  Beloved, 105
  The Bluest Eye, 101–102, 103,
    106–107
  colonization and, 100, 102–105
  Jazz, 103, 106–109
  periodization of works of, 99–100
  Song of Solomon, 103
  Sula, 103
  Tar Baby, 100–101, 103, 103–105,
    110
Moses, Michael, 218
Mountjoy, Lord, 160
Murdoch, H. Adlai, 231
Mycanae, 84–86
"My Kinsman, Major Molineux"
  (Hawthorne), 115–122
"Myth of Sisyphus, The" (Camus),
  63
mythology, 153–154, 158

N

national Indian literature, 7–14

nationalism
   black cultural, 102
   in India, 138
   Native American, 9
Native American culture, oral
   tradition in, 10–14
Native American literature
   Christian religious rituals and,
      8–11
   nationalism in, 9
Native Americans
   Columbus's writings on, 21–24
natives. *See* indigenous people
neocolonialism, 123–124, 125, 128,
   130
Neruda, Pablo, 201–210
   Canto General, 201–210
   diplomatic posts, 202
   fame of, 210
   indigenous people and, 206–208
   as political poet, 208–209
   Spain in My Heart, 202
   "United Fruit Co.," 201–210
Nestor (*Iliad*), 91
Newman, Lea Bertani Vozar, 115
New World
   British colonialism in, 187–189
   writing of Columbus in discovery
      of, 15–30
Nigeria, 152–153, 155–156
   British colonialism in, 191–199
   missionaries in, 195–196
nonlinear time, 129–130
Northern Ireland. *See also* Ireland
   British exploitation in, 40–41
   Catholic-Protestant divide in, 38
   colonization of, 36
   The Cure at Troy and, 34–39
   political discourse in, 32–34
   postcolonial discourse and, 34,
      52–53
   reconciliation and, 52–53

O

Odysseus, xv–xvi
   in *Cure at Troy*, 40–42, 43–46
   in *The Iliad*, 91–92
   in *Philoctetes*, 39–40
Odyssey (Homer), xv
Ogun myth, 154
Okigbo, Christopher, 152–153
One Hundred Years of Solitude
   (Márquez), 123–131
   depiction of power in, 127–128
   magic realism in, 123, 124
   repetition in, 129
   representation of history in,
      124–129
   time in, 128–130
O'Neill, Hugh, 160
Opera Wonyosi (Soyinka), 156
oppression, 166–167
oral tradition, in Native culture, 7–14
Other/Otherness, 34, 38, 39, 40, 42,
   50, 57, 215, 218
Ovid, 165–166

P

pain, 216, 218
Paradise Lost (Milton), xv–xvi
Passage to India, A (Forster), 133–145
   Aziz in, 134–135, 136, 137–139,
      141–143
   bigotry exposed in, 134–135
   critique of imperialism in, 133–
      145
   friendship theme in, 133–134, 136,
      138–143
   Hinduism in, 142
   historical references in, 138–139
   Mrs. Moore in, 141
   power relationships in, 135–137
Peacock, Alan, 50
periodization, 99–100, 110n1

Philoctetes (Sophocles), 32, 33
  allegorical readings of, 36–38
  animalism in, 39–40, 42
  colonial discourse in, 49–50
  friendship theme in, 137–138
  revisions, 34–39
Pinochet, August, 210
Plague, The (Camus), 63
Poems from Prison (Soyinka), 153
postcolonial consciousness, 47, 49
postcolonial discourse, 52–53
postcolonialism, 39, 50, 51, 57
postcolonial mythology, 34
power
  depiction of, 127–128
power relationships, 215–216, 220–221
prayer narratives, 9–10
"Primitive, The" (Lee), 102
Proposal for the Universal Use of Irish Manufacture, A (Swift), 163–166, 168–169
Protestants
  in Northern Ireland, 33–34, 36

R

racial beauty, 101–105
racism, 80, 81, 231–232
Radford, Michael, 210
Ramos Pérez, Demetrio, 17–18, 19, 26
reading
  act of, 16
rebellion, 58–59
resistance
  to colonization, 10–14
Rhys, Jean, 225–232
Rich, Adrienne, 235–236
Rich, Paul, 219
Rivera, Diego, 201
Road, The (Soyinka), 155
Robinson, Mary, 32

Robinson Crusoe (Defoe), 147–150, 171
ruler-ruled conflict, 94
Rumeu de Armas, Antonio, 17, 18–19

S

Sánchez, Rafaél, 16–17
Santa María (ship), 20
Santángel, Luis de, 16–17, 19, 27
Savage, Derek S., 140
Scarry, Elaine, 216, 218
Scotland, 176
Season of Anomy (Soyinka), 156
self-representation, 236–237, 240
Sepulveda, 4
Shakespeare, William, 179–189
Shuttle in the Crypt (Soyinka), 153
signification, 106–107
Silko, Leslie Marmon, 12–14
Siquieros, David Alfaro, 201
slavery, 39
social contract, 177
socialism, 202
Somoza, Anastasio, 204–205
Song of Myself (Whitman), 207
Song of Solomon (Morrison), 103
Sophocles, 32, 34
South Africa, 219, 222
Southern Exposure (Hall), 13
Soyinka, Wole, 151–158
  prison writings of, 153
  use of mythology by, 153–154, 158
Spain in My Heart (Neruda), 202
Spanish
  in New World, 8–11
  reception of, by Native Americans, 21–23
Spanish Civil War, 202, 208
Spanish Conquest
  motivations for, 25–27

speechlessness, 246–247
Spivak, Gayatri Chakravorty, 232
Stalin, Josef, 209
state
    individual's relationship with, 94
storytelling, 237–238
Stranger, The (Camus), 58, 63
Sula (Morrison), 103
Sunningdale Agreement, 37
Swift, Jonathan, 159–178
    Drapier Letters, The , 170–171,
        175–176
    Gulliver's Travels, 167–168, 170–
        171, 174–175, 177
    Ireland and, 162–166, 170–172,
        176–178
    Letter to Harding , 172–174
    madness metaphor and, 166–168
    *Proposal for the Universal Use of
        Irish Manufacture*, 163–166,
        168–169
    satire of, 164, 165, 168
    Tale of a Tub, A, 164, 167

T

Tale of a Tub, A (Swift), 164, 167
Tar Baby (Morrison), 100–101, 103,
    103–105, 110
Tarrow, Susan, 58
Tempest, The (Shakespeare), 179–189
    Adrian in, 184
    Antonio in, 182–186, 187
    Caliban in, 179–180
    Gonzalo in, 181–187, 189
    island as penal colony in, 180–181
    Prospero in, 180, 181
    Sebastian in, 182–186, 187
    stereotypes in, 180
    utopian ideal and, 186–187
Tennyson, Alfred Lord, xv–xvi
themes, xi–xiii

Things Fall Apart (Achebe), 191–199
Thomas, Sue, 228
topos, xi–xii
torture, 220, 222
Trilling, Lionel, 135
Trojan War, 84–86, 92, 93–94
trope, xi–xiii
Trujillo, Rafael, 204
*Twenty Love Poems and a Song of
    Despair* (Neruda), 202

U

Ubico, Jorge, 204
Ulysses. *See* Odysseus
Ulysses (Joyce), xvi
Ulysses (Tennyson), xv–xvi
"United Fruit Co." (Neruda), 201–210
United Fruit Company, 125, 202–
    203, 205
United States, 209
    exploitation of Latin America by,
        203
    interference in Latin America by,
        209–210
    neocolonialism and, 123–124
utopian ideal, 186–187

V

victim-oppressor relationships,
    215–216
Virginia Company, 187–189

W

Waiting for the Barbarians (Coetzee),
    213–222
    ambivalence in, 219–220
    conclusion of, 219
    crisis of conscience in, 214–215
    ethical sensibility in, 217–218

narrative devices, 213–214, 222
power relationships in, 215–216, 220–221
storytelling in, 238–240
Walcott, Derek, 34
Western Region crisis (Nigeria), 155–156
white female beauty, 103–105, 106, 108–109
Whitman, Walt, 207
Wide Sargasso Sea (Rhys), 225–232
Wind from an Enemy Sky (McNickle), 11
Woman Warrior, The (Kingston), 235–252
  Brave Orchid in, 237–241, 243–246, 250–252

female victimization in, 244–245, 248–249
female voice in, 246–250
Moon Orchid in, 242–243, 244, 245
mother-daughter relationship in, 240–241
narrative structure, 237
storytelling in, 237–238, 250–252
traditions in, 243–244
Wool Act (1699), 162, 163
worker alienation, 206
Wright, Laura, 221–222

Y

Yeats, William Butler, 34